# LIVING
## LANGUAGE

# LIVING LANGUAGE
## Exploring Kiwitalk

## Elizabeth Gordon

CANTERBURY UNIVERSITY PRESS

UNIVERSITY OF
CANTERBURY
Te Whare Wānanga o Waitaha
CHRISTCHURCH NEW ZEALAND

First published in 2010 by
CANTERBURY UNIVERSITY PRESS
University of Canterbury
Private Bag 4800, Christchurch
NEW ZEALAND
www.cup.canterbury.ac.nz

ISBN 978-1-877257-87-2

A catalogue record for this book is available from the National Library of New Zealand.

Author photograph, back cover: Duncan Shaw-Brown
Cover design and layout: Sarah Healey
Book design and page layout: Quentin Wilson
Printed by Toltech Print Ltd, Christchurch

# Contents

# Introduction

In May 2007 I was holidaying in Malaysia when I received an invitation to write a weekly column on language for *The Press*. At the time I thought I would continue for only a few months, but this book is the product of over two years' writing. I kept going was because *The Press* gave me a completely free hand to write on any aspect of language I wished, and because there has been so much to write about.

From the beginning I have been grateful for the support of colleagues from the University of Canterbury. Tony Deverson has willingly advised me about earlier periods of English; as the editor of *The New Zealand Oxford Dictionary* he has also been a generous source of information on New Zealand vocabulary. Heidi Quinn has extracted data for me from the Canterbury Corpus of recorded present-day New Zealand English. Andrew Carstairs-McCarthy, Margaret Maclagan, Alex D'Arcy, Robin Barrett, Kon Kuiper, David Gough and Ronnie Davey have also given me their academic expertise.

Peter Trudgill, a foremost British sociolinguist, comes to New Zealand every year with his wife Jean Hannah. We have had long and useful discussions about some of the topics in these columns. They have also alerted me to examples where New Zealand English differs from British English. We need outside observers to provide this information – without it we can be unaware that some everyday New Zealand usages are unique to this country.

I wish to thank those who have given me help with examples from other languages: Jeanette King with Maori, my daughter-in-law Marie Ualese with Samoan, and Bill Willmott with Chinese.

I have also been assisted by the resources of the internet, the online reference books available through Christchurch City Libraries, and Michael Quinion at www.worldwidewords.org.

My own family have been a useful source of language material. My husband Derry gives me constant support and constructive criticism every week. My children – John, Susannah, Margaret and Charlotte – give me suggestions for columns and language examples from a younger age group. I needed them to tell me about bogans, emo chicks and muffin-tops. My grandchildren have delighted me with their different stages of language development.

Above all I am grateful to the many readers of *The Press* who have taken time to contact me. I have been surprised and heartened by the generosity and kindness of those who have encouraged me to keep writing the columns, and given me queries or suggestions to follow up.

I would like to acknowledge the support from *The Press*: Geoff Collett, Mark Wilson, Paul McIntyre and Ewan Sergent. Cate Hogan was the sub-editor responsible for my favourite headline, 'The bell tolls for whom'.

Finally I wish to thank Rachel Scott from Canterbury University Press. This book was her idea; she has been a competent and sympathetic editor and a pleasure to work with.

I know that my columns have not always pleased everyone, and some have written to tell me so. But everyone agrees that language is a fascinating subject. When I invited readers to work out the rule to explain why I could live 'in' or 'at' Brighton but only 'in' Fendalton I was sent a number of suggestions. One reader said she had picked up her pencil at the breakfast table and tried to work it out. She hadn't had so much fun for ages. I hope that people reading this book will see language not as a linguistic minefield of rules for correctness, but as a subject that is intensely interesting, that tells us about ourselves as New Zealanders, and which can be fun.

# Delighting in our English

11 August 2007

WHEN I WAS AT SCHOOL, our English teacher told us to listen to a radio programme called *The Queen's English*.

This was in the 1950s and the speaker was Professor Arnold Wall, formerly Professor of English at Canterbury University College, who used this programme to answer listeners' questions. Wall had a deep knowledge of the English language and its history, and he had no patience with time-wasters and people who sent in silly questions such as: 'If someone in Scotland calls a mouse a 'moose' what do they call a moose?'

The popularity of *The Queen's English* came not just from Wall's ability to reprimand adults sternly and publicly, but because he could confidently answer all questions about the English language.

Wall was one in a long line of language experts who over the years have set out the rules of right and wrong in English for the linguistically anxious. He also affirmed those who wanted to hear English language miscreants publicly chastised. We thought his services were helpful because when I was at school we were often given exercises beginning: 'State what is wrong with the following sentences.' The English language was a minefield for the insecure.

Wall also wrote about pronunciation in a book called *New Zealand English: How it should be spoken*. Here he gives an accurate description of features of New Zealand English as it was spoken in the 1930s and '40s but under the heading 'Essential Faults in New Zealand Speech'.

In the 1960s I studied linguistics at University College London. When I came home to New Zealand and told people what I had been doing, some would say, 'Oh, I'll have to be very careful how I speak to you', thinking I would want to correct their grammar or complain about their vowels.

In London I was shown a different way of looking at language. People in my linguistics class did not describe my New Zealand accent as ugly, or even funny, and there was no mention of 'essential faults'. They thought the way I said words like 'pin' and 'pen' and 'pan' was extremely interesting and kept asking me to repeat them. This began for me a lifelong interest in New Zealand English.

In writing this column I am following Frank Haden, a man with a deep love of the English language. During my university study of New Zealand English, Haden gave us valuable evidence of language change in his columns, although I'm sure this wasn't his intention when he was writing them. For example, two years ago he wrote that people getting off the bus were saying 'Thank you Jiver' for 'Thank you Driver'. We had been hearing 'jiver' for some years but we hadn't seen any comment about it in print.

'Thank you Jiver' dismayed Haden, whereas for me it was an excellent example of a change in the pronunciation of New Zealand English. Whatever their views, one thing is certain: New Zealanders are interested in the English language, and I hope this column will continue the discussion.

# The ear that we breathe

*18 August 2007*

A VISITING ENGLISHMAN IN THE 1980S thought it was very funny when a New Zealand TV commentator said, 'This is a rear view of the Queen' when the Queen was clearly facing the camera. Those of us working on New Zealand English were not shrieking with laughter because this was just another example of a sound change called the 'ear/air merger'.

Old-fashioned people like me pronounce 'ear' and 'air' differently, and the same for words like cheer and chair, sheer and share, fear and fair, and so on. New-fashioned people have only one pronunciation. They say only ear, cheer, sheer and fear.

A few, like F. Phelps (Letters, 18 July), have gone the other way. Phelps was pulled up recently for saying 'fair' instead of 'fear'.

Back in 1983 we pursued the ear/air merger and recorded fourth-formers in Christchurch schools. Our sample included private schools and state schools, and we had equal numbers of girls and boys. A research assistant asked these students to read sentences like, 'He sat on a chair and gave a loud cheer.' 'Come here and I'll brush your hair.' 'He should have known that he would need his spare spear.'

In 1983, 16 per cent of the students said 'ear' for all the words with 'air'. We repeated this experiment every five years and by 1998 it was 80 per cent. Because we needed to demonstrate that this was a recent sound change, we also tested some people over the age of 80. Although one fell asleep and another refused to read our sentences because they were silly, to our great surprise we found that some of these old New Zealanders also used 'ear' for some 'air' words.

When people notice this change, some get anxious and some get annoyed. Julie Newsum (Letters, 20 July) complained about newscasters talking about the 'shear' market and says this is lazy. F. Phelps also asks if this is laziness or a generational change.

In the 17th century there were probably parents and teachers complaining that their children were lazy because they were not making a distinction between words like sea and see, meat and meet. And, just as bad, their children were saying nose and knows in the same way, or days and daze. The words in these pairs were also once pronounced differently, as we can see from the spelling.

At some point in history they too have merged and the sky hasn't fallen.

Christchurch hair salons are well up with the play with the ear/air merger – Hair 'n' Beyond, Stop Hair Design, The Look Hair Studio, Hair We R, and Why Not Hair. We know from our research that people have been commenting on it for well over 30 years and it's probably been around for much longer than this.

Like all sound changes, the ear/air merger has not been greeted with delight, and some people find it deeply distressing. But it's here to stay, it's part of New Zealand English, and I don't think anyone has missed a plane because they were flying on 'Ear New Zealand'.

# Relishing Maori input

*25 August 2007*

MY BROTHER JOHN [OSMERS] HAS spent all his working life in southern and central Africa. On the rare occasions when he comes back to New Zealand he is always struck by the changes he sees – large houses in holiday places where there used to be only baches; cafés and bistros where there used to be tearooms and milkbars. The videoshop was his great discovery.

We are always surprised by his reactions because we've scarcely noticed these changes ourselves. They just creep up on us. Was there ever life before videoshops?

John's visits have also been useful to me as a register of language change. In a visit in the 1980s he was very puzzled to hear someone described as 'very laid back'. He didn't know what it meant when people said, 'He just couldn't hack it' or 'I was really hacked off'.

Two years ago he was back in New Zealand and this time he was amazed by the number of Maori words that had come into New Zealand English in his absence. He had no idea what they meant. He didn't know what an iwi or a hapu were; he didn't even know words like whanau, kaumatua, mokopuna, koha or taonga.

John left New Zealand in 1958, a time when the Maori words in New Zealand English related mainly to flora and fauna – kowhai, rimu, rata, tui, kea, katipo, pipi; in addition to words like haka, tangi, marae, tiki. These words had been borrowed into English at the beginning of European settlement. After about 1860 almost no more Maori words came into New Zealand English, and that's how it was for over a hundred years.

The turnaround came in about 1970, and since then more and more have been moving across every year. In 1998 I was asked to help with the revision of the *Collins New Zealand School Dictionary*. The edition that needed updating had only 24 Maori words in it, all early borrowings.

15

Now Collins has a Maori consultant because of the influx of Maori words into present-day New Zealand English. Oxford University Press has also responded and in 2005 published *A Dictionary of Maori Words in New Zealand English*, edited by John McAlister. It has 190 pages and the long vowels are not marked with macrons or double letters because these words are part of New Zealand English.

In Maori Language Week we recently heard the announcers on radio and television using Maori words and greetings in a totally unselfconscious way. It seemed natural and appropriate and I hope they will continue to use them because in the end it's the Maori input that makes New Zealand English so distinctive.

As a mark of how far we have come, I have on my kitchen shelf a small laminated card with a guide to Maori pronunciation on one side (to be sung to the tune of 'Stupid Cupid') and the words of the New Zealand national anthem in Maori on the other. I was given this card when I attended a meeting of the Ferrymead Rotary Club. I'll make sure I keep it handy for my brother's next visit.

# Good as gold

*1 September 2007*

We've had New Zealand slang expressions on our T-shirts and tea-towels and now it's time to have them on our stamps. Ivor Masters, from New Zealand Post, said it was 'hard yakka' to choose 20 different sayings. They had gone through loads of books and dictionaries and then 'whittled the list down to what we felt were still most commonly used'.

If you don't know the meaning of any of these phrases, then you can put your finger on a small black square and the English translations will be revealed. Or so they say. Maybe my finger wasn't warm enough to work the magic, but then it had been cold.

The slang words and phrases on the stamps are mostly familiar, such as 'she'll be right', which the great New Zealand dictionary writer Harry Orsman tracks back to 1947; and 'good as gold' – not just with the English sense of 'well behaved' but 'fine, OK, no worries'. (When my husband was growing up in Northland in the 1940s this was reduced to 'she's a goldie', although I wasn't aware of that phrase in Christchurch.)

Other phrases on the stamps include 'wop-wops', 'away laughing', 'boots and all', 'sparrow fart' and 'shark and taties' (acknowledging that a main ingredient of New Zealand fish and chips is the euphemistically named lemonfish).

'Tiki tour' comes from the name of a New Zealand tourism organisation, but 'hard yakker' (or 'yakka' or 'yacker') came here across the ditch from an Aboriginal word *yaga* meaning 'work'.

And this is the difficulty with identifying New Zealand slang, because we share a lot of it with Australia and quite a bit with the rest of the English-speaking world.

It probably seems a bit picky to point out that some of the slang selected for our New Zealand stamps actually came from somewhere else.

'Hissy fit' is American, and 'knackered' is British or Irish slang for exhausted and tired out – ready for the knacker's yard. The 'dreaded lurgy' first made its appearance on *The Goon Show* in the 1950s as a dangerous disease, cured only by the playing of brass band instruments.

But in the end it doesn't really matter that these slang expressions are not entirely home grown. We use them here, and it's part of New Zealand English to say that someone is 'a bit of a dag', or something is 'cod's wallop'.

If people from overseas don't understand, then there must be a tea-towel somewhere with a translation. If all else fails, they can try the hot-finger technique on this issue of stamps.

Sweet as.

# Growen accustomed

*8 September 2007*

When we're talking about New Zealand English, there is always a point when someone will announce with great passion that they really hate it when people say 'knowen' or 'growen' when they should say 'known' or 'grown'.

This complaint has turned up in the letters to *The Press*. Raymond Welsh (20 July) describes it as 'the worst of all' and says 'it makes me wince'.

When this happens, I always observe that some people will nod in agreement and say, 'Yes, shocking, lazy, disgraceful!' But there will be just as many people looking quite puzzled and wondering what the problem is.

One thing is certain. Those who say 'grown' believe they're absolutely right because this is the traditional pronunciation and anything else is incorrect; but the people who say 'growen' believe they're absolutely right because they are making a clear distinction between 'grown' and 'groan', and other similar pairs.

The 'growen' pronunciation has been around in New Zealand for a long time. In the 1930s broadcaster Clive Drummond pencilled a warning in the margin of the first pronunciation guide for New Zealand radio announcers: 'Blown not blow-en c.f. known, grown, flown.'

Now, thanks to the Radio New Zealand Sound Archives, we can go back even further and listen to speakers born in New Zealand between the 1860s and 1890s. A few of them also use the 'growen' pronunciation from time to time.

So where did it come from? We'll discount laziness, unless you want to argue that the names 'Owen' and 'Bowen' are also lazy. One possibility is that it survives from the Old English spoken around the time of King Arthur. The past participle 'known' was 'cnawen', 'grown' was 'growen' and 'blown' was 'blawen'. Perhaps these forms survived in dialects spoken in

19

remote parts of Britain and were transported here by immigrants from rural areas. This would also explain why you hear the 'growen' pronunciation in Australia and parts of South Africa too, where those British immigrants also settled.

A different explanation is that this is a more recent change – a change by analogy. We have other past participles ending in '-en' – fallen, eaten, given, taken, written. So 'grow/growen', 'know/knowen', 'blow/blowen' and the rest are just following suit.

Whatever people think about 'grown' or 'growen', we know from our research that the New Zealand population is evenly divided. Our two women prime ministers, Jenny Shipley and Helen Clark, both say 'growen', and you will hear it from people in all walks of life.

At Princess Diana's funeral Tony Blair read the lesson from St Paul's Epistle to the Corinthians. When he said, 'I shall know even as also I am known,' New Zealand linguists became excited because he too said 'knowen'.

So perhaps in New Zealand (and Australia and South Africa) we are ahead of the rest of the English-speaking world. Maybe one day, people in Britain will start to complain about 'lazy' and 'sloppy' speech for pronunciations used by half the New Zealand population.

# Gladly the cross-eyed bear

*15 September 2007*

MY BEST FRIEND AT SCHOOL once told me that when her mother was a child she had a teddy bear called Gladly. She explained that her mother had misheard the lines in the children's hymn, 'Gladly My Cross I'd Bear', for 'Gladly, my cross-eyed bear'.

A few years later someone else told me that his aunt had a bear called Gladly, and then another person said her cousin's bear was called Gladly. Since then that bear called Gladly has popped up several times in print.

The human brain works hard to make sense of things, even the strangest things. I once asked a university class about the lyrics in the 1970s song 'Killing Me Softly', sung by Roberta Flack.

For the line 'Strumming my pain with his fingers' quite a few thought the words were 'Strumming my face with his fingers' and a few thought they were 'Strumming my faith with his fingers'.

There is a name for these misinterpretations. They are called mondegreens, a word the *Collins English Dictionary* defines as 'a word or phrase that is misinterpreted as another word or phrase, usually with amusing result'.

The word mondegreen was invented in 1954 by Sylvia Wright, who wrote an article in *Harper's Magazine* where she described as a child hearing a Scottish ballad with the words 'Thay hae slain the Earl o' Murray/ and laid him on the green'. She had always thought it was a tragically romantic story in which the Earl of Murray was killed beside his lover: 'Thay hae slain the Earl o' Murray/And Lady Mondegreen.'

Friends used to collect mondegreens for me from the wall of the Daily Bagel café in Christchurch's Victoria Street. There was the line from the Creedence Clearwater Revival song: 'There's a bad moon on the rise' misheard as 'there's a bathroom on the right'; and the Beatles' song in which 'she's got a ticket to ride' was heard as 'she's got a tick in her eye'.

Someone thought Boney M's line 'How can you sing the Lord's song in a strange land?' was 'How can you sing the Lord's song in Australia?'

I discovered my youngest child had a mondegreen in the Christmas carol 'Away in a Manger'. For the verse beginning 'The cattle are lowing/ The baby awakes', she was singing 'The kettle is blowing/The baby awakes'. It throws new light on the nativity story. 'I'm sorry, Joseph and Mary, there's no room in the inn, but we have an annex with tea-making facilities.'

There must be many archaic phrases for which children have created their own mondegreens. Some have made grammatical if not theological sense out of the line in the Lord's Prayer: 'Hallowed be thy name' understood as 'Hello, what's your name?' or 'Harold be thy name.'

The *Guardian* newspaper in England invited readers to send in their favourite mondegreens and there was a huge response. There are now web pages devoted to them and even a book of them. And I wonder how many other people have had teddy bears called Gladly?

# Emos and petticoats

*22 September 2007*

MY ELDERLY AUNTS LIVED IN a retirement home. Sometimes when residents died my aunts would help to pack up their clothes for charity. Once a great-niece was visiting and saw some boxes of these clothes. She went home with a selection of vests and petticoats. Soon afterwards these appeared as outer garments in the layered look. The great-aunts looked appropriately shocked and wondered what the young people of today were coming to.

The phrase 'slave to fashion' also applies to language. One of the most fashionable and changeable forms of language is slang, and for teenagers it's important to keep up with the latest words and phrases.

Sociolinguists talk about 'age grading', which means using language appropriate to your stage in life. When Jo Seagar says her recipes are 'easy peasy' we know she's using kindergarten language. If I press my thumb to my forehead when the phone goes and say, 'Bags not I', I'm using children's language.

The great-niece now goes to work wearing a suit, and the old vests and petticoats have become dusters; in the same way there comes a point when we don't bother to keep up with the latest slang. Then the next generation comes along with something new.

In July, Houston Paea, a Year 12 student from Linwood College, wrote an article in *The Press* called 'Gin breath isn't cool'. It was a lively piece of writing and I hope we hear more from this student. But some words I had difficulty with. Sometimes Houston helped, as with 'crunk (crazy drunk for those of you who don't speak hood)'. So I could work out 'crunked up homies'. 'Homies' is in the *New Zealand Oxford Dictionary* as 'members of one's own gang'.

I also worked out that 'getting on the maggot' meant getting drunk – and that's not in the dictionary. I asked my youngest daughter to help with 'emo chick'. She tells me that emo is a very 'right now' word describing a teenage subculture. It comes from the word emotional and is a genre of music (a mixture of Goth and punk) as well as fashion (skinny black jeans, black hair with long fringes). She says that the music and the fashion have the 'feel my pain thing'.

There are emo jokes. How many emos does it take to change a lightbulb? None – they just cry in the dark.

For those of us who carry our gold card, these slang terms are a foreign language. It's probably useful to know what they mean, but on no account should we use them ourselves. I can still remember my surprise when a school friend's mother told me in 1956 that 'Jeremy had pranged his bomb'. She might as well have come out wearing tartan trousers. She was far too old to be saying 'pranged' or 'bomb'.

In moments of enthusiasm I still say that things are 'super' or 'beaut'. My father would have said they were 'extra curly'; my children would say they're 'cool'; my great-nephew says they 'rock'.

I'm happy to leave it like that. After all, no one in their right mind would want to see a grandmother with a muffin top.

# Changing political correctness

*29 September 2007*

I'VE FOUND AN OLD COPY of the *New Zealand Free Lance* – the Coronation Souvenir Edition. It shows that in 1953 people all over New Zealand were in a high state of excitement over the crowning of a British monarch. There were Empire Society balls, bonfires and bands, special coronation dinners in hospitals, a coronation pageant in Invercargill and coronation debutantes in Waipukurau.

But the picture that caught my eye was of a group of young Maori women, under the heading 'Dusky Maidens'. Just imagine the outcry if that appeared in a newspaper today.

We have come some way since 1953 to avoid language that gives offence. That's why you don't see references any more to 'Red Indians' or 'Chinamen', and when an unspecified person is mentioned we allow that it could be 'he' or 'she'.

This kind of change was named, somewhat ironically, 'political correctness'. *Collins English Dictionary* defines 'politically correct' as 'demonstrating progressive ideals, especially by avoiding vocabulary that is considered offensive, discriminatory, or judgmental, especially concerning race and gender'. If we accept this definition, then it follows that those opposed to political correctness don't mind if language is offensive.

If political correctness is a term for linguistic politeness and good manners, why has it become such a dirty word? Why did the National Party need to appoint Wayne Mapp as their political correctness watchdog?

I think it might have something to do with the way these linguistic changes were promoted.

Usually language change takes place naturally and without a fuss. Often we don't even notice it. But those calling for changes away from sexist and racist language wanted it urgently. They were shouting for it. And it's not always easy to change the habits of a lifetime. People felt uncomfortably pressured and resented the implication that they might be racist or sexist if they used the old language.

My father was stationed in Guadalcanal in the Pacific during World War 2 and he referred to the locals there as 'natives'. It wasn't his choice – it was the word everyone used at that time. Years later we put it to him that calling them 'natives' wasn't such a good idea any more and he did his best.

Others were less flexible and we started to hear about the 'language police' and 'social engineering'. Silly invented words like 'personipulate' or 'personhole cover' were put forward as examples of the stupidity of political correctness and it became a joke.

Today the term politically correct is almost meaningless. I have seen it used in relation to the fuss over GE crops and efforts to control water use and microchip dogs. It's become a general term of abuse for any vaguely left-wing concern.

We can't undo the semantic degeneration of the term political correctness, but I feel sad that a worthwhile attempt to remove racist and sexist language should have come to such a sticky end.

Yet there has been success also. Since 1953, people have become more careful in their language use and we don't call Maori women 'dusky maidens' any more.

# Unstoppable changes

6 October 2007

IN THE 1980S I WAS on a committee of the Anglican Church that was set up to revise the prayer book. The task involved converting the language into modern English and writing specifically for New Zealand.

Some of the more interesting discussions were not about theology; they were about language.

On one occasion I remember a politely heated debate about the meaning of the word 'minister'. The new text had the instruction that a prayer would be said by the minister. I asked why a lay member of the congregation could not say that particular prayer. The answer came that of course a lay member could say the prayer because the word 'minister' really meant a servant, someone who ministers, and this didn't just mean the vicar or priest.

So there was a debate, some saying that the true meaning of the word was its original meaning, and others arguing that the meaning of the word was its present-day usage.

'Minister' meaning 'servant' came into the English language in the 13th century, with many other French words after the Norman conquest. You can see the Latin word 'minus' meaning 'less' – the original minister was a lowly servant. But if you went into Cathedral Square today and asked people what ministers in a church did, I don't think they would say they were just ordinary members of the congregation.

The Ancient Greeks believed that the true meanings of words were their original meanings and went looking for these basic meanings or *etumon* (where we get our word 'etymology'). While this is a fascinating study, it doesn't necessarily help us with today's word meanings. I'm delighted to know that 'alcohol' was once Arabic eye-shadow – you can see the Arabic word *khol* in there. But it doesn't help me when I'm talking about alcohol today.

Some people insist that you can't 'aggravate' your friends with your annoying habits. You can only aggravate a situation or a wound. They say the word means 'to make something worse' because it comes from the Latin *aggravare*, which meant 'to make heavy'. But those arguing in this way must be consistent and go for the alcoholic Arabic eye-shadow as well.

Where it gets tricky is when a word has changed its meaning in more recent times. I can remember when the word 'gay' meant happy and cheerful. Some people look back with nostalgia and wish it still did. But it's changed, and, like it or not, one of the meanings of 'gay' today is homosexual.

I was taught at school that 'disinterested' meant impartial. Today it also means 'uninterested'. People now use 'enormity' to refer to largeness of size rather than an act of wickedness. That's the way the change has gone and we can't turn back the clock. If we could we would find some interesting old meanings: 'silly' meaning 'blessed', 'hussy' meaning 'house-wife', 'cretin' meaning 'Christian' and 'treacle' being an 'antidote to poison'.

And that's what they are – interesting old meanings.

# A place for the passive

*13 October 2007*

AT THE STORY-WRITING CLASS I attend, the teacher advises us not to use passive verbs. My computer has a grammar checker that doesn't like passive verbs either, and they come out underlined in green.

For people whose grammar is a bit rusty, I'll explain. The most common sentence structure in English is subject-verb-object: the boss (subject) dismissed (verb) the tea-lady (object).

In this sentence 'dismissed' is an active verb. But I can change the words around and write: 'The tea-lady was dismissed by the boss.'

Here, the boss, who was the subject in the active sentence, is now the agent in a passive sentence. 'John ate the apple' (active). 'The apple was eaten by John' (passive).

So what's wrong with passive verbs? This isn't really a question of grammar but a question of style. The difference between an active sentence and a passive one is subtle and relates to emphasis.

When we say a sentence out loud we can add emphasis by saying a word a bit more loudly. 'The BOSS dismissed the tea-lady.' But we can't do this when we're writing, so we have to do it in different ways. We could say, 'It was the boss who dismissed the tea-lady.' Or we could use a passive verb and say, 'The tea lady was dismissed by the boss'.

Sentences with passive verbs have a handy characteristic. You can delete the agent and still have a sensible sentence. If I were describing a restaurant meal, I could write: 'The lamb was drizzled with olive oil and seasoned with tarragon'. Someone wanting to know about that meal doesn't needed to know that the lamb was drizzled with olive oil by the head chef and seasoned with tarragon by one of the chef's more beautiful assistants.

This is why passive verbs are useful in reports. The reader doesn't need to know the name of the person who added the sodium chloride or the organisation that built the bridge in 1930.

But because you can delete the agent, passive sentences can also be tricky. An active sentence must have a subject, so we know straight away who performed the action. But what if you wanted to keep this secret? The way around it is to use a passive verb without an agent. Perhaps the boss wants people to know that the tea-lady was dismissed but he doesn't want them to know that he was the one who did the dastardly deed. So he writes the official notice with a passive verb without an agent: 'The tea-lady has been dismissed.'

I think we need to keep our eyes open for those passive verbs without agents. Many times students have written in their essays, 'It has been said that' or 'It is widely agreed that' and the red pencil comes out: 'Who said this?' or 'Agreed by whom?'

If you change a passive verb to an active one it requires a statement of responsibility.

A recent correspondent to *The Press* queried another correspondent's claim that the government 'has been described as the most corrupt'. It's that passive verb without an agent again, and, as he pointed out, it is important in this instance to know who did the describing.

# An age-old downhill slide

*20 October 2007*

In September we were driving along the Desert Road listening to Kathryn Ryan on the *Nine to Noon* radio programme.

She was interviewing a London University lecturer in genetics, but I didn't hear his name as our car radio cut out every time we went under the power lines. But I managed to hear most of the discussion.

Mr Geneticist was concerned about a decline in the literacy of his students and their lack of grammatical knowledge. He had published an article about this in a magazine devoted to the Queen's English. He was certain that things were much worse now, that the rot had begun in the 1960s and that it was the fault of school teachers.

Like Mr Geneticist, I too have spent time considering student literacy, but unlike him I enjoy student howlers. They relieve the tedium of exam marking.

'The Anglo-Saxons had no language apart from occasional words picked up in battle.' This gets an exclamation mark in the margin and is shared with other exam markers over morning tea. 'Quarantine was the name of the desert where Christ went to pray for 40 days.' A colleague was told that the Vikings came to Britain and engaged in 'pillaging, raping and word-borrowing'.

Mr Geneticist doesn't think such things are at all funny. They make him grind his teeth and kick the cat, and he adds them to his collection of evidence for the shocking decline in student literacy.

Is there evidence that student writing is getting worse? Did Mr Geneticist have any longitudinal data for comparison? Maybe some statistics?

When I began my university teaching in 1967 I kept lists of student errors. After about 10 years I gave up my list-making because the same old errors were showing up – the comma splice, 'it's' for the possessive, and the inability to spell 'pronunciation' or 'Scandinavian'.

I came to the conclusion that there were always students who would leave essay writing to the last minute and hand in work entirely unsullied by proofreading. There would always be students who got into muddles in exams and wrote silly things.

But there are also students who write remarkably well and we are reassured when visiting academics from famous overseas universities tell us that some of our student essays are among the best they have read.

There's a belief that there was once a golden age when teachers taught grammar and students wrote and spoke impeccable English. Mr Geneticist believed that this was some time before 1960.

But is it true? From the 1880s on, New Zealand school inspectors' reports contained many complaints about children's grammar. Professor Rutherford, of the History Department of Auckland University, complained in the *New Zealand Listener* that a quarter of his first-year class of 147 students were illiterate – and that was in 1944.

Since 1967 I have spent many hours correcting students' use of language, and, like my colleagues, I demand clear, accurate writing. If it's true that the standard of student writing has declined, then this claim should be supported by evidence and not just by loud assertions and an attack on English teachers.

By the way, did you know that Pidgin English was spoken in the Gilbert and Sullivan Islands?

# Aunt Maude knew best

27 October 2007

MY AUNT MAUDE WAS A woman with strong convictions. When she was in her nineties there was one subject she kept returning to. She was convinced that the design of the modern pushchair was quite wrong, with the child facing the wrong way.

'Look at that,' she would say as a mother walked past with a fancy new pushchair. 'It's all wrong. That poor child doesn't want to look at the scenery – she wants to see her mother.'

It was even worse if the pushchair had three wheels, was covered with shade-cloth and propelled by a runner wearing a sweatband.

'That mother isn't taking her child for a walk – she's just going for a run with a baby attached.'

Aunt Maude had good credentials. She was a trained maternity nurse, and during World War 2 she ran a baby home in Papanui. Babies who were cranky or didn't 'thrive' were sent to Aunt Maude, and in a week or so they were returned in a calm and contented state. Her contribution to the war effort was to take over screaming babies when their fathers came home on leave.

In her later years she could point to several Christchurch citizens who she had sorted out in the bassinet.

Why do Aunt Maude's views on the design of pushchairs feature in a language column? The reason is that Aunt Maude knew instinctively about the importance of talking to babies and little children and responding to them. Her gripe with modern pushchairs was that with the child facing the front there was no possibility for the child and the mother (or, of course, any other carer) to communicate with each other. Taking a small child for a walk was a lost opportunity.

If she had been a social psychologist she could have talked about 'face-to-face communicative needs'. We now know more about this, and about

33

the importance of face-to-face communication in the early development of language. We can see the beginning of conversational turn taking when the baby smiles, and the mother smiles back. When the baby yawns the mother says, 'Are you feeling sleepy?'

As the child gets older, objects, animals and people are named and questions get asked. And it's also building up relationships.

My grandchildren don't live in Christchurch but we are well prepared for them when they visit. We found an elderly but sturdy twin pushchair in a second-hand shop in Ferry Road. It was the Oxley brand and cost $50. Most importantly, it was facing what Aunt Maude would have called 'the right way'.

When we go for walks with Kathleen and Frankie we comment on seagulls, dogs, interesting letterboxes, pretty gardens, and the leaking water pump that the council is fixing.

Sometimes 'Baa Baa Black Sheep' gets in there, too, and there's lots of reciprocal smiling. If the sun gets in their eyes, we don't have to cover them with shade-cloth – we adjust the hood of the pushchair.

And by the time we get home I know that Aunt Maude was quite right about pushchairs and small children and communication. We've been for a walk together and it really was together.

# From Pommy to popcorn

*3 November 2007*

I KNOW AN ANAESTHETIST WHO TOOK early retirement to work on his hobby – genealogy. When family members get married he gives them a framed family tree.

All over New Zealand this kind of research is going on into whakapapa and family history. We can work out family trees for some words, too. It's not quite the same as with people because words don't get born, have children and die – but they can have relationships and connections.

'Corn' and 'grain' are English words with similar meanings and they are related to each other. They have both descended from the same prehistoric ancestral language called Indo-European, spoken about 4000 years ago.

Scholars have worked out that there could have been an Indo-European word for grain that was something like *grnom*. The word corn came down the Germanic branch of the Indo-European family tree; it's had a sound change along the way. The Germanic branch is where English belongs, along with other Germanic languages such as German, Dutch, Swedish, Danish. The word 'grain' came down the Celto-Italic branch, which includes Latin and the languages that evolved from Latin – French, Italian, Spanish etc.

The original waving corn growing in cornfields was wheat. In New Zealand today corn is a variety of maize, giving us sweetcorn, corn syrup, popcorn. (I see on my old packet of cornflour that it was made from wheat. Today cornflour is made from corn.) A peppercorn is a grain of pepper and corned beef was preserved with peppercorns and other things.

The word 'grain' was borrowed from French after the Norman Conquest. Some other related French words came into English at the same time. One is pomegranate – literally a 'grainy apple'. Another is grange. Houses named The Grange sound posh but the original grange was just a storehouse for grain.

We've also borrowed words from Latin – when I was a child we had a breakfast cereal called Granose. Words such as granular, granulate and granule were borrowed into English in the 17th century when it was fashionable for educated people to use a Latinate vocabulary. One 17th-century borrowing from Italian was granite – a rock with a grainy appearance.

The word pomegranate is a linguistically productive member of the corn–grain family tree. In the 16th century grenades were named after pomegranates, and the men who threw them were Grenadiers. Garnet, the semi-precious stone, was given its name because it was the colour of a pomegranate.

The pomegranate sub-branch of the family tree left its mark in Australia and New Zealand. There have been lots of ideas about the origins of the word Pom. One theory is that it was short for Port of Melbourne, another that it came from POHM – prisoner of Her Majesty, or POME – prisoner of Mother England.

The experts tell us that Pommy came from pomegranate. It's a play on the word 'immigrant'. Immigrants were called jimmy grants or pomegranates, later shortened to pommies.

I once went to a family reunion in the Waipara community hall. Most of us had nothing in common apart from having the same great-great-grandparents. The same could be said for popcorn, corned beef, granite, garnet, grenade and Pommy.

# Let's talk Strine

*10 November 2007*

WHEN I WAS STUDYING AT University College London in the 1960s my supervisor was Professor Randolph Quirk, a world authority on the English language. On one occasion he went on an academic fact-finding tour of Australian universities and returned full of enthusiasm for Australian English. 'They have a wonderful use of metaphor,' he said. 'Their vocabulary is rich with imagery.'

In my brief stay in Sydney, metaphor and imagery hadn't been foremost in my mind, so I asked Quirk to elaborate. 'They use the example of the tide going in and out. When Australians are hungry they say that they have an 'ebb-tide'. Quirk was a man of certain brilliance but uncertain temper, so I wondered if I should explain about Australians and their appetites.

In 1965 'Afferbeck Lauder, Professor of Strine Studies, University of Sinny,' wrote a book called *Let Stalk Strine*. In the introduction the author described an incident when the English author Monica Dickens was autographing copies of her latest book in a Sydney bookshop. A woman came up and said, 'Emma Chisit' and Dickens duly inscribed the book to Emma Chisit with her best wishes. The woman looked puzzled and asked again, 'No, Emma chisit? What does it cost?'

So Afferbeck Lauder decided that 'while Strines are able to understand and read English, they usually speak only Strine', and his book was written to help 'visitors, students, New Strines and people who speak only English'. So we are told that 'baked necks' is Strine for a popular cooked breakfast, 'furry tiles' are stories for children that begin with the words 'One spawner time', and 'garbler mince' means in the next half hour ('I'll be with you in a garbler mince').

Strine quickly caught on, especially in New Zealand, where people could now legitimately laugh at the way Australians spoke. Similar books appeared.

I have a book called *Bristle: The correct way to speak Bristol*. Apparently in Bristol 'hard tack' means cardiac failure, and 'miniature' means 'the very instant', as in 'Miniature back sterned, summonse upto summit'.

In 1966 Arch Acker wrote *New Zild and How to Speak It*. We were told 'Brem barder' meant either a simple meal or principal means of support, as in 'I carnivore Toulouse me drive licence it's me brem barder'. 'Mitre swell' signalled a sensible but disappointing course of action, as in 'We mitre swell go home.'

A more recent book is *Kiwese* by Alex Buzo, described on its cover as 'A Ductionary and A Shearing of Unsights'.

In a letter to *The Press* in August, Tom Taylor gave some examples of New Zild. He was confounded by the question 'Rennum pebble?' when he was buying a Lotto ticket. It fooled me too, and I'm glad he told us it meant 'random Powerball'.

He came to New Zealand seven years ago from Pomgolia, but he's still having problems with the local dialect. In 1965 I found the little book on Strine funny, and I can laugh at Bristle, but New Zild is different. I don't mind other people laughing at us, but don't expect me to join in. This is the way I speak, and my friends and family speak, and that's no joking matter.

# 20 odd people

*17 November 2007*

A FORMER STUDENT OF MINE ASKED me to review a book she had written. It was on punctuation and was called *Punc Rocks*, written by Jenny Buxton and Susan Carter.

It's a lively little book – one of the chapters is headed 'The comma sutra'. I'm sure it will be useful for people who have punctuation queries.

I especially wanted to see what they had written about hyphens, as these sometimes give trouble, and I found some relaxed advice. 'Hyphens are really tricky,' they wrote, 'and their usage is constantly changing, so use them with common sense.'

Later on in the book they say that 'your eye and your common sense must prevail' and 'it's a matter of personal fancy'. So they allow lunch break, lunch-break and lunchbreak; fairy tales, fairy-tales and fairytales. You can take your pick.

This year has seen an important five-yearly event with the publication of the new edition of the *Shorter Oxford English Dictionary*. (The diction-ary isn't short at all – it's two volumes and more than 3700 pages, but I guess that's short compared with the 20 volumes of the full *Oxford English Dictionary*.)

The fate of the hyphen is still a hot topic with the arrival of the sixth edition.

The Oxford Dictionaries' web page warns: 'Lovers of the hyphen, look away now: it seems to be on the way out. Drawing on the evidence of the Oxford Reading Programme and our two billion-word Oxford English Corpus, we removed something like 16,000 hyphens from the text of the *Shorter*. So it's double bass, not double-bass, ice cream not ice-cream, makeover instead of make-over, and postmodern rather than post-modern.'

The editor of the *Shorter OED*, Angus Stevenson, believes that people have lost confidence about using hyphens. Buxton and Carter give readers a choice and tell them to use their common sense, but people are not always sure how to proceed.

Maybe this is why, according to dictionary writers, people have been using the hyphen less and less.

And not just this year. In the fifth edition of the dictionary five years ago the authors remarked that the hyphen was being used only half as much as it had been 10 years earlier. Angus Stevenson also recognises the effect of email and text messaging and he acknowledges the influence of designers.

'Printed writing is very much design-led these days, and people feel that hyphens mess up the look of a nice bit of typography. The hyphen is seen as messy looking and old-fashioned.'

So the new dictionary might make things a bit easier. Hyphens have been dropped from many compound nouns. Some are now two single words: pot belly, fig leaf, hobby horse, test tube, fire drill, pin money and water bed.

Others have been made into a single word: crybaby, pigeonhole, bumblebee, chickpea, lowlife, touchline, upmarket and leapfrog.

But the hyphen hasn't completely disappeared. The *Shorter OED* editor allows it in cases where there might be ambiguity. So we're back to using our common sense.

After all, there is a difference between 20-odd people coming to your party and 20 odd people turning up.

# Altering our world view

*24 November 2007*

A FRIEND WHO IS AN ANGLICAN clergyman turned 70 this year. In the birthday speeches his son said he always remembered a poster in his father's study that read: 'God is a verb.'

That poster raises an interesting language question. Would we think of God differently if God were a verb? Does our language influence the way we see things?

In the 1930s a man called Benjamin Lee Whorf went to Arizona to study the language of the Hopi Indians. He came to the conclusion that the Hopi language was very different from any Western language, and therefore the Hopi viewed the world around them differently from Westerners.

They saw objects, time and activities differently. Whorf concluded that this was because of their language.

In English we divide most of our words into two classes – they are either nouns (like 'book' or 'cup') or they are verbs (like 'turn' or 'run'). But sometimes it is not clear cut.

Words like 'striking', 'turning' or 'running' are obviously verbs. The word 'fist' is a noun. Yet 'fist' could also be a verb – 'fisting' – referring to the tight closing of the hand. We can see a 'fist' as an action when it's pointed out to us, but we think of a fist first of all as a thing (like a cup or a book) because it's categorised as a noun.

Thus our language influences the way we see it.

Today, people still question whether Whorf got it right about the Hopi language, but he did raise some interesting questions about language and the way we see the world. The language we speak is not neutral – it imposes a pattern on things. In Hopi, words like 'lightning', 'wave', 'flame', 'meteor', 'puff of smoke' are all verbs.

So do the Hopi actually think of lightning and flames and meteors differently from speakers of English, for whom they are nouns?

Do things exist for us if we don't have words for them?

Linguist and anthropologist Edward Sapir wrote, 'Would we be so ready to die for "liberty", to struggle for "ideals", if the words were not ringing within us?' Well, would we?

If you have an extensive vocabulary of colour words do you actually see colours differently from someone who has not heard of 'yellow ochre' or 'cerulean blue' or 'brown madder' – they're just yellow, blue and brown?

You can see the power of words when the doctor gives your vague but miserable ailment a name. There will be a sigh of relief when you say, 'Ah, so I've got bi gemini arrhythmia. Well, thank goodness for that. Now I can deal with it.'

The other side of the coin is that names can also be fetters. When a family is labelled 'dysfunctional' how much of what happens is determined by the labelling? Can the children who are 'terrible twos' or their brothers and sisters who are 'moody adolescents' easily break away from their labels? And would we think about God differently if God were a verb?

# Of bowsers and wowsers

*1 December 2007*

S OME YEARS AGO CARA WEIR, a University of Canterbury student, devised a slang questionnaire that she tested on three generations of an Oamaru family – Daughter, (aged 24), Mother (48) and Grandmother (74).

She found (predictably) that slang changes over the generations. Only Grandmother knew the words 'bowser' and 'stumer' (a horse 'fixed' not to be placed).

Only Grandmother and Mother knew 'wowser' and 'tinny', and only Mother and Daughter knew 'ankle biter' (small child), 'chunder', 'geek', 'kai' and 'nerd'.

I was interested in the word 'bowser' because it was familiar to me in my childhood. On Saturday mornings, my father would say, 'I'm off to the bowser', and for some reason I thought this had something to do with alcoholic beverages. I was glad to find that he was only going to the petrol station, because he was a vicar. My husband uses the word 'bowser' for the actual petrol pump; for me it's the whole petrol station.

The word 'bowser' comes from Mr Sylvanus Bowser, of Fort Wayne, Indiana, who invented what he described as 'a self-measuring gasoline storage pump'. 'Bowser' did good business in Australia and New Zealand. In places where there was only one bowser, you can see how the name could be extended in meaning by synecdoche so that the whole enterprise was called a bowser.

Later S. F. Bowser & Co. moved on to make mobile fuel-storage tanks. Harry Orsman's *Oxford Dictionary of New Zealand English* cites an ad in the *Hawke's Bay Herald* in 1918: 'All Benzine and Oils are now retailed from the famous Bowser Steel Tanks'.

Bowsers were used during World War 2 to refuel aeroplanes.

In September I was asked to come out of retirement briefly to give some lectures to a first-year linguistics class. I used the opportunity to ask them if anyone knew the word 'bowser'. The result was a class of blank faces: out of about 50 students only three claimed to know the word. An older student said afterwards that she hadn't heard it for years.

From this unscientific experiment, and from Cara Weir's study, it looks as if 'bowsers' are fondly remembered by people of my age but are otherwise now unknown.

However, when I checked with Tony Deverson, editor of the *New Zealand Oxford Dictionary*, he assured me that the word has not died out completely in New Zealand, and they have citations from the 2000s in their dictionary database. He gave an example from the *Evening Post* in 2002: '[The government] won't upset motorists more by playing wowser at the bowser.' (Younger people might have a few problems with wowser, too). And I have been told that bowser is still in use in Sydney.

I read of a report from the BBC during the floods in Britain this year where the word 'bowser' turned up, but not as a petrol pump. It announced that water was being brought into the flood affected areas by 'bowsers'. So we are back to the mobile tankers invented by Sylvanus Bowser. Maybe Fonterra might start using bowsers and bring the word back to life.

# Change of address

*8 December 2007*

I SPENT MY FIRST YEARS IN Christchurch's South Brighton. Bombs were falling in Europe, but my existence was secure. I can still remember the names of people living in our street – Mr and Mrs Buxton over the road, Mr and Mrs Clark, Miss McLintock and her mother Mrs McLintock at the corner shop. That's how we always addressed our elders. If you asked me about their first names I'd have no idea.

In my first university tutorial the professor asked me for my name and I replied, 'Elizabeth.' That was the wrong answer. He didn't want my first name.

All students were addressed by title and last name, and of course that's how we addressed the staff, too. We might talk about 'Archie' behind his back but he was 'Mr Stockwell' to his face.

I left New Zealand in 1963. When I came back in 1967 there had been changes at the university. Academics still wore gowns, but senior students were now addressed by their first names. Then gowns disappeared and all students were addressed by their first names. Soon students were using first names for younger staff, and even some older staff.

A visiting professor from London recently told me how startled she was when a student addressed her as 'Jenny'.

Names once reflected power relationships, even within a family. When Jane Austen's Emma married Mr Knightley she continued to call him Mr Knightley.

The way we name people today still tells something about relationships. If my doctor is a personal friend I'll call him 'Paul' – otherwise he's 'Dr Smith'.

Using a person's first name is familiar and friendly; using a title and last name is more formal and shows respect; using the last name only is impersonal. New Zealand prisoners are addressed by their last names.

The changes that have occurred in naming customs can cause discomfort to older people. When a teenager who is totally unknown to me addresses me as 'Elizabeth' it feels uncomfortably familiar, and worse if I'm called 'Liz'. But the friendly young one doesn't realise this.

My uncle directed an engineering firm and was always 'Mr Davies'. In his last years in a retirement home the young nurses called him 'John' or even 'Johnny'. Respect had changed to familiarity whether he liked it or not.

I asked my son about the naming practices in the law firm where he works. He told me that the partners are addressed by their first names – Ross, Graeme and Prue.

However, the solicitors call them Rocky, Quiggles and Mum (though not necessarily to their faces). Among the junior male lawyers there's a 'boys' boarding school mentality' – they use last names only. Clients almost always address my son as 'John'. 'Mr Gordon' might be used ironically, or it might be used by a foreigner or a cold caller. In John's view there are social rules governing the use of names, but there are a lot of factors in play.

I think he's right. When I retired and was clearing out papers I found a note that a student had once pinned to my door with an excuse for a late essay. It was addressed 'Dear Liz' and signed 'Mr A. Brown'. Perhaps there was another message there.

# Mixing of languages

*15 December 2007*

MY DAUGHTER-IN-LAW MARIE IS BILINGUAL. Marie's parents came to New Zealand from Samoa in the 1960s and all their children were born in Auckland. When Marie was growing up, her family usually spoke Samoan at home because they had grandparents living with them. At school and everywhere else Marie spoke English. Today she speaks much more English than Samoan. (My son speaks only English.)

Most days Marie phones her parents, who live close by, and her conversation is a mix of Samoan and English. Marie's mother says, 'O a mai oe?' (How are you?) Marie replies, 'I'm fine, thanks. O a mai oe?' Sometimes she will switch languages in mid-sentence. She might say to her children, 'O le a le mea e fai on your toast?' (What do you want on your toast?)

Marie says she is conscious of language switching, but it's not something she means to do – it just seems to happen. She says other New Zealand-born Samoans of her generation do it all the time.

When I visit the university I often hear this mixing of languages. Chinese students will walk past speaking Chinese with snatches of English. At Verkerk's butchery in Christchurch I used to hear Dutch customers and the Dutch-speaking assistants mixing English and Dutch. We can see this language mixing in *Te Timatanga Tatau Tatau*, a book of early stories from founding members of the Maori Women's Welfare League. The written stories are transcriptions of oral accounts. Some are in English, some in Maori, and some mix Maori and English.

The technical name for this switching between languages is 'code-switching', and since the 1970s it's been a hot topic among sociolinguists. In some situations code-switching has a social function. Sociolinguist Susan Gal studied language use in a town in eastern Austria, near the Hungarian border, where speakers used both Hungarian and German. If an argument was being carried out in Hungarian, then a switch to German would add extra force – like having the last word. If speakers wanted to sound particularly knowledgeable then they would switch to German. But this doesn't explain Marie's English/Samoan code-switching.

Some code-switching is considered quite sophisticated. There's elite code-switching, where a person has chosen to learn a European language and can interpose a foreign phrase – 'je ne sais quoi' or 'sine qua non'.

But generally code-switching is not so favoured and is more likely to be seen as a muddle or a mish-mash. I heard of a case in Britain where a doctor advised a Punjabi woman not to mix Urdu and English when she was talking to her child. That was silly, ignorant advice. The doctor didn't understand that code-switching is a highly skilled use of language among bilingual speakers, and absolutely normal.

There's still much to learn about code-switching. We can't predict the places where Marie will use Samoan and when she will switch to English. What we can predict is that she will use both languages when she's speaking to another Samoan-speaking person.

Now that her children go to a Samoan pre-school and can speak both Samoan and English, this language mixing is happening all the time at home.

# To boldly go ...

*22 December 2007*

A T   U N I V E R S I T Y   T H E   T E A C H I N G   S T A F F   are offered all sorts of courses to help them become effective teachers. It wasn't always like that. For many years advice on teaching was restricted to a single day at the beginning of each year.

One year it was decided that we should learn from observation. Who better to show us how to lecture than the vice-chancellor himself? So Professor Brownlie gave a demonstration stage one economics lecture. It was polished, well organised and entertaining – and delivered without notes.

Afterwards, while we were considering our own lecturing inadequacies over tea and biscuits, I overheard one professor say to another, 'Brilliant lecture, but did you notice that he split an infinitive?'

There are still people around, like that professor, who seem to have special antennae for detecting split infinitives. In case these have passed you by in school grammar lessons, an infinitive is a base verb like 'love' preceded by the particle 'to'. The rule is that you mustn't put another word between the 'to' and 'love'. So you can decide 'to replant your garden gradually', but, according to the rule, on no account may you decide 'to gradually replant your garden'. That would be a split infinitive.

Where did this rule come from? Like a number of rules taught in school grammar books it came from Latin. Those writing traditional grammars of English believed that rules for Latin could also be applied to English. This produced some very peculiar outcomes because Latin and English are different languages.

Have you ever wondered about the grammar rule that says we must say 'It is I' and not 'It's me'? Blame a Latin rule for that.

Because the infinitive was a single word in Latin – *amare* (to love) – the grammarians decided that 'to love' in English must also be taken as a single unit. And that's where the rule forbidding split infinitives came from.

In my experience, the split infinitive is a topic that still seems to inflame passions. I suppose those who had this rule drilled into them at school feel justified in seeking out split infinitives and condemning those who use them.

In the 1990s I wrote a grammar of English for New Zealand school teachers. In it I remarked that the ban on the split infinitive was misguided. I explained that some adverbs need to go before the verb: I ought to flatly refuse. She decided to gradually sell the books she had collected. He has failed to adequately provide for his children.

At the end of this section I wrote (tongue in cheek): 'We have to sometimes revise old grammatical rules.' This did not please the woman who edited the grammar for the publisher and she tried to change it to: 'We have sometimes to revise.'

How many people know about split infinitives today? Justin is 16. I asked him if he knew what a split infinitive was and he replied, 'Wouldn't have a clue.' If Justin is typical, then the rule about split infinitives won't be troubling people in future. We will all be able to boldly go where no one has gone before.

# To Mum of Kaitaia

*29 December 2007*

SINCE I BEGAN WRITING THIS column in August, two topics have produced a particularly lively response.

One was about the design of modern pushchairs, where the child can't communicate with the person doing the pushing. It seems that lots of grandparents have been complaining about this for a long time.

Some were especially bothered by children being covered in plastic or under a shade-cloth – 'in a plastic cell' – as one writer put it. Another correspondent wrote, 'I've spent 14 months full time as personal assistant to my granddaughter. The pushchair outings were spoilt by not being able to talk face to face. I continually stop to stand in front and have a conversation.'

I think if an enterprising manufacturer developed a pushchair facing the other way, which could also be folded up easily, there would be money in it. If it were advertised as 'the pushchair where you can talk to your child', the grannies would certainly be out there promoting sales.

The second topic that produced an interesting postbag was on mondegreens – where people mishear words, often a line from a song or a poem or a hymn. Alan Tunnicliffe always thought the coal range was a 'cold range', even though it got hot. I liked the story about the children burying a dead sparrow in the garden with the prayer: 'In the name of the Father and of the Son, and into the hole 'e goes.'

Alice was sent a tea-towel from Scotland with the words of 'Auld Lang Syne'. She found to her surprise that the words were: 'We'll take a cup of kindness yet.' For years she'd been singing, 'We'll take a cup of wine midships.'

Some people had some quite creative versions of Sunday School hymns. Ruth Yusaf sang the line: 'Pity my simplicity' as 'Pity mice in Plicity'. She wrote, 'I did not know where or what Plicity was, but believed my Sunday School teacher would know, and I didn't need to ask.'

These are examples of the human ability to work hard to make sense of things – and perhaps also to accept some quite strange possibilities. I remember some from my own children. My son John once asked us what 'oily' meant. He was about five and my husband had a happy time explaining the difference between oil and water, with practical demonstrations. John looked puzzled. 'Then why are the children in Sunday School oily?' He had been singing 'Praise Him, praise Him, all ye little children' as 'Praise Him, praise Him, oily little children'.

My youngest daughter, Charlotte, once asked me to sing the song about the little girl. 'You know. The one about little Thought Eye.' That was a puzzle. We found it was 'The Ashgrove' – 'Ah then, little thought I how soon we should part.'

Do you remember Paul McCartney's song 'Mull of Kintyre'? 'O mist rolling in from the sea'? Paul Edwards described listening to a Sunday request session on the radio.

'A lady rang up asking for a song dear to her heart. Please play the song by Paul McCartney dedicated to Mum of Kaitaia, and Mr Rowling's in from the sea.' Now there's a genuinely New Zealand mondegreen.

# Vanished into the darkness

*5 January 2008*

IN THE 1960s ENGLISH WAS a popular university subject. If you wanted to continue in English there was a compulsory unit called Early English Language Studies, commonly known as EELS. Here we learnt about Old English (sometimes called Anglo-Saxon) and Middle English, the language of the time of Chaucer. In the MA course there was another compulsory paper – on *Beowulf*, the great Anglo-Saxon epic poem.

Compulsion produces grumblers, and I was a grumbler.

At that time I was studying English to understand poetry, novels and plays, not to learn about verbs in an ancient language that would be no use in later life. But I can now look back with a different view. Elements from those Early English language classes keep coming back.

I remember how Anglo-Saxon speech-makers didn't just speak – they 'unlocked their word hoards'.

Years later, in university faculty meetings, I observed important men unlocking their word-hoards. I remember the poem called 'The Dream of the Rood' – a moving account of the crucifixion from the viewpoint of the cross – and there were stories about Anglo-Saxon saints such as Caedmon, Cuthbert and Edmund.

*Beowulf* was a stirring poem about a legendary Scandinavian hero: it was based on Germanic myths mixed with Christian elements. It had graphic accounts of battles; swords and shields had secret inscriptions and magical powers. There was Grendel, the monster in human form living in the fens, and, even more frightening, Grendel's mother.

I'm not surprised that *The Lord of the Rings* has been so popular. Tolkien was a professor of Anglo-Saxon. When you've studied *Beowulf*, *The Lord of the Rings* seems very familiar.

I was fortunate to be able to read the literature of this early stage of the English language. It's part of my culture. Students today are not so lucky.

53

It has been some years since Old English and Middle English were taught in the University of Canterbury English programme. This period of English language and literature went out of fashion. Perhaps people thought it was no longer relevant.

Maybe one day Old English and Middle English will be rediscovered. I hope so. Students might once again read stories in the earliest form of the English language. They would learn about those dwellers in the British Isles over a thousand years ago and discover what people living then thought about life.

I'll give you a taste. Here's an extract from a book written by the Venerable Bede in 731, translated from Old English. He describes an Anglo-Saxon council debating whether to accept Christianity. One of the chiefs stands up to speak:

'The present life of man ... is like the swift flight of a lone sparrow through the banqueting hall ... Inside there is a comforting fire to warm the room; outside, the wintry storms of snow and rain are raging. While he is inside, he is safe from the winter storms; but after a few moments of comfort, he vanishes from sight into the darkness whence he came. Similarly, man appears on earth for a little while, but we know nothing of what went before this life, and what follows. Therefore if this new teaching can reveal any more certain knowledge, it seems only right we should follow it.'

# The long and short of A

*12 January 2008*

AT A THEATRE IN NEW YORK there is going to be a revival of George Bernard Shaw's play *Pygmalion* – the story of Eliza Doolittle, the London flower girl who became socially elevated by way of speech lessons. Apparently they've brought in a dialect coach from England to assist.

Jefferson Mays, who is playing Professor Henry Higgins, has been listening to archival recordings from the Edwardian period – to Lord Baden-Powell, Lord Asquith and Sir Arthur Conan Doyle. According to the *New Yorker*,

> the drawback in using archival material as a guide was that not every old Brit was consistent in his accent. Mays noticed, for example, that Conan Doyle waffled between 'ask' and 'ahsk'.

Jefferson Mays obviously doesn't know about language change. Conan Doyle said both 'ask' and 'ahsk' not because he was a waffler, but because that's what happens when sounds change. You get variation.

In the 18th century 'ask' had a short vowel, like the vowel in 'hat'. (You still hear this in the north of England today). By the end of the century, in the south of England, it was changing, and people began to use the long 'a' that we use in New Zealand today.

New Zealanders were commenting on the vowel in 'ask' in the early 1900s. In 1909 there was a letter in the literary journal the *Triad*:

> Many people, especially those who boast a college education, give such words as grass, brass, casting, class, master, aspect, the absurd pronunciation of grarse, brarse, carsting, clarse, marster, arspect. Why is this thus?

*Truth* newspaper responded:

> Dance pronounced 'dahnce' is as good English as dance pronounced with the so called 'short a'. May the Lord preserve the English language from prigs and pedants.

It's interesting that *Truth* mentions 'dance'. Words with 'a' before 'n' retained the short 'a' for much longer. We know this from recordings of old New Zealanders in the Radio New Zealand Sound Archives. Many old New Zealanders used to pronounce words like chance and dance to rhyme with 'ants'. My father did. There are elderly members of my husband's family who still pronounce names like Francis or Alexandra with the short 'a'.

In 1936 Arnold Wall said the two pronunciations of chance and dance were equally good, but the short 'a' was more common in New Zealand.

Since the 1930s things have changed. New Zealanders now say chance and dance to rhyme with 'aunts'. If you use the ants pronunciation, people will ask which part of Australia you come from. We've changed to the new form; Australians have retained the old. Was this because we were deliberately trying to sound different from Australians? Who knows?

By the 1930s the particular way New Zealanders pronounced the long 'a' had become a characteristic feature of our accent. Today, it still makes the New Zealand accent distinctive. Visitors have commented on it over the years – and never favourably. Here's Mr A. N. Fitzgerald, an Englishman writing in the *Education Gazette* in 1934: 'It was illuminating to hear the young voices attempting such exercises as "Arthur has parked his large car in Armagh Street". It sounded too much like the sound of the lamb.'

And I say baa to him too.

# What do you know?

*19 January 2008*

I HAVE A GOOD FRIEND WHO for this column I'll call Myrtle. She takes care with her appearance, wears gloves and a hat when she goes to town and complains about the way people 'misuse' the English language.

At the top of her list of linguistic miscreants are those who say 'you know' and 'you see' in their conversations. I think she has the vain hope that I might be able to do something about this.

Another friend, Jonathan, agrees with Myrtle. ' "You know" annoys me because it's redundant,' he says.

Jonathan is a logical man. I'd been telling him about our bach, where rainwater had been seeping in through the back wall (you know?) and we've had problems with the drains (you know?). Maybe Jonathan has a point. I don't need to ask him if he knows – he's stayed in our bach when it rained.

But I'm not going to wage a campaign against 'you know' and 'you see' because I think they're valuable little language devices. People like Myrtle and Jonathan don't realise it, but they're basing their objections on conventions of written language.

You don't see 'you knows' in writing. Our education system devotes hundreds of hours to reading and writing, so it's natural that Myrtle and Jonathan think written language is the 'proper' form. They think features that appear only when we speak must somehow be wrong, or at least not so good.

Conversations involve at least two people – a speaker and a listener; with turn-taking these roles are then reversed. There are people who are wonderful conversationalists. They have the ability to draw you in, so you want to be part of the conversation. They don't harangue you or talk *at* you. One of the ways they bring you in is to use connecting devices – 'you know?' They're saying, 'Are you with me?'

There are other connecting devices we can use in conversation. Asking a question is one, or using a tag-question. 'It was shocking, wasn't it?'

Some useful linguistic conversational supports have a bad press too. They get on lists of 'things I hate in language use'. One is the little particle 'eh'. This has a number of functions in speech and one is to act like a tag question. 'It was shocking, eh?'

Another connecting device has the grand-sounding title of 'high rising terminal contour', or HRT for short. (In Canada it's called 'uptalk'.) This is when the voice goes up at the end of a statement. It's not a question, it's a connecting device. 'Are you with me?'

Sometimes the literal meaning of what we're saying is less important than its function. When you say, 'It's a lovely day today' to a shopkeeper you're not telling that shopkeeper something new. Both you and the shopkeeper know it's a lovely day, so why bother to say it? The function of your greeting is not to give meteorological information – it's to show friendliness.

It's another way of making connections with people.

When I next see Myrtle and tell her about our problems with the bach in the rain, it's possible she might respond: 'You've done it again – you've just said "you know" '. Now that's a real conversation killer, eh?

# Pulling the rules apart

*26 January 2008*

Twenty years ago my husband and I went to teach in China. A fellowship had been set up at the time of the University of Canterbury's centenary, so university staff could teach in a developing country.

In 1986 we packed our bags and went to the Wuhan Technical University of Surveying and Mapping, where I taught English and my husband taught surveying.

But the authorities in Wuhan also gave my husband an English class – after all, he was a native English speaker so they assumed it would be easy for him to teach a bit of English on the side.

It wasn't long before he was in trouble.

When you're a native speaker of a language you learn the rules of your language without anyone sitting down and teaching them to you. But if someone asks you to explain one of these rules, that's another matter.

We found the students in China had difficulty with the English articles – when to use the definite article 'the' and the indefinite article 'a', and when not to use an article at all.

They don't have articles in Chinese.

A student called Shi Jian wrote an essay about an earthquake, and described how his family moved into a tent that was lit by a lamp at night.

Shi Jian wrote: 'Very often gale came up and blew out light.'

A native English speaker could easily get a pencil and correct that sentence. As my husband found out, that bit was easy. The hard part was when Shi Jian asked him to explain why we say 'a gale', but 'the light'.

My husband had been using his articles perfectly all his life but he had never had to think about them consciously.

I spent time with my students in Wuhan teaching them place names – they were students of surveying and mapping. I had to teach them the rules of English that produce 'Mount Cook' without an article but 'the

Southern Alps' with one. 'Lake Tekapo' without an article but 'the river Avon' or 'the Avon River' with one.

In language nothing appears by chance; nothing is haphazard; everything is governed by rules.

This is why we can recognise older British tourists, and not just by their socks under their sandals. They say they have been travelling 'in North Island' when every New Zealander knows that we travel 'in the North Island'.

A year ago we moved to live in New Brighton. I can say that I now live 'in New Brighton' and I can also say I live 'at New Brighton'. I have friends who live 'in Sumner' or 'at Sumner'. My daughter used to live 'in Leeston' or 'at Leeston'.

But what if we'd moved to Fendalton?

We could live 'in Fendalton', but we certainly couldn't live 'at Fendalton'. That sounds wrong.

So there must be a rule that native speakers know, that tells them which places they can live both 'in' or 'at', and which places they can only live 'in'.

I haven't worked it out yet, but it's something to puzzle about while I'm waiting for the bus. Any suggestions?

# Watching speech grow

*2 February 2008*

It's been a good summer and we've spent time with our grandchildren. They live in other cities, so we see them only intermittently. Every time we meet we're amazed at the changes that have taken place, and I'm especially interested in their language development.

Makerita was born in December. She's the fourth child in her family and the older children treat her with aggressive affection. For the most part she sleeps and feeds, with periods of wakefulness when she stares around her and sometimes cries. We lean over her bassinette telling her she's lovely.

Annabel is nine months old, and is the first child in her family. She can crawl and pull herself up on furniture. She waves and claps her hands. Her language is at the babbling stage: 'bub bub bub, mum mum mum'. Her parents like to think she's naming them but it's a bit soon for that. When she babbles, variations in pitch make it sound rather like talking and we respond by saying: 'Is that so, Annabel?'

Christopher is 18 months old, walking and feeding himself. He understands lots of language and can follow simple requests – 'go and sit on the beanbag'. He's at the one-word stage in language development and has useful food words – bread, apple, honey, juice – and animal words – dog, duck, cow. People name things for him and he tries to copy them. 'Look, Christopher, it's a giraffe!' And he will say 'raff'.

Frankie is three. He can run and jump and climb and ask questions and tell us about events at his preschool. He knows some of his favourite books by heart. He speaks with a lisp so that Christmas is 'Chrithmath' but I expect this won't last. He still uses regular verb inflections for irregular verbs: 'I eated it', 'I holded it'.

Kathleen is almost five. She can play simple card games, she likes 'knock knock' jokes and is constantly asking questions. And she can

61

produce an annoying tone of voice that all parents recognise as whining. Kathleen likes stories: 'Tell me a story from your head, Granny.'

When I tell her about when her father was a little boy she wants to know where she was at that time. She hasn't yet mastered passive verbs. If I say, 'The car is bumped by the truck,' she thinks the car bumped the truck. If I ask her to show me teddy being patted by dolly, she will make the teddy do the patting. But this is a trivial matter that will be sorted within a year or so. Kathleen is now a fluent English speaker.

These children are all at different stages on the language development road.

Some reach milestones sooner than others. Kathleen reached the one-word stage at a year; Christopher didn't get there until he was 18 months. They progress at their own speed. They are not exceptional – they're doing what all humans are programmed to do: learn language.

I know how hard it is to learn a foreign language. Yet tiny children who can't do up their own shoelaces can pick up language so easily. I know it's not fashionable to believe in miracles, but this seems close to a miracle to me.

# The bell tolls for 'whom'

*9 February 2008*

When I was a student in London in the 1960s I worked as a tutor at the University of London Summer School of English. Looking back now, I think I probably learned more about the English language than my foreign students did.

There were times when I needed help, such as when students asked me about use of the word 'whom'. I went to the professor for advice because he was an expert on the English language. He said I should tell the students that they needn't worry about using 'whom' because it was no longer necessary in English. If they avoided it they wouldn't make mistakes.

I remembered this advice when I received a message from R. L. Clough from the Chatham Islands. I wasn't surprised to hear from Clough because he keeps a close eye on what's written in the newspaper.

He wrote a complaint to *The Press*:

> In her column (January 21), she starts with, 'I have a good friend who, for this column I'll call ...' That sentence should read, '... good friend whom for this column I'll call ...'

He asked me to comment on this.

I'm afraid Clough won't like my response, and traditionalists will be annoyed, but I still follow the 1960s advice of my London professor. For the most part 'whom' is now dead.

Are there any circumstances when I might use 'whom'?

I would normally say: 'Ben Watson was the man who I addressed the letter to.' If I wanted to be formal I could write: 'Ben Watson was the man to whom I addressed the letter.'

I would normally say: 'Emily's the child who I knitted the socks for.' In formal English I could write: 'Emily is the child for whom I knitted the socks.'

When George Bush used the slogan 'Who do you trust?' he was taken to task and told it should be 'Whom do you trust?' But what politician today would say 'whom'? It might please English traditionalists but it sounds like something out of the ark.

The problem with 'whom' is that for many English speakers now it's not part of their native language. We can manage perfectly well without it.

But there are some people who think they should use it and when they do they sometimes get it wrong. So you find people writing things like: 'The man whom he had been talking to', or 'We discussed whom should be invited to the wedding.'

It's as if 'whom' is rather grand, so people add it in an attempt to raise the tone – but then get it wrong.

It's the sort of hyper-correction that Hyacinth Bucket in the TV series *Keeping Up Appearances* might use. She answers the phone: 'Whom shall I say is speaking?'

So my advice is that unless you're certain you can use 'whom' appropriately it's better to avoid it. In everyday language you can get by perfectly well without it.

This newspaper column on language is not written in a formal style, so you probably won't find me using 'whom', unless of course the sub-editor decides to change the text in order to protect me from the complaints of the traditionalists.

# Breakfast from a melting pot

16 February 2008

I MET GRANT IN TOWN AND he asked me if I would write more about the origins of words. He also mentioned that he reads this column while he's eating his breakfast. So I thought I'd look for the origins of words relating to breakfast.

I'm not sure what Grant has for breakfast, but he might begin with cereal. 'Cereal' is a 19th-century borrowing from Latin *cerealis*, pertaining to agriculture. You can see the name of Ceres, the Roman goddess of agriculture. Porridge is a variant of *pottage*, Old French for the contents of a pot. Muesli, on the other hand, is Swiss German. Cornflakes have the English word 'corn', but 'flake' comes from the Scandinavian word *flak*. (Many Scandinavian words were borrowed into English after the Viking raids and settlements up to the 11th century.)

Grant might prefer rice bubbles. 'Rice' is a very old borrowing via French from Greek *oruza*, and 'bubbles' is a 14th-century Scandinavian borrowing. (Kelloggs' Rice Bubbles were first produced in America in 1928.) Cereals are better with milk, which is a home-grown English word from Old English 'milc'.

Perhaps Grant eats toast and marmalade. Toast came from Old French (after the Norman invasion in 1066), derived originally from the Latin *tostus* meaning parched or baked. (Our words 'thirst' and 'torrid' come from the same source.) Toast is better with butter, a borrowing from Latin, or maybe margarine, a 19th-century word derived from the Greek word *margaron*, a pearl. Marmalade came into English from Portuguese via French, from *marmelo*, a quince. (The original marmalade was made of quinces cooked with honey.)

Grant might prefer honey on his toast, and that's a true English word from Old English 'huneg'. On special occasions he might have a croissant, the French word for a crescent.

Some places serve a breakfast that I've seen called 'the works'. There's bacon (from Old French) and eggs (an early Scandinavian loan word). Tomatoes came via Spanish from Nahuatl, an Uto Aztecan language, and if Grant has yesterday's cold potatoes fried up they came via Spanish from Taino, an Arawakan language. Mushrooms are a good addition – a 15th-century borrowing from Old French *mousseron*. In America I had waffles and they come from the Dutch.

What does Grant drink at breakfast? His cup of tea comes from Chinese 't'e'. Sugar comes from Old French. If he drinks coffee, that came via Italian and Turkish from Arabic. For his orange juice, the orange came via French from Persian *narang*, and juice came from French. You see the French word *jus* used in posh restaurants.

When I began looking up breakfast words I was sure many would turn out to be borrowed from other languages but I was surprised just how many were. Pure English words are hard to find – the biblical 'milk' and 'honey'. But the word 'breakfast' is English. It comes from the Old English words 'break' and 'fast', the meal where you break the fast of the night.

The history of the English language is a story about contact with other languages. I hope I've demonstrated that most of our words for kai come from somewhere else.

# Words doing double duty

*23 February 2008*

SOMETIMES I GET LETTERS FROM people who are concerned about the meanings of words. One Greymouth writer was troubled by the word 'critical'. To her the idea of someone in a critical condition in hospital conjured up a picture of an 'annoyed, carping and downright argumentative patient'.

But words can have more than one meaning. The critical condition in hospital doesn't mean being negative. It relates to 'crisis' and involves risk.

Another correspondent to *The Press* complained about a 'hard man' of a criminal family being described as 'staunch'. The letter-writer wrote: 'What being trustworthy or loyal have to do with being a feared hard man I don't know.' The adjective 'staunch' has another meaning in gang culture, where it refers to someone who is dependable, especially in a fight or a tough spot.

I have read about words in other languages that have unusual meanings. For example there is a word in Tzeltal (a branch of the Maya language of Mexico) for a kind of language use that is 'speech by someone who comes to another's house and spends time talking even though the other is quite ill'. There is a word in the Fuegian language spoken in southern Argentina for two people looking at each other without speaking but each hoping the other will offer to do something that both parties desire but neither is willing to do.

These words have complex single meanings. But many words are like 'critical' and 'staunch', with more than one meaning.

In Samuel Johnson's *Dictionary of the English Language* published in 1755, he gives 64 senses for the verb 'to fall'. At the end he wrote: 'This is one of those general words of which it is very difficult to ascertain or detail the full signification.'

The problem with writing definitions for words came up in an episode of the TV series *Blackadder*. Blackadder's master, Prince George, was thinking of becoming the patron of Samuel Johnson. Unfortunately Baldrick, Blackadder's servant, used Johnson's dictionary to light a fire and it was the only copy. (Johnson in this episode said that making copies 'is like fitting wheels to a tomato – time-consuming and completely unnecessary'.)

So Blackadder sets about writing a new dictionary to replace the lost one. He starts with 'Aardvark: a medium-sized insectivore with protruding nasal implement'. Baldrick tries to help. He suggests that 'C' is 'a big blue wobbly thing that mermaids live in'. He is especially pleased with his definition of 'dog' – 'not a cat'.

The problem is resolved when they find that the dictionary wasn't burnt after all. But the episode demonstrates some of the challenges for lexicographers. At times they must feel a bit like St Augustine writing about the meaning of 'time': 'I know what it is until someone asks me.'

And words change their meanings or acquire additional meanings. I remember being surprised years ago to hear my bacon-and-egg pie described as 'wicked'. I have recently been told that for surfers a 'sick' wave is a good one, and a 'sick' party is really good.

Samuel Johnson defined a lexicographer as 'a writer of dictionaries, a harmless drudge'. We know he was joking.

# Cheerio to the cheerio

*1 March 2008*

WHEN I WAS GROWING UP there was a box in the wash-house containing shoe-cleaning materials – brushes, polishing pads and tins of nugget. Some of these tins were labelled Kiwi Shoe Polish, but we called the contents 'nugget', using the name of a different brand of shoe polish. When my mother cleaned the house she did the electroluxing. I understand that in Southland people still 'lux' their floors. Other people used to 'hoover'. These brand names have made their way into everyday language.

The English language has a long history of converting proper names into common nouns. Among the dried fruit are currants, which were raisins from Corinth, and muscatels, those flat dried grapes in boxes covered with cellophane that appear at Christmas-time, which came from Muscat in the Persian Gulf. Denim came from a French town and was originally 'serge de Nîmes'; bayonets came from another French town – Bayonne. Milliners originally came from Milan; sandwiches were named after the Earl of Sandwich, who used to eat them at the gaming table so he could keep on gambling. I remember seeing a bus in Ireland destined for Donnybrook, although you don't hear that word for a fight so often today.

The ease with which proper nouns can slip into everyday language can cause problems. I understand there are people in our Ministry of Foreign Affairs and Trade who spend time dealing with names like champagne and parmesan. Should these words be restricted to wine from the Champagne Ardenne region of France, or cheese from Parma in Italy, or can we produce champagne and parmesan in New Zealand? Does sherry have to come from Jerez in Spain, and port from Oporto in Portugal?

In 2005 I gave a public lecture in Christchurch where I referred to 'cheerios' – those small pink sausages so loved at children's parties.

The name 'cheerio' was devised by the manager of J. C. Huttons, manufacturers of Swan bacon, because he always said cheerio rather than goodbye. I had noticed these were now being labelled 'cocktail sausages'. When I asked my butcher about this, he told me they called them 'cheerios' in the back of the shop but 'cocktail sausages' in the window.

In my talk I expressed regret that the New Zealand cheerio was being chased out by the interloping cocktail sausage.

Soon after this I received a four-page lawyer's letter telling me that 'cheerio' was a trademark registered to Mainland Products, and I must always refer to them as 'CHEERIOS™ – cocktail sausages'. I wasn't the only one. Children at Christchurch's Parkside Preschool Kindergarten and Nursery had shared a multicultural lunch that included sushi and cheerios. This had been commended in a newsletter of the Human Rights Commission. The preschool also received a lawyer's letter telling them not to use the word cheerios.

Unfortunately for Mainland Products, every New Zealand dictionary gives 'cheerio' as a generic, and not as a registered trademark. There are citations dating from 1953. It's also used in Australia. I can see that French people might want to preserve their champagne brand name because it's an expensive wine. But cheerios are hardly in the same league. I think it's sad that big business can kill off a fine little New Zealand word.

# The power of a name

*8 March 2008*

'MARGARET GORDON, PLEASE.' WHEN A receptionist announces this it still takes me a moment to register that the call is for me.

For some strange reason my parents gave me two names – Margaret Elizabeth – but then went on to call me Elizabeth. Was this confusion or was it fashion? And I'm not alone. I know a number of people of my age and older who are addressed by their second name. And we all complain about the complications it causes.

The strange thing is that I sometimes get addressed as Margaret by people who couldn't possibly know that it's my first name.

When I explained to a WEA tutor last year that my name was actually Elizabeth she replied that she knew it was but she always thought I 'seemed like a Margaret'.

What does this mean? Is there some kind of natural connection between me and the name Margaret? The tutor thinks so, although I know very well that I was named after my mother.

The question about the origin of words was one that interested the Ancient Greeks and they had lively debates about it. Plato's dialogue *The Cratylus* was on this very subject.

On the one side were those who said there was a natural connection between a referent and its name and people should try to find it. ('Etymology' was the search for *etumon* – true word meanings.)

On the other side were those who argued that there was no such natural connection – we name things as we do because there is a general agreement to do so.

If you ask a small child why that animal that says 'woof woof' is called a dog, the child will probably reply, 'Because it *is* a dog.'

In other words the child thinks that 'dog' is its right and natural name. But with experience the child will learn that our English word 'dog' is arbitrary and is different in other languages – in French it's *chien*, in Maori it's kuri.

These names are the creations of the human mind that we use by general agreement. And because there's no natural connection between words and their referents there's nothing to stop us changing them.

You might decide not to use the word dog. Maybe you'll call the animal a 'drig', but I doubt you'll get very far.

'Dog' works perfectly well, so why bother to change it? As the Swiss linguist Ferdinand de Saussure wrote, 'Collective inertia prevents innovation.'

The argument that language is arbitrary and that word meanings are just the result of an agreed convention is a powerful one. Aristotle taught it and linguists today adopt it. But it doesn't stop some people believing in their hearts that there really is a natural connection between some names and their referents.

A student once told me that she and her husband had chosen the name Emma for their forthcoming child. When the baby was born they looked at her and realised that she wasn't an Emma at all, so they named her Lucy.

What makes a baby seem like a Lucy and not an Emma?

And why do people keep calling me Margaret? I wish I knew.

# Women on air

*15 March 2008*

EARLY IN MY UNIVERSITY TEACHING life, a student asked me if there were differences between the way men and women speak. I said I thought they were pretty much the same. I feel embarrassed about my answer now. The difference between the language of women and men has been a lively research topic for the past 40 years.

A lot of what lay people write and say about women's language comes into the category of folk-linguistics. This works on the principle that if you say something often enough, in the end people will believe it's true, even if there's no evidence to back it up. You can see this with jokes about talkative women. 'I haven't spoken to my wife for 18 months – I don't like to interrupt her.'

In kindergarten my children sang about 'the wheels on the bus'. The mothers on the bus went 'chat chat chat' while the fathers on the bus went 'nod nod nod'. I thought things might have changed but I've heard my grandchildren singing this.

The generalisation that women always talk more than men isn't true. It's folk-linguistics. Research has shown that in public men talk more than women; women are more likely to talk more in private and at home.

In early copies of the *New Zealand Listener* you can find discussions about women's language. The burning issue then was whether women's voices should be allowed at all over the airwaves. The general opinion in the 1940s was that they shouldn't.

One article was illustrated by Russell Clark. He showed a woman standing in front of a microphone surrounded by people pointing their fingers at her and laughing.

The arguments against women broadcasters also come into the category of folk-linguistics. Women's voices were said to be unsuitable. One man wrote: 'Most women tend to produce a flat impersonal feeling on air, a lack of vocal variety.' Another said: 'Nearly all women let their maternal instincts creep into their voices.'

They also said that women broadcasters might offend people from other countries, especially from 'certain Asian communities'. One man wrote: 'News or commentaries given in a female voice would be objectionable to these communities, but a male voice is acceptable everywhere.'

A Presbyterian minister joined the debate: 'I find it seldom that a woman speaker is as impressive as a man, and I do feel that women are more inclined to listen to men than men are inclined to listen to women.'

Someone from commercial broadcasting said there were always many objections if they 'put a woman on for announcing', but this didn't apply to 'talks on domestic subjects – cooking, children's care and so on, which are without doubt best done by women'.

This debate took place long ago and women have long since taken their place with men in front of the microphone. But it's easy to forget that this took a struggle. There were no women announcers on the BBC until 1976, when Anne Every was allowed to read the news for the first time. I once wrote the script for a broadcast talk about attitudes towards women's language and broadcasting. It was rejected. It wasn't considered a suitable topic for the Concert Programme. That was in 1988.

# Valuing the visual

*22 March 2008*

IN 1994 THERE WAS A major event in the English teaching world in New Zealand: the launch of a new English curriculum.

At the time there was concern that some English teachers in New Zealand didn't know enough about the English language, so the Department of Education commissioned a book called *Exploring Language*. I was called in to help, and before I knew it I was elevated to principal developer. The task was a daunting one. The small group working on this project were asked to produce a book containing 'everything we would like teachers to know about language'. It was to be written in non-academic language for secondary English teachers and all primary teachers. It wasn't an easy task, but over about three years we worked closely with many teachers and the book was written.

The new English curriculum recognised three strands of language – oral, written and visual. In the beginning I was unsure about 'visual language' but I became converted to its importance.

When I was growing up, education concentrated on reading and writing. The new curriculum recognised that the world had changed since then. By 1994 it was obvious that film, television, print advertising, computer games and other strongly visual media were playing an important part in the lives of school pupils. So the question was being asked – shouldn't we be giving these pupils the skills and terminology to describe, analyse and evaluate the visual aspects of language as well as the spoken and written aspects?

The concept of 'visual language' quickly came under attack. Critics said the English classroom should be concerned only with reading and writing. The Education Forum commissioned a highly critical report.

In 1994 we had no idea of the changes that would take place over the next 14 years. Now it seems that those who wrote that new English curriculum were visionary. What does literacy mean for children today? It's not just reading books and writing essays. The students' world today has been described as 'media saturated'. They sit in front of computer screens, watch films and TV, create web pages, read and write blogs, get involved with social network sites such as Bebo, Facebook and MySpace. Today those three strands of language – oral, written and visual – are completely integrated in ways we could not have imagined in 1994. (I've been told that this integration has been recognised in the revised national curriculum, which will appear in a few years.)

All this has led to significant developments in English teaching. There are so many more new and different possibilities than there were when I sat in a classroom over 50 years ago. All we had then were written texts, which we sometimes read aloud.

It makes me sad that the university departments of film studies and American studies in the College of Arts at the University of Canterbury might be closed. This is where the effects of visual language are taught and studied. This is where future teachers are being educated so that they can teach children whose world is so vastly different from mine. I can't think why anyone would want to turn back the clock and return to the English lessons in textbooks like *Plain Sailing*. I hope it doesn't happen.

# Ins and ats of suburbia

*29 March 2008*

IN JANUARY I WROTE ABOUT language rules – those rules that children learn when they learn to speak. I explained that all language is governed by rules – we don't just make things up.

When we think something 'sounds wrong' there must be a rule that's been broken. Linguists have a happy time working out what these rules are.

I mentioned that I now live 'in' New Brighton but I can also say that I live 'at' New Brighton. If I'd moved to Fendalton I could only live 'in' Fendalton.

I wondered what the rule was and asked for suggestions. Several people told me they got out their pencils and paper and tried to work it out. Some sent their suggestions.

Chris Goodyear thought 'in' referred to a general area but 'at' to a more specific locale. The Woolworths supermarket is 'at' Ferrymead but they live 'in' Brookhaven.

Anne Godfrey suggested that we live 'out at' New Brighton, which is on the periphery of the city, whereas Fendalton is within the city.

John Ewan wrote:

> It's to do with whether a place is seen as a stand-alone entity.
> We ourselves live both 'in' and 'at' Sumner (which in its earlier
> days was a borough separate from the city, and was, until quite
> recently seen as a long way away from the city). Similarly, with
> New Brighton …
>
> People live 'in' Fendalton, or St Martins or Hornby because
> they're part of the greater whole, i.e. Christchurch.

A place in the middle of change is Prebbleton. It was a hamlet a distance out of Christchurch, and people would live 'at' Prebbleton. Now, with a number of subdivisions and many houses being built there, I am not surprised when people tell me that they live 'in' Prebbleton.

Maurice Cook wrote:

'I live at Lincoln' means I live in the vicinity of Lincoln, but 'I live in Lincoln' means 'I live in Lincoln township'. Perhaps if you wait 50 years then Lincoln will be part of Christchurch and everyone will say 'I live in Lincoln'.

I discussed this question with my former colleague Robin Barrett. He once taught English to German students and he still has his old textbook.

The rule in his book was that choice of preposition depended on size. You live 'in' a larger town or city, and 'at' a smaller place. So you live in London but at Stratford-on-Avon.

So this more or less fits with some of the answers I received. You can live in Timaru, but at Fairlie.

Within Christchurch there were once outlying boroughs – Brighton, Sumner, Riccarton. My grandparents lived 'at' Riccarton. Their property on Middleton Road was sold after the war because it was too far out from the city.

The fact that Brighton and Sumner now have a choice of 'in' or 'at' has been explained by John Ewan. The old usage 'at Brighton' or 'out at Sumner' dates from an earlier time but it's still heard.

But there's also a newer usage that follows the general pattern of suburbs within the city – in Linwood, in Aranui, in Brighton.

George wrote: 'You're lucky to have a choice. I live *on* St Andrews Hill.'

# Linguistic extinction

*5 April 2008*

IN JANUARY AN 89-YEAR-OLD WOMAN called Marie Smith Jones died in Anchorage, Alaska. She was blind, had been a heavy smoker and drinker and was the mother of nine children. She had worked in a salmon-canning factory.

The British newspaper the *Guardian Weekly* has devoted two pages to Marie Smith Jones. There is an article about her in the *Economist*.

So what was so special about this old woman?

The answer is that she was the last full-blooded member of the Eyak people of southern Alaska. And she was the last speaker of the Eyak language. Her language was known to be endangered – when she was born there were only 38 speakers of Eyak left. Her people had suffered from smallpox, measles and influenza, and from colonialism.

At school Marie was prevented from using her language. When she married a white man, she didn't pass her language on to her children. Her sister died in the early 1990s and since then she'd had no one to talk to in her mother tongue.

This is a familiar story to people who are concerned about language death.

We are fortunate that Marie Smith Jones trusted a linguist called Michael Krauss, of the University of Alaska. She spent hours working with Krauss to record her language, and there is now a dictionary and a grammar.

The subject of endangered languages and language death has been of great concern to linguists.

At the University of Canterbury, Lyle Campbell was a professor in the Linguistics Department for 10 years. He's a world expert on American Indian languages and was awarded the Bloomfield Medal twice for his work. (In the linguistic world this is the equivalent of the Nobel Prize and as far as I know he's the only person to have received this honour twice.)

Campbell had spent much of his earlier working life in remote and difficult places recording languages that were in danger of being lost. In New Zealand he had a special interest in the Maori language and was concerned about its survival. In 2004 he moved to Salt Lake City, Utah, where he became director of the Centre for American Indian Languages. Today he is documenting three endangered languages in northern Argentina, and doing the same for several Mesoamerican languages that are near to extinction.

I wonder if linguistic students at the University of Canterbury realised how lucky they were to have had such a teacher. I remember him lecturing on language death, and the sense of urgency he conveyed about the need to save and revitalise endangered languages. With the death of a language we lose valuable linguistic information. We also lose information about culture, stories, and knowledge of plants with medicinal value. As Krauss said about the death of Eyak: 'Every language is a treasury of human experience.'

In a world where languages are dying every year, the survival of the Maori language in New Zealand is a success story. The story of kohanga reo is an example of what can be done. This is important not just for New Zealand but for the world.

# Clarification of an article

*12 April 2008*

A FEW WEEKS AGO I WROTE a column about language rules. I explained that when we were teaching in China my husband was asked to teach an English class. His students asked him the rule for using the definite article 'the' and the indefinite article 'a'.

He couldn't explain this to them, even though he uses these articles appropriately every day of his life.

One student had written about an earthquake when his family slept in a tent lit by a lamp. He wrote: 'Gale came and blew out lamp.'

Wendy Floyd has written to ask me why we say 'a gale' came and blew out 'the lamp'. Bill is helping a Thai student with his English and he has asked the same question.

The rules for this are complex. I looked up Sir Randolph Quirk's 1770-page book, *A Comprehensive Grammar of English*, and found over 60 pages devoted to the word class 'determiner' where articles belong. So my response in 500 words will be simple and basic and certainly not the whole story.

We use the definite article 'the' when something has already been mentioned, or we know what's being talked about.

If I say: 'The cat knocked over a pot plant' we know about the cat, but it's a vague pot plant.

If I said: 'A cat knocked over the pot plant' then I don't know which cat did it, but I know which pot plant it was.

When new information is first added we use 'a' but after that we change to 'the'.

I'll write my own version of the Chinese student's story to illustrate how this works. 'The family lived in A tent. THE tent was lit by A lamp. A gale blew out THE lamp. THE gale also blew over A chair. THE chair was broken.'

There are other times when we use 'the'. One is called *the unique use of* 'the'. We use it for objects, people or places that are unique in the world: the North Pole, the Earth, the equator, the sea, the beach, the Renaissance, the Queen, the Prime Minister.

We also use 'the' for institutions shared by the community. He read it in the paper. I saw it on the television. We caught the train to Picton.

In some examples the use or non-use of 'the' can change a noun from specific to generic. 'Pass the butter please' (specific). When it's omitted it becomes generic: 'Butter has become much more expensive.'

The singing was wonderful (specific). She loves singing and dancing (generic). Look at the cows (specific). Cows are very lucrative animals (generic).

When I began this column I thought it would be straightforward. Then I began to read more about the use of articles in English and I realised that there are complex rules involved in their use.

These rules are part of the grammar of English that you won't find in school grammar books – because we don't need them. Native speakers learn these rules without instruction when they learn their language, and they get them right. It's the Chinese students who need to learn the rules because they don't have articles in Chinese.

I sometimes hear people saying that children today don't know any grammar. Yeah, right!

# The old vers the new

THIS COLUMN HAS PRODUCED SOME interesting correspondence. Sometimes there's more than I can answer, and I can't always respond with the detail that some writers would like.

Some people have written with suggestions for columns and I've filed these away for the future. What I have very much enjoyed are the observations of people who have noticed changes in New Zealand English.

Some of these are new to me – I obviously move in different circles from the writers.

David Small has alerted me to a new transitive verb, 'to vers'. He has heard: 'Who are you versing? We versed them last week. We were going to vers them but it got cancelled.'

Small says he's never heard a sports commentator use it (yet) but he wrote: 'Every Kiwi kid knows and uses it and so do lots of adults.'

Well, this is a new verb for me – I'm out of touch with the age group and the people who are using it. I thought I should get some expert help so I asked Tony Deverson if he had come across it.

Deverson is co-editor of the *New Zealand Oxford Dictionary* and the senior lexicographer at the New Zealand Dictionary Centre at Victoria University in Wellington, where they manage a database of New Zealand English that is always being updated.

The verb 'to vers' is familiar to Deverson. He's heard it used by an eight-year-old boy playing computer games.

Of course the story begins with 'versus'. 'It's Canterbury versus Otago.' (Versus comes from the Latin word *vertere* – to turn.)

This preposition has now been shortened in everyday language and you will hear: 'It's Canterbury vers Otago.' Deverson believes that this usage has been around for a long time and I've certainly heard it. The shift from preposition to verb, however, is more recent.

The New Zealand Dictionary Centre database has this citation from the *Dominion Post*, September 2004: 'Schoolboy rugby is reported to have given us the charming neologism 'versing'. Cameron Williamson writes that his nine-year-old son's mates are in the habit of bursting in through the back door, yelling, "Who are we versing on Saturday?" Then attention is likely to turn to Gameboy or PlayStation, in which contestants are locked in battle, "versing" each other to death.'

The verb 'vers' is now part of New Zealand English, but Deverson also reports that it's being heard in Australia. So far it is not in any British dictionary.

So I've learned something new. But the processes that have produced vers, versed and versing are not new.

Many words have been shortened, and others change their word class – in this case from a preposition to a verb. This is the process that produced the verbs in these sentences: They downed tools when the boss shouted at them. She will off and do her own thing. The actor was outed.

Deverson gave me another example of a word that has had a recent change of function. Apparently there's now a verb 'to podium'. You can use it if you come first, second or third on the podium.

Maybe we'll hear more about athletes podiuming around the time of the Olympics.

# The tomato problem

*26 April 2008*

WHEN MY CHILDREN WERE SMALL we devised games we could play on car journeys.

One game they used to enjoy we called fruit and vegetables. We would call out a word and they had to say whether it was a fruit or a vegetable. The reason they enjoyed this game was because it was easy.

They seemed to have no trouble categorising items. Someone from outer space might think that a pumpkin and a rock melon were similar, but little children know that one is a vegetable and the other is a fruit. The one big difficulty was always with tomato. They said this was a fruit, whereas I think it's a vegetable.

I used this exercise with my university students. I asked them to work out the criteria they used to distinguish fruit and vegetables in everyday usage. This always resulted in long and lively discussions. They would bring forward various criteria – some were botanical, some were functional. Does it grow on trees? Do you eat it for dinner or for pudding? Does it grow in the vegetable garden? Is pineapple on your ham steak a vegetable?

Every method of categorisation had its difficulties. The dictionary defines 'cucumber' as edible fruit. But my students insisted it was a vegetable. Tomato was a tricky one for them, too.

This exercise shows some of the complexities involved in the classifications we make every day.

If I ask, 'What is a chair?' I usually get an answer that involves a structure with four legs and a back, designed for a person to sit on. But what about a rocking chair, a deckchair, a dentist's chair and even a beanbag chair? They don't exactly fit the definition.

And we don't refer to objects with the same function in a picture theatre or in a car as chairs – they're seats.

A child of five has no trouble in deciding what is a chair and what is a seat, yet when you think about it, this process of naming involves amazing feats of generalisation.

So when you think of a chair, do you have a set of defining characteristics in your mind that you can tick off – back, seat, legs etc – or do you picture a prototypical chair in your mind – the most 'chairy' chair you can think of?

If you do it that way, I'm pretty sure your prototype will be more like a kitchen chair than a rocking chair, and certainly not a beanbag chair.

Defining characteristics are very useful when we want to categorise things like sets of odd or even numbers – we need to be exact.

But when it comes to chairs it's more likely that we have a picture of a typical chair somewhere in our memory and we match other seating devices to it. Some will be close to our prototype and some will be very different, but they will still have something in common.

I'm amazed at the way little children can name things.

How do they know that the St Bernard and the chihuahua are both dogs?

How do they know that lettuces, carrots and pumpkins are all vegetables? And why is the tomato always a problem?

# Lost in translation

*3 May 2008*

I HAVE A FRIEND CALLED DAVID Cooke who trained as a linguist. He worked in language education in Mozambique when that country became independent. Determining a national language policy for a newly independent country is important – it's easy to have conflict over language issues.

A country with a difficult language situation today is East Timor. We've heard much about New Zealand's peacekeeping efforts there over the past nine years. There are still many problems and some of these relate directly to language policies.

East Timor was under Portuguese rule until 1975, with a small Portuguese-educated elite. Then came 24 years of Indonesian domination when education and government was conducted in Bahasa Indonesian. In the law courts, schools, hospitals and in government everyone used Indonesian. In homes most people spoke indigenous languages. Tetum was the language used in Dili, and it was also the language of the Catholic Church.

When East Timor became independent in 1999 the new leaders (such as Xanana Gusmao and Jose Ramos-Horta) had been part of the Portuguese-speaking elite. They decreed that East Timor would have two standard languages – Portuguese and Tetum. The reasons for the choice involved national identity. The freedom fighters had been resisting Indonesian domination and were opposed to using the Indonesian language. There was also an underlying belief that Portuguese was a superior European language and Tetum was inferior. So Tetum remained a language for the home, and where formerly people had used Indonesian they had now to use Portuguese. (Linguists say that all languages are capable of doing whatever their speakers want to do, and there was no linguistic reason why Tetum could not have been used as an official language, but that's not how the Portuguese speakers saw it.)

This meant that teachers who had taught in Indonesian for 24 years suddenly had to teach in Portuguese, even though only 5 per cent of teachers, parents and children could speak it. East Timorese law had to be translated from Indonesian into Portuguese. Judges and court officials were sent to Portugal for language courses; lawyers from Portugal were sent out to East Timor to be judges. Delays in hearings were caused by a lack of Portuguese-speaking judges; litigants and lawyers struggled with the language.

Some members of the government resisted this language policy. The first Minister of Health after independence, Rui Aranjo, had trained at the University of Otago. He allowed the health sector to continue to work in Indonesian. (A friend of mine said: 'How sensible – I'd prefer that my surgeon could understand what was being said.') But Armindo Maia, the Minister of Education, a graduate of Massey University, championed the introduction of Portuguese from grade one.

Linguists cannot solve the problems of East Timor, but they can give advice. They can point out the importance of the mother tongue in early education. They can study prevailing attitudes to different languages and consider questions of language and national identity. In my view, the language policy in East Timor is hampering its efforts to achieve peaceful nationhood.

# Sledging and floordrobes

*10 May 2008*

IT WAS ALMOST EMBARRASSING WATCHING the cricket earlier in the year with the English visitors who were staying with us. As Jesse Ryder and Brendon McCullum hit their way to a 10-wicket victory our visitors became quieter and quieter. We changed the subject to sledging, which was a word they hadn't heard, although it's now in the main dictionaries.

We'd heard about sledging in reports of the confrontation between members of the Australian and Indian cricket teams. Apparently taunts and nasty comments were being exchanged. There's a report that former English cricketer Geoff Boycott was heard to say on the BBC that umpires who wanted a quiet life were 'turning a blind ear' to sledging.

Our visitors wanted to know where the word came from. My dictionaries suggest that it's a shortened form of 'sledgehammer'. But how did the word sledgehammer come to be used for taunts in a cricket match?

Michael Quinion (www.worldwidewords.org) has an excellent newsletter which I recommend, called *Worldwide Words*. It has all kinds of information about international English words from a British point of view. People write in with their queries and observations, and 'sledging' has cropped up there.

Quinion gave the dictionary derivation as being from sledgehammer, but contributors to his newsletter suggested a different origin. They said it was used by the Australian team captained by Ian Chappell in the 1970s, and came from the name of soul singer Percy Sledge. Sledge had a hit song in 1966, 'When a Man Loves a Woman', and he was popular with the cricketers at that time. The connection with abusive comments is that these were often attacks on mothers, lovers or sisters.

Quinion's newsletter also alerted me to the Words of the Year, a contest run by the Macquarie Dictionary in Sydney where readers can vote for their favourite new words from a given list. Some of the words

I recognised. There was a category called 'carbon terms' with words and phrases familiar in New Zealand such as 'carbon footprint' and 'carbon sequestration'. The category of travel included 'health travel' and 'slow travel'.

My favourites, however, were words that were new to me. I asked my husband if he knew what a 'floordrobe' was. He didn't, but he could easily guess. When our children were teenagers several of the bedroom floors in our house were floordrobes. Another new term with a transparent meaning was 'slummy mummy', which I guess is the opposite of a 'yummy mummy' – the attractive well-dressed mother. I also hadn't heard the term 'salad dodger' for an overweight person.

New words can be reflections of changes in society. I'd heard of the Australian 'white-shoe brigade' for unscrupulous Queensland property developers in the 1980s. Now Australia has a 'green-shoe brigade', for people who are looking for dubious ways to make a profit from the cause of protecting the environment.

Is nothing sacred?

# Somethink and nothink

*17 May 2008*

ONE OF THE HIGHLIGHTS OF our recent TV viewing was the BBC production of Charles Dickens' *Bleak House*. (Why on earth was this scheduled so late on Sunday evening? Thank goodness for the DVD recorder.)

One of the characters is a poor young London crossing sweeper called Jo. When Jo is questioned he always answers, 'I don't know nothink.'

I've checked in my copy of *Bleak House*. In the written text Jo says, 'I don't know nothink about no plans. I don't know nothink about nothink at all.'

Sometimes I talk about language to community groups and when it gets around to question time I can guarantee someone will stand up and say, 'What I really hate is ...' And 'nothink' and 'somethink' are always there.

Just say the word 'nothink' and eyes are rolled upwards and there's visible shuddering.

I can remember when I was in the primers at Sydenham School in the 1940s, teachers were growling about 'nothink'. Maybe they still are. So it seems remarkable that in the face of such hostility 'nothink' hasn't gone away.

A few years ago in one of his Saturday morning radio talks about language Max Cryer responded to a question from a listener who wanted to know about 'everythink' and 'nothink'.

Cryer gave his personal theory that this was caused by laziness.

Cryer is very much in line here with other language commentators. Laziness is the most common explanation for those language usages that people dislike.

In the early reports of New Zealand school inspectors there are many complaints about poor language habits. The inspectors always said these were the result of laziness: children were not making the physical effort to articulate clearly.

The problem with that explanation is that it cannot be defended. It actually takes more physical effort to say 'think' than it does to say 'thing'. If it were lazy, then presumably in a fit of indolence I might say I have a 'rink' on my finger, or someone was 'runnink' down the road.

But I wouldn't say this because the '-ink' variant appears on four words only – nothing, something, anything and everything.

If 'nothink' is caused by laziness, why is laziness so unevenly distributed? Why is it that lower-class speakers are lazy but middle-class speakers are not?

We know that 'nothink' is an old variant. It was used by lower-class characters in novels by Dickens and Thackeray.

In New Zealand it was reported in 1887 by Samuel McBurney, a visiting singing teacher. We have audio recordings of Mr W. Wylie, born in Oamaru in 1862, who definitely says 'nothink'. So the evidence shows that 'nothink' has been around for a long time. Some say it could go back even as far as the 8th century. It was certainly used in parts of Britain in the 19th century, especially around London.

And from there it was transported to Australia and New Zealand, where it continues to survive today. I think this shows the remarkable power of people (especially children) to preserve and transmit ancient forms – and in a way that challenges the respectable and the conventional.

So I'll defend 'nothink' from the criticisms of those who say it's bad language. I see 'somethink', 'nothink', 'everythink' and 'anythink' as small reminders of that remarkable ability of non-standard variants to survive against the odds.

And there's nothing lazy about that.

# Bread of life

24 May 2008

ONE OF MY DAUGHTERS HAS been on a diet in which she avoids bread in all its forms. This seems to me a great sacrifice when there are so many different types of delicious bread around today.

When I was growing up there were just two kinds of bread – brown and white. You bought bread by the quarter or by the half, which consisted of two joined quarters. When these were pulled apart, this produced the kissing or kiss crust – the most desirable part of the bread, which we fought over.

We bought our bread from the corner shop and carried it home in a calico bag. On the walk home we would always be seduced by that kissing crust. A few small strips of fresh white bread were pulled off and eaten, and then a few more, and a misshapen loaf was eventually handed over. 'Sorry, Mum, the grocer says he has rats in his shop.'

When I visited an aunt in Tauranga I was sent out to buy 'half a white' and returned with two quarters. My aunt was most surprised. This was my first experience of dialect differences in New Zealand. What was called a quarter loaf in the South Island was called a half loaf in the North Island.

Another bread memory from my childhood was the plate of thin bread and butter on the afternoon tea trolley.

Bread is one of our oldest foods – apparently people were making solid cakes from stone-crushed barley and wheat in the Stone Age. In the British Museum in London you can see actual loaves baked in Egypt over 5000 years ago.

Our word 'bread' is common to many Germanic languages. In Dutch it's *brood*; in German it's *Brot*; in Swedish it's *bröd*. However, in Old English (the earliest form of English) the generic word for bread was 'hlaf'.

This became our word 'loaf'. In the Old English version of the Lord's

Prayer, Anglo-Saxons prayed to be given 'our daily loaf'. The word 'loaf' remained the common English term for bread until the 12th century.

Surprisingly, 'loaf' is connected to the words 'lord' and 'lady'. In Old English, 'lord' was 'hlaford', from 'hlaf weard', which meant 'guardian of the loaf'.

'Lady' came from 'hlaf dige' – the loaf kneader. I suppose because bread was so important in the diet of the Anglo-Saxons, those who made it and controlled it gained power and importance.

Names for specialty breads come from many languages. One of the first variants I can remember was the Vienna loaf. Today we have Italian ciabatta (literally a carpet slipper, because of its shape), French baguette (little rod), Italian focaccia (flat bread cooked on the ashes – from Latin *focus* meaning hearth) and German pumpernickel.

Some dictionaries suggest that *pumpen* was an old German word for flatulence, and 'nickel' referred to Old Nick. But the *Oxford Dictionary* is more reticent. It doesn't accept the etymology for pumpernickel as 'devil's fart'. It just says 'origin uncertain'. The other day I saw a sign up in Aranui advertising rewena – Maori bread. The young people selling it said the loaves had been baked by their mum and it was wonderful. Forget about diets – I'm hoping that sign will appear again.

# Our priceless oral archive

*31 May 2008*

WHEN I WENT TO LONDON University in the 1960s people were puzzled about the subject I had chosen to study.

Linguistics wasn't a subject taught in any New Zealand university at that time and no one at home seemed to know what it was.

Some would ask: 'What are linguistics?' Some thought it involved speaking lots of languages. Others thought linguists guarded the language against people who broke the rules.

I had to tell people that linguistics was the scientific study of language. And it had sub-categories. You could study syntax – the arrangement of words within a sentence; you could look at morphology – the structure of words; you could study the sounds of the language – phonetics and phonology; or the meaning of language – semantics.

Today I call myself a sociolinguist. Sociolinguistics is a branch of linguistics that studies the relationship between language and society. It's a broad subject and it means different things to different people.

Some sociolinguists study the language situations in different countries. Others look at the language used by different groups in our society. We might look at the language of men and women, or of older people and younger, or of Maori and Pakeha. Some sociolinguists study conversation. Some are interested in what people feel about language varieties – why people like some varieties and hate others. Theoretical linguists can sit in their studies and think deeply. Sociolinguists often go out with tape recorders and collect recordings, which is not as easy as it might seem.

I first became interested in this subject in 1973 when I read a small book called *Sociolinguistics* by Professor Peter Trudgill. Today, Trudgill is Britain's leading sociolinguist and dialectologist. Twenty years ago he visited Christchurch. He was especially interested in an archive of New

Zealand recordings collected by the New Zealand National Broadcasting Service in the 1940s.

Many of the speakers recorded in this archive were old: some were born in New Zealand as early as the 1850s and 1860s. It wasn't long before Trudgill was coming to New Zealand every summer to study this archive, and he's been part of a team at the University of Canterbury ever since.

In the past two decades New Zealand English has become a popular subject in sociolinguistics. I attended a conference in Cardiff a few years ago where there were more papers on New Zealand English than on any other variety of English.

One of the reasons for this interest is that ours is the only native speaker variety of English in the world where there is recorded evidence of its entire history. And for this we must thank the people at Radio New Zealand Sound Archives, who preserved the 1940s archive of recordings.

When the New Zealand accent was first noticed people thought it was appalling. They called it an 'odious colonial twang' and said that the government should do something about it. Now world experts are coming to New Zealand to study the way we speak.

Trudgill was back again this summer. As he came out of the Lyttelton farmers' market with his bread, goat's cheese and salad for lunch he said, 'I'm a happy man. I have some wonderful food and I've been listening to such interesting vowel sounds.' What more could a professor of sociolinguistics want?

# Gestures of goodwill

*7 June 2008*

A YOUNG ASIAN WOMAN IN MY university tutorial told me this story. She'd been working during the holidays in a factory where she became increasingly unhappy about the way she was being treated by her supervisor.

When the supervisor wanted her to come to him he beckoned to her with his forefinger. Where my student came from this was a highly insulting gesture. It was the equivalent of saying, 'You are a filthy pig.'

My student was about to hand in her notice when she realised that the supervisor was using the same gesture to New Zealand workers, who were not a bit bothered by it.

The technical name for this is 'non-verbal communication' – communication without words. And the problem is that this differs in different societies, and what is perfectly acceptable in one country might be offensive in another.

In an Australian TV programme about border control, a young man from the Philippines was being questioned by officials. He responded by laughing. The officials became irate: 'So you think it's funny, do you?'

My daughter, who had lived in Vietnam, pointed out that they had completely misunderstood the man's reaction. In many Asian countries laughter is often a sign of nervousness. The man wasn't laughing because he didn't care – he was laughing because he was embarrassed.

There are significant differences between the non-verbal communication of New Zealanders and Pacific Islanders. We're taught that it's polite to stand up when an older person comes into the room. If we go into someone's office, we wait until we're invited to sit down.

The Samoan custom is the opposite. It's considered rude to be higher than the other person: you must make yourself lower and sit down immediately. When my Samoan daughter-in-law visits us I notice that if there are older members of our family present she doesn't talk.

97

I thought this was a sign of shyness or discomfort. But she explained to me that in her culture children are trained not to talk in the presence of adults, and she is still affected by this custom.

Our grandchildren are not allowed to eat while they walk. Even if it's only an apple or a biscuit, they must sit down to eat it. It would be unthinkable for my daughter-in-law to walk along the street eating an icecream.

Sometimes individual gestures have different meanings in different cultures. In Britain and New Zealand the nose tap is a sign that something is secret. In Italy it's a friendly warning. If we tap our forehead with our forefinger we're signifying craziness, but in some places this is a sign of high intelligence.

When we're dealing with non-native speakers we're usually quite forgiving when they make mistakes in grammar or pronunciation. After all, it's hard to learn a foreign language. But because we're usually not aware of differences in non-verbal communication we are not so understanding about them.

This point was well made by M. Davies in a letter to *The Press* (29 May). The writer was concerned about the lack of understanding of Samoan culture by a *Press* reporter writing about the Edgeware Road tragedy in which two teenage girls died. The reporter had interpreted the accused man's reluctance to look the parents of his victims in the eye as a sign of disrespect. M. Davies wrote: 'It is common knowledge that, in Pacific culture, to look someone in the eye in such a situation is extremely disrespectful. In bowing his head, Sila was trying to avoid being disrespectful.'

Misunderstandings can be avoided if people make allowances for possible differences in interpretation of non-verbal communication. With more and more cross-cultural mixing today this kind of understanding is important. Even Margaret Thatcher needed some training when she used the 'V' for victory sign the wrong way. I'm sure she didn't mean to give the British public an obscene gesture.

# The place of pidgin

*14 June 2008*

THIS SUMMER JULIET JOHNSTON HAD some visitors from Solomon Islands. She noticed that the men (with New Zealand university degrees) were speaking to their children in Pidgin English, even though the children were confident English speakers. She's asked me if I'd write about Pidgin English.

About forty years ago my interest in Pidgin English was awakened by R. A. Hall's book *Hands off Pidgin English!* This book was written in the 1950s to defend Pidgin English in Papua New Guinea when there was an attempt to ban it. Hall argued that Pidgin was a legitimate language, not just broken English or baby talk. You couldn't make it up on the spot, or toss in a few words like 'bilong' ('belong') or 'pela' ('fellow'). Pidgin English had its own rules and you had to learn them.

Today Pidgin English (Tok Pisin) has survived in Papua New Guinea and it is one of the three official languages there. It's frequently used in the national parliament. Radio Australia has a Tok Pisin Service.

Where did the word 'pidgin' come from? Possibly it came from Chinese Pidgin English and was the Chinese pronunciation of 'business' – *bishin*. 'Business English' is a good description of a pidgin. Pidgins function as auxiliary trade languages for people speaking different languages who need to communicate.

Pidgins are hybrid languages that are not anyone's mother tongue. They have simplified grammar. 'Man i-go' can be 'the man is going' or 'the men were going'. If number is important we add words: 'wanpela man' for one, or 'plentiman' for more than one. If time is important we can say 'nau i-go' (present) or 'i-go baimbai' (future). 'Bilong' is the possessive 'my', 'your' and 'our'. So 'my father' is 'papa bilong mi', 'your house' is 'haus bilong yupela'.

Pidgins have a small vocabulary so an individual word can have a wider meaning. You can see the word 'gras' is English 'grass'. But it also has an extended meaning. 'Gras bilong het' is hair, 'gras bilong pisin' are feathers, 'gras bilong solwara' (salt water) is seaweed, and 'gras nogut' are weeds. If someone is hairy it's 'i-gat gras'.

Because pidgins have restricted functions they don't need to express personal thoughts and emotions. They don't need elaborate politeness forms. It's as if the language is stripped to its essentials for the sake of communication.

You find pidgins throughout the world. They often appear along trade routes through contact between European languages and indigenous languages. So there's Pidgin French, Pidgin Dutch, Pidgin Portuguese, Pidgin Spanish as well as Pidgin English. (Chinese Pidgin English gave us phrases like 'long time no see' and have a 'look see'.)

Pidgins can disappear without a trace. In the Korean War there was Korean Bamboo English; there was Vietnamese Pidgin English in the Vietnam War. It's believed that there was once Maori Pidgin English. Because pidgins are spoken and not written, they are not generally preserved.

One pidgin that did survive was Sabir, the language of the Franks. It was probably used by the Crusaders in the Middle Ages and was still around in Portugal in the 15th and 16th centuries. Today we use its name – 'lingua franca' – for a common means of communication between people who speak different languages.

You'll also find pidgins in countries where there are many languages. In the Pacific region Pidgin English is used in Solomon Islands, where there are about 120 languages, in PNG with over 800 languages, and in Vanuatu with around 100. These countries need a lingua franca.

Over time pidgins can develop into full languages. Once that happens they're known as creoles. This has happened in the Pacific. In some places now Pidgin English is spoken by children as their first language. Linguists have been getting themselves to PNG to study the significant changes that take place when a pidgin becomes a creole. This is one way new languages are born.

# Once upon a time there was a dream house

*21 June 2008*

WHEN THE GRANDCHILDREN WERE LAST visiting I read them fairy stories. One they liked was about a giant who ate children for breakfast, and the brave little girl who escaped from him across a bridge made from a single hair. At the end they always ask if I'll read it all over again.

As I tell them about old crones who wend their way through forests and say things like 'Prithee, good sir', I'm delighted at their unquestioning acceptance of an older form of English.

They sit on my knee to hear these stories with a potent combination of security and terror. With my rational mind I ask if this material is suitable for small children. But they are protected by the magical words 'Once upon a time'.

I've been thinking about the similarity between fairy stories and real estate advertisements, because one of my daughters has been interested in buying a house. So we've been actively looking at the property pages of *The Press* and any other advertising literature that comes our way.

The advertisements give certain factual information – how many bedrooms, the size of the section, and whether the sale is by auction, tender or given price.

Then come the descriptions. My daughter wants a house that is sound and affordable, and she can't afford very much. But according to the advertisements she will be blown away, awe-inspired and generally thrilled by hidden delights, magical views and stunning treasures.

There are dreams, too – the dream home, the handyman's dream (sounds dodgy), the discerning person's dream, and, of course, the dream come true.

If they tell us a house is in 'Christchurch's dress circle', is that a defined place? Do estate agents decide which streets qualify? Do some try to sneak in streets outside the dress circle? We don't see so many advertisements now for the 'gentleman's desirable residence'. Is that because there's a shortage of gentlemen or is it a reflection of the changed position of women in our society?

We once had a German professor of linguistics staying with us. Professor Manfred Gorlach was looking through an estate agent's brochure. He wanted to know what was meant by a 'character house'. So we told him about verandas and bay windows, leadlight glass and wooden floors. Then he found an advertisement for a 'character character house'. No doubt he went back to Germany to write a learned academic paper on character houses and the innovative iterative intensifier.

The language of estate agents is poetic. We lived for many years in a house on Mount Pleasant that was advertised in 1970 with metaphor promising 'fairy-land views day and night'. (Someone asked at the time whether the fairy-land views were seen by people looking out or looking in.)

There's alliteration and assonance as well as ellipsis in 'Magic on Madras', 'Glamour on Glandovey', 'Perfection on Perry', 'Countrified on Cunliffe'.

Even the architect's name can get into a rhyming couplet: 'Your heaven, by Beaven'.

It's like the fairy stories – there has to be a suspension of belief. I think the newspaper heading 'Property' has the same function as the words 'Once upon a time'. We know that 'perfect' 'amazing' 'stunning' 'immaculate' all have to be taken with a bag of salt. I'm still wondering about the house described as having 'charisma'.

And what about the advertisement I saw in Auckland, inviting me to 'languish on the sun-drenched deck'? I'd always thought languishing involved a certain amount of pain and suffering over a period of time. You languish in hospital or in prison. So are estate agents taking 'languish' along the road of 'wicked' and 'sick', which have become terms of approval? Can we now languish by the pool with a glass of wine?

My daughter has had her offer on a house accepted. It was advertised as 'a real cutie-pie – one of Christchurch's best-kept secrets'. Maybe she'll remember this when she's paying for the rewiring and trying to get the floor levelled.

# How to address you

*28 June 2008*

In French lessons at school I was puzzled by the two pronouns for 'you'. The singular is *tu* and the plural is *vous*.

However, it's more complicated than this. If someone is close to you, you address that person as 'tu'. But if an individual is more distant or you want to be more formal you use 'vous'. This means sometimes you have to make a decision about your relationship. Is a person close enough to you to be 'tu' or would that be too familiar?

In English there are no such options. We have only one pronoun – 'you' – and it's both singular and plural. We don't differentiate between people who are close or distant.

It wasn't always like this. In Shakespeare's time English had two pronouns for 'you'. One person was 'thou' and more than one was 'you'. And as with French 'tu' and 'vous' today, 'thou' was also used for someone you felt close to, and singular 'you' was used for someone more distant.

In Shakespeare's play *Henry IV, Part 1* the king sometimes addresses Hotspur as 'thou', showing he is an equal and a friend, and sometimes as 'you', when he's giving orders. This switching of pronouns was not random. It conveyed an added meaning that Elizabethans watching the play would have picked up at once.

Over time, whether you used 'you' or 'thou' became a marker of your social class. Upper-class people all used 'you' among themselves; middle-class people quickly followed suit. They kept 'thou' for people who they thought were their inferiors, but they would have been highly insulted if one of those inferiors turned around and addressed them back as 'thou'. (In the trial of Sir Walter Raleigh in 1603 the prosecutor tries to insult him by saying, 'I thou thee thou traitor!') Lower-class people continued to use 'thou', 'thee' and 'thy' to each other.

By about 1650 the use of 'thou' and 'thee' was disappearing in English.

Everyone was using 'you'.

There was, however, a small group of people who still used 'thou' in their everyday speech. They were members of the Religious Society of Friends (commonly known as Quakers), founded in England in the 17th century.

Why did Quakers keep on saying 'thou' and 'thee' long after these pronouns had gone from everyday English?

It was a deliberate attempt at egalitarianism. Quakers were known for their refusal to acknowledge differences in class, race and gender. They were pacifists, and were foremost in the move to abolish slavery. They instituted co-educational schools before anyone else. Quaker reformer Elizabeth Fry worked with women convicts. The founder of the Religious Society of Friends, George Fox, refused to take off his hat in front of judges – even in front of the king. He refused to accept that any one person was superior to another.

So his followers carried this through into their language use. They avoided the higher-class singular 'you' and used the old lower-class 'thou' and 'thee'. My mother-in-law, Hayden Gordon, grew up in a Quaker family. Her grandfather and great-grandfather were members of the nonconformist Albertland settlement in Northland in the 1860s. Hayden told me that as a child she saw family letters from England where the writers used 'thee' and 'thy'. I've heard that there are a few Quakers in the rural mid-west of America who still use 'thee' but this is not general Quaker practice today.

Today, Quakers still express their belief in equality linguistically by refusing to use honorifics or titles. No one in the Religious Society of Friends is Mr, Mrs or Miss, Doctor or Professor. They are just plain John Morrison and Muriel Morrison.

# Serviettes and table napkins

5 July 2008

IN THESE COLUMNS I HAVE sometimes commented on new words and usages. Like others of my age I sometimes find it hard to keep up with language changes. But I'm also sometimes surprised to find that some of my own familiar words or phrases are completely unknown to younger people.

I found this once in a university tutorial where we were discussing language and social class. I'd used the terms 'U' and 'non-U' and then realised that the students had absolutely no idea what I was talking about.

'U' and 'non-U' were introduced to the British public in 1956 by Nancy Mitford in a book called *Noblesse Oblige*. (I expect my students wouldn't have heard of Nancy Mitford either.) But while Mitford always gets the credit, the terms were actually the invention of Professor A. S. C. Ross, who, in 1954, published an article entitled 'Linguistic Class Indicators in Present-day English'.

It appeared in a Finnish journal where it would normally have remained unnoticed as another obscure piece of academic writing. But he allowed Nancy Mitford to use his material and those terms became famous.

In his article Ross argued that traditional class markers were disappearing, and the upper class in Britain were becoming harder to distinguish from other classes. He concluded that the only way you could identify members of the upper class was by the language they used. Language was the most reliable indicator of social class. He invented the term 'U' for the upper class, and 'Non-U' for those who were not upper class.

The U/non-U categorisation attracted a huge amount of attention at that time. I'm sure it was partly because anxious people wanted to know where they fitted in on the social ladder. The socially insecure could then make appropriate linguistic changes.

Ross decreed that it was U to be 'rich' and non-U to be 'wealthy'. The U people said, 'Have some more tea.' The non-U said, 'How's your cup?'

U people said, 'They've a very nice house.' The non-U said, 'They have a lovely home.' U women put on scent, the non-U used perfume; U people wore spectacles, the non-U put on their glasses.

U people 'remembered' where the non-U 'recalled'. They had 'relations', not 'relatives'.

U women carried 'bags', and used a 'looking glass'; the non-U had 'handbags' and 'mirrors'. U people wrote on 'writing paper', never on 'note-paper', and when they played cards they referred to 'knaves' and not 'jacks'.

The most celebrated non-U indicators were 'serviette' and 'toilet'. Your choice of word here was a real social giveaway. U people only ever used 'table napkins' and went to the 'lavatory'.

Ross wrote this half a century ago, but he produced updates from time to time. In 1968 he allowed that not even U women wore 'stays' any more or had 'counterpanes' on their beds. He accepted that people of all classes were listening to the non-U 'radio' rather than the U 'wireless'.

In some ways I'm glad my students didn't know about these social-class indicators. I feel sorry for those socially aspiring English people in the 1950s and '60s who clutched Ross's categories as their checklist. They made sure they always sat on sofas, ate pudding and wore mackintoshes, unlike common people who sat on couches or settees, wore raincoats and ate dessert.

In the early planned settlements of New Zealand the intention was to reproduce the British class system without either the very top level or the very bottom. Perhaps much of this discussion was therefore irrelevant here.

But I would like to challenge the assumption that 'U' language was somehow better. We were told that if you bumped into someone it was non-U to say, 'I beg your pardon' or 'Sorry'. It was U to say nothing at all.

To me that's just plain bad manners, whatever social class you think you belong to.

# Chicken roll, ham roll, dog roll ...

*12 July 2008*

I WAS ONCE INVITED TO TALK to a school class in Christchurch on the topic of New Zealand English. A 16-year-old girl put up her hand. 'I don't have a New Zealand accent. The way I speak is normal.'

I can understand why she thought this, even though the evidence of her New Zealand accent was there for anyone to hear. She'd lived all her life in Christchurch. She'd heard only New Zealand English spoken around her. So it's perfectly natural that she thought her speech was 'normal'.

I'm sure also that when that girl went overseas she would have people commenting on the way she spoke. Sometimes they wouldn't understand her. When she asked for a pen they'd give her a pin. She'd be asked which part of Australia she came from.

She would become aware that she did indeed have a New Zealand accent.

New Zealand friends have told me how they are struck by the New Zealand vowels of customs officials and airport workers when they arrive home. You have to go away to notice them.

It's easy for us to think the language we use is 'normal', too. Sometimes it takes overseas visitors to point out differences.

I remember when Professor Brian Joseph from Ohio State University came to the University of Canterbury for a few weeks. He went around taking photos of advertisements for dog roll. He thought these were very funny. Where he came from you could eat ham roll, chicken roll and turkey roll, but never dog roll.

An English visitor was puzzled by the notice on a van for 'smallgoods'. I explained that this referred to sausages and salami and other preserved meat products. When I checked my dictionary I found that this was an Australia and New Zealand term, but I hadn't known that until my friend asked me what it meant.

Another term visitors have noticed is the verb 'to go flatting'. I had assumed that when all young English-speaking people left home they could 'go flatting', but this is not the case. It's only in New Zealand that we go flatting, and here you don't need to live in a flat to go flatting. My son 'flatted' in a large decaying house in Dunedin when he was a student.

Earlier this year I saw a headline in the *Southland Times*: 'Grannies go flatting'. The article was about three elderly women who had moved into a house together.

But the headline was a joke because old people don't go flatting. To go flatting is a rite of passage for young people. It involves leaving home and living independently with other young people and discovering that the toilet paper roll isn't replaced by magic.

This summer a visiting linguist became excited when my husband asked, 'I wonder if they brew beer in Hokitika any more?'

The linguist asked him to repeat it. 'That's amazing! You're using the positive "any more".' Apparently in parts of America and Canada you can say, 'They brew good beer any more.'

We can't say that in New Zealand but we can have a positive interrogative (as they also have in parts of America and Canada). 'Do they brew beer in Hokitika any more?' Our linguist friend (who comes from England) couldn't say that. He could only use 'any more' with a negative: 'They *don't* brew beer in Hokitika any more.'

We didn't know (until then) that New Zealanders used the positive interrogative 'any more', or that many other English speakers don't. We didn't know that other people don't buy smallgoods or go flatting, and that some people might find 'dog roll' funny. It takes visitors to point these things out. For us it's just normal.

# Nothing new under the thumb

*19 July 2008*

W E  W E R E  A T T E N D I N G  A  B A P T I S M A L  service in South Auckland. The minister was preaching and in fine flow when I noticed a girl in the pew in front of us busy texting. Then I saw that a young man at the other end of the same pew was also texting, and it became apparent that there was a private communication going on between the two of them. I suppose in my day we passed notes.

Text messaging is a form of communication that has crept up on us. I watch with admiration as my daughter uses both thumbs to send a message *while* keeping up a lively conversation.

I'm still at the stage where I have to search for each letter. 'Where's "r" gone?' But I've found it a useful way of letting people know when the meeting's ended or when we've reached Ashburton on the way home.

In talks to community groups I encounter a considerable amount of anxiety among older people about text messaging. The concern is that texting will somehow corrupt the language, and that children will no longer be able to write or spell properly.

Is this a genuine difficulty? Perhaps the negative response is just a normal reaction to a new method of communication, and especially one that the young are so much better using than the rest of us.

We've had similar reactions in the past to new developments. I found some correspondence in some early New Zealand school inspectors' reports where people were arguing strongly against the intro- duction of typewriters into schools. They said it would be detrimental to handwriting.

The basis of text messaging isn't new. The use of 'c' for 'see' or 'L8' for 'late' is another form of the rebuses we used to get in puzzles when we were children.

I have an autograph book from my time in primary school. My friend

Deborah wrote this: '2 Ys U R/ 2 Ys U B/ I C U R/ 2 Ys 4 me. Deborah could have been sending me the first text message!

In my student days, when I was taking lecture notes, the word 'character' was always 'Xter'; 'sociolinguistics' was 'slx'; 'language' was 'lg'. When time is short we produce our own shorthand. There's nothing new about this – people have been doing it for years. When there are only 160 characters per message you need to drop vowels and punctuation and use rebuses.

So I'll continue to admire the ability of young people to communicate electronically with their flying thumbs. But I don't admire those who come for dinner and spend their time at the table silently fiddling with their phones.

We belong to Servas, an organisation devoted to international understanding, where people offer free hospitality to travellers for a couple of nights. I received an email message from a young European woman asking if she could stay with us. It was written in text language. As she was leaving I explained to her that using text language in such a letter would be seen as impolite by many New Zealand hosts. She was most surprised. As with all forms of communication there are questions of acceptability and etiquette. And it's not acceptable to write letters of this nature in text language – or, for that matter, school essays.

Text language has many practical uses but it also has creative possibilities. The British newspaper the *Guardian* had a text message poetry competition. I liked this poem by Emma Passmore, one of the winners:

I left my pictur on th ground wher u walk
so that somday if th sun was jst right
& th rain didn't wash me awa
u might c me out of the corner of yr i & pic me up

110

# Embracing Maori language

*26 July 2008*

WHEN I STUDIED IN LONDON in the 1960s I was an 'international student'. Sometimes we would be asked to a function and told to wear native costume and be prepared to perform a native song or dance. The costume was an impossibility, and for the song or dance Pakeha New Zealanders would stand in an embarrassed line and sing 'Pokarekare Ana'. What made New Zealand students different was that we came from a bicultural society made up of Maori and Pakeha.

When I returned to New Zealand in 1966 there was little evidence of this biculturalism. In 1984 Naida Glavish, a Maori toll operator in Auckland, was demoted for answering a call with 'Kia ora'.

In 1987, when I was on a committee of the National Library, we had a debate about whether the library should have a Maori name. In the end Russell Marshall, Minister responsible for the National Library, intervened and two names were made official: the National Library of New Zealand and Te Puna Matauranga o Aotearoa. That year the Maori Language Act was passed, giving Maori official status, equal with English. In that year also the Maori Language Commission was set up. From this point the Maori language began to appear publicly beside English.

I'm a New Zealander who has not learned Maori. The Maori greetings and phrases that are being used increasingly on radio and TV sound familiar to me, but I don't know what they mean. So I asked Dr Jeanette King to help me here. She has taught in the School of Maori and Indigenous Studies at the University of Canterbury for many years.

Probably the most common greeting is 'kia ora' which means 'be well'. Another is 'ata marie' – good morning (literally 'peaceful morning'). 'Ko te purongo o te ata nei': 'This is the morning news'. In Kim Hill's Saturday morning radio show she says: 'Nga mihi o te ata' – 'good morning' (literally 'greetings of the morning').

111

On *Morning Report* you can hear, 'Ko Geoff Robinson tenei', which means 'This is Geoff Robinson'. He then says, 'Ko te pitopito korero': 'It is the news'. The word 'pitopito' means 'a snippet' and 'korero' means 'speech'. 'Pitopito korero' is a longstanding compound phrase for 'news'.

A continuity phrase is 'Kei te whakarongo koe ki te reo irirangi o Aotearoa', which means 'you are listening to National Radio'. 'Reo irirangi' (radio) comes from 'reo' (voice) and irirangi (spirit voice).

On TV3 John Campbell starts his show *Campbell Live* with 'Gidday, haere mai, welcome' a mixture of New Zealand English slang, Maori and formal English. 'Haere mai' means 'welcome' (literally 'come here') and is a traditional greeting. Campbell ends his show with 'ka kite' – 'see you', a modern expression based on the English equivalent.

The increasing popularity of Maori Television cannot be overlooked, and in Maori Language Week for the past few years both TV One and TV3 have incorporated te reo into their main news programmes. Mereana Hond and Mihingarangi Forbes, of TV3, have presented news items in Maori with English subtitles.

How surprised and delighted Bishop Bennett, former Anglican Bishop of Aotearoa, would have been to hear this. In 1947 he wrote to the *New Zealand Listener* asking the authorities politely: 'Would it be possible to allot more time for the Maori broadcast. Twenty minutes a week only for the world news and home news as well is too little.' His letter ended: 'Of course there are bound to be difficulties, but I hope some big effort will be made by the authorities to meet the wishes of a very large circle of Maori listeners. Meanwhile, we of the Maori race are very grateful for what has been given to us already, and wish to assure the authorities that our Maori broadcast is very highly appreciated.'

In this Maori Language Week the bishop's request is a useful reminder of how things were in the past, and it shows us that progress is possible.

# Malay words spice up English

This is an anniversary. The Living Language column has now been going for a year. At first I was anxious about the commitment of writing a weekly column and worried that I wouldn't have enough topics to write about.

I was also nervous about following in the footsteps of Frank Haden, a man whose views on language I often disagreed with. But I've received warm encouragement from many people, and even those who want to quarrel with me admit that language is a wonderfully complex and interesting subject.

I was in Malaysia when I received the email from *The Press* asking me to write this column. My daughter's first child was born in Kuala Lumpur and we were there to admire our granddaughter.

In Kuala Lumpur there's an excellent museum called the Islamic Arts Museum. At the time of our visit it had an exhibition highlighting the importance of the spice trade to Western Europe. In the 15th century Arab traders looking to buy spices came to the Malayan town of Malacca, which was a major port. Malacca was captured by the Portuguese early in the 16th century, and over a century later it was captured again by the Dutch.

You can see the evidence of both European countries in Malacca today, and of course there was the later presence of the British by way of the British East India Company in the late 18th century.

A pidginised form of Malay known as Bazaar Malay dates from before European contact. This became the lingua franca throughout the Indonesian archipelago. The contact with Malay over the centuries has left its mark on the English language, and some quite common English words have been borrowed from Malay.

As you might expect, some of the Malay words taken into English related to trade. The first traders set up permanent trading stations, which had the Malay name *kampong*, meaning an enclosure. This has given us the word 'compound'. To protect their compounds they made stockades, using a local plant called *bambu*, which has come into English as bamboo.

Some of the names for the items that were traded have also made their way into English. I remember when I was a child our pillows were filled with kapok. The material called gingham comes from Malay *ginggang*, which meant 'striped cloth', and the national garment of Malaysia, the sarong, is worn in many places today.

Sago pudding used to appear regularly on our family dinner table, and this comes from a Malay word *sagu*. Another Malay borrowing is *rattan*. Do people still have rattan blinds? And there's *gong*, an onomatopoeic Malay word for a musical instrument.

Things were not always easy for the traders. The local people sometimes ran 'amok' (or amuck), from *amoq* meaning a murderous attack. Some carried a dagger with a scalloped edge called a *kris*. I was surprised to find that the name of the heavy leather whip called the 'sjambok' also came from Malay. I had associated this with South Africa. But then those East Indian traders went to South Africa as well.

Among our animal names comes the 'orangutan', which means 'a man from the forest' in Malay. That language has also given us the cockatoo, the cassowary and the gecko.

Some of the Malay words in English came by way of Chinese. One of these is the Malay word *kechap*, which you might not recognise as our word 'ketchup'. The original ketchup was apparently a kind of fish sauce. We also associate paddyfields with China. The word *padi* is Malay for rice that has been harvested but not yet milled.

It was my first visit to Malaysia, and I've enjoyed looking for Malay words in English. They add to the wonderful mongrel mixture that makes up the language we speak.

# No such thing as a primitive language

I WAS STAYING WITH MY BROTHER in Lesotho when an English-man came to visit. He told me about a primitive tribe, somewhere in the depths of Africa, that had no proper language. The people communicated only with clicks and grunts and gestures. When I asked him where this tribe lived he was rather vague, but he assured me that he had heard about it from a reliable source and that it was true.

No one has ever found such a tribe, but myths about them keep turning up.

One of the first things I learnt when I began studying linguistics in the 1960s was that all languages are complex. It doesn't matter where speakers live or what kind of lifestyle they have, the language they use has internal structures that are systematically ordered by rules. So this means there's no such thing as a primitive language.

I was taught another principle of linguistics: all languages are equally well equipped to say the things their speakers want to say. If a language can't do this, then it will change, it will adapt. When computers appeared, people were not suddenly rendered speechless because they didn't have the words to describe the new technology.

I'm old enough to remember the arrival in New Zealand of the word 'smorgasbord'. There was a new trendy custom to lay the food out on a table so people could help themselves. This didn't mean food had never been laid out on tables before so people in the past could not describe this. But frequency of occurrence produced a more convenient name.

I am not saying that all languages are equal in all situations. An Arab might have a complex vocabulary for describing different kinds of camel. A New Zealand farmer will have many words for different breeds of sheep and New Zealand urban dwellers might not know these words.

People living in the Kalahari Desert might not have the vocabulary to deal with life in Christchurch, but then we might not cope linguistically with aspects of life in the Kalahari Desert. And that's the point: languages are well equipped to say the things their speakers need to say.

Languages can vary in the degree of convenience with which they describe things. I have two brothers who are older than me. How do I refer to David, who is younger than John but older than me?

He's neither my older brother nor my younger brother. So I have to use a sentence explaining the position of my brothers in my family. In Chinese, my brother John would be 'da go' (big older brother) and my brother David would be 'er ge' (second older brother). So we can say that both Chinese and English can describe this position in the family, but Chinese is far more convenient and economical.

There is one area of life today where I think the use of language is not yet sorted out. I have two women friends who recently celebrated their civil union. Their families referred to it as a wedding, but they themselves didn't want to use that word so it was a civil union. How do they describe their relationship? They can't say they're married; they have to use the longer explanation about civil union. And how do they refer to each other?

This was a question in the past for people who weren't married but who lived together. We've got away from 'living in sin', thank goodness. And it seemed rather chilling to say, 'We are in a de facto relationship', or for Tom to say that Mary was his 'common-law wife' or his 'de facto'.

At present all these things seem to be covered by the word 'partner'. But there can still be the possibility of confusion between an emotional partner and a business partner. Is there a better word?

# Naming fads and fashions

*23 August 2008*

CHILDREN'S NAMES HAVE BEEN IN the news lately, thanks to Judge Rob Murfitt's concerns about the name Talula Does the Hula from Hawaii.

Chris Martin from Coldplay supported Nicole Kidman's decision to call her baby Sunday. He said a name was just a noise, that Chewbacca was no stranger than Sarah. Is he right? Is a name just a noise? I haven't noticed any babies named Adolf lately.

Children's names have changed over the years. It's a topic of conversation for grandparents who named their own children Peter, Michael, Sarah and Jane, that they now have grandchildren named Mickela, Taylah or Soozy.

Over the history of the English language, naming customs have changed. The Anglo-Saxons used names made up of two parts, like Alfred, a compound of 'elf' and 'counsel', or Edgar – 'prosperity' and 'spear'.

Then came the Norman Conquest, bringing new names: Geoffrey, Hugh, Ralph, Richard, Robert, Roger, William, and for females Alice, Cicely, Emma and Matilda.

It wasn't long before ordinary people started using those names too. Did they hope their little William would gain some advantage from this?

When earthly patronage wasn't forthcoming, people switched to possibly more reliable heavenly patron saints' names, such as Matthew, Mark, Luke and John – and most of the other apostles: Andrew, James, Peter, Phillip, Simon, Thomas etc. They also liked some non-scriptural saints: Nicholas, Martin, Maurice, Lawrence.

For girls the most popular name was Mary, her mother Anne, and the mother of John the Baptist, Elizabeth. There were also feminised versions of saints' names: Johanna, from John, was a favourite. Early martyrs were Margaret, Agnes and Katherine.

At the time of the Reformation, people chose Old Testament names such as Abigail, Deborah, Esther, Rebecca, Sarah, Susannah, or Benjamin, Joshua, Isaac, Samuel.

The Puritans used names from virtues – Faith, Hope and Charity, Felicity and Grace. (Some poor children were named Temperance, Repentance, Obedience and Perseverance.)

And there were the classical names from Latin and Greek: Julia, Sophia, Diana, Penelope, Anthea.

Some of these names continued to be used for centuries. John has been constantly popular. Some get rediscovered. We named our youngest daughter Charlotte, thinking it was an uncommon name, but it seems many other people had the same thought at the same time. Our daughter Margaret insists that she is the only person in her generation with that name. When I was growing up it was a popular girl's name at my school.

Florence Nightingale was named after the city of her birth, which was unusual at the time. Today I see more children named after places: Chelsea, Sydney, Savannah, India, Paris, Asia. My grandson Franklyne was named after the street his mother grew up in. His aunt is Tara, shortened from Otara.

So there are different ways of naming children. There are names that are commonly heard, and have been used before in the same family. There is also a desire often to create something new: to give a child a name that's different. I see this kind of creativity now with different spellings Alicia/Aleesha, Georgia/Jorja, Jessica/Jesekah. (I heard of a child in South Auckland with the same name as my grandson, but spelt Phranklyne.)

So is a name just a noise? Like other teachers, I learnt the importance of getting names right. It mattered to 'Sandra' how you pronounced the vowel in her name.

When I look at the spam messages I receive every day on my computer, where I'm offered fake university degrees or Rolex watches and pills that will bring me hours of sensual pleasure, perhaps I can expect this sort of thing from Garifo or Markita, Philana or Deneen.

But Edith, Ethel, Mavis and Thelma? They should know better.

# Semantic degradation

*30 August 2008*

A YEAR AGO I WROTE ABOUT political correctness. I explained that during World War 2, when my father was stationed in Guadalcanal in the Pacific, he always referred to the local inhabitants as 'the natives'. It wasn't a racist term – it was what everyone used at that time. But in later years, with encouragement from his family, he stopped using the term.

This received a response from Sir Bob Jones, who thought I was being prissy about the word 'native'. He wrote that he could cheerfully talk about a Glaswegian native. Of course Jones is right. I, too, can say 'he's a native of Birmingham' or 'I have native plants in my garden'. The word 'native' has more than one meaning and we don't need to avoid them all.

In my column I was talking about the use of 'native' with the meaning given by the *New Zealand Oxford Dictionary* of 'a member of a non-white indigenous people, as regarded by colonial settlers'. The dictionary adds: 'often offensive'. In early New Zealand writings, Maori were sometimes referred to as 'natives'. There were 'native schools' in New Zealand. This usage would be offensive today.

I think some people want a word to have one single, clear meaning. But words are not like this. In his dictionary written in 1755 Dr Johnson gave 64 meanings for the verb 'to fall'. If you say you are a political liberal, the meaning of 'liberal' depends on where you live. It has a different meaning in Australia (where it means conservative) from its meaning in Britain. In South Africa, during the apartheid era, a liberal was considered close to being a communist.

A word that has changed in meaning is 'feminist'. In the 1970s many of my women university students wore the label 'feminist' with pride. It referred to someone who advocated women's rights on the grounds of equality of the sexes. Three decades later when I asked women students if they would like to be called 'feminists' they said they certainly would not.

When I asked why, they told me that a feminist was a hairy-legged man-hater. Yet these same women also advocated women's rights on the grounds of equality of the sexes.

So we can say that the meaning of the word 'feminist' has degenerated. It has developed negative connotations. Semantic degeneration is common with words relating to women: a 'hussy' was once just a housewife, a 'courtesan' was the female equivalent of a courtier, and 'tart' was a short-ened form of 'sweetheart'.

A word that interests me is 'victim'. We hear this word a lot today, with victims' rights, victim support, victims of abuse and so on. At a dinner to commemorate 10 years of restorative justice in Christchurch, every speaker who used the word 'victim' added 'I really dislike that word'.

My dictionary defines 'victim' as 'a person injured or killed as a result of an event or circumstance'. That meaning is factual and unemotive.

So I asked some of those who objected to this word why they did. One person said that 'victim' now denotes powerlessness. Another said that when you're a victim you continue to suffer.

Discomfort with the word 'victim' is not being heard only in New Zealand. In the British newspaper the *Guardian Weekly* Libby Brooks wrote an article on rapists. She wrote about political candidate Jill Saward, who two decades after the event is still identified in Britain as 'the Ealing vic-arage rape victim'. Brooks suggested that 'survivor' would be a preferable term.

I once met some refugees in Zambia who had escaped there from the slaughter in Rwanda. One young man had seen his entire family butch-ered. In New Zealand he would have high victim status, but as I talked to him there was no sense of self-pity or powerlessness – he was indeed a survivor. Perhaps if the people in the Sensible Sentencing Trust used the word 'survivors' rather than 'victims', this could help some unfortunate people to be healed.

# A little lexical diffusion

*6 September 2008*

I'VE BEEN GOING BACK THROUGH old copies of the *New Zealand Listener*. People in the 1940s believed that broadcasting should set the standard for correct English in New Zealand. And they were quick to point out instances when it failed to do so.

Richard Rae, of Wadestown, was deeply troubled by people who pronounced 'romance' with a stress on the first syllable. He wrote:

> The only way of curing this evil would be for the NBS to employ specialists to listen to every broadcast, and to record every mispronunciation by speakers, actors in radio plays, and announcers. If these were not able or willing to mend their ways, their voices should cease to be heard on the air.!!

So, if you said 'ROM-ance' you should be sacked.

People learning English as a second language are taught that every English word with more than one syllable has a set place for the stress and we can't change it around.

Some words are stressed on the first syllable – father, any, obstinacy, reasonableness; some are stressed on the second syllable – about, before, attractive, beginning. Some words have two stressed syllables – fourteen, disbelieve, contradiction.

In some languages you always know where the stress will go because there is a rule. This is not the case with English; think of photo, photography, photographic. There's no simple way of knowing which syllable or syllables in an English word must be stressed.

It's something that has to be learned with every new word, and it's important to get it right. The foreigner who says 'e-CONomics' for 'economics' will not be understood.

121

But there are some exceptions. There are a few English words where you do have a choice: CON-troversy and con-TROversy, KIL-ometre and kil-Ometre, HAR-ass and har-ASS.

But some people don't like choice. It makes them cross. They want to know which one is *right* and which is *wrong*.

Lynette Elphick, of Greymouth, has heard words like 'protest' (as a verb) and 'research' with the accent on the first syllable. She finds this annoying.

Like Richard Rae in the 1940s, this writer has identified a change that is creeping through the English language, one word at a time. It's been happening since the 16th century and it's still continuing. It has the fancy academic name of 'lexical diffusion'.

Early in the 16th century the words 'rebel' and 'record' had the stress on the second syllable for both nouns and verbs. By the end of the 16th century the verb was still 're-CORD' but the noun had become 'RE-cord'.

Since then, this change of stress to the first syllable has been slowly and quietly affecting other words in our English vocabulary.

I used to give my university students a small test. I'd write the following sentence on the blackboard: 'There's a recess in the wall.' I asked them where they would put the stress in 'recess'. The answer was always unanimous: it was always on the first syllable.

Yet the 1982 edition of the *Concise Oxford Dictionary* gives only one possibility: stress on the second syllable. Whether you are interested in 'research' or you wish to 'research' your family tree, the word 'research' always used to be stressed on the second syllable. That's not what Lynette Elphick hears in New Zealand today.

The noun and even the verb can be heard with the stress on the first syllable. And the same thing has happened to protest, resource and decrease. You can blame it on lexical diffusion.

There are still plenty of words that have not been affected by this sound change: mistake, report, dislike and so on. But maybe one day they'll get caught up in the change too.

One word that has changed in American English is 'address'. I thought I wouldn't hear 'ADD-ress' in New Zealand – it sounds too American. But recently I have heard it. I've also heard rugby commentators talking about the 'DE-fence'. That's not how I'd say it, but it's that lexical diffusion again, and, like rust, it never sleeps.

# Linguistic imperialism

*13 September 2008*

THIS YEAR I WAS ASKED to go to the Christchurch Polytechnic to talk to a group of school teachers from Spain. They were in New Zealand for a few weeks on Spanish government scholarships. When I met them they had just spent time on the West Coast, where it had rained heavily. But despite the weather they were enthusiastic about New Zealand.

I was to talk to them about New Zealand English. When I asked them what they had noticed, they told me they were especially confused by words such as 'best' and 'beast', 'men' and 'mean'. They thought everything sounded like 'beast' and 'mean'.

I explained some New Zealand English vowel changes. But it was when I asked them about the language situation in their own country that the group became animated. They all wanted to talk about it.

They came from Catalonia and Valencia and, as well as speaking Spanish, they also spoke Catalan, a language that is as closely related to French as it is to Spanish.

The Catalan language has a history of oppression. It used to be the official language in Catalonia before that area was annexed by Castile at the beginning of the 18th century. Then things changed. The government insisted that only Spanish be used in schools, and all political documents and legal contracts had to be in Spanish.

There was a respite between 1931 to 1939 under the Spanish republic, during which the Catalan language was allowed. Then General Franco came to power and it was banned again, in favour of Spanish.

The visiting teachers wanted to talk about that time under the Franco government. It was a bad time for speakers of Catalan. Because the language was banned from schools, children came to school unable to understand what the Spanish-speaking teacher was saying, and they grew up unable to read or write their own language.

123

The chairs of Catalan language and literature at the University of Barcelona were abolished. The teachers had stories of people being imprisoned for promoting Catalan, and told me how their parents tried to keep the language alive in secret at home.

I asked if anything had been published in Catalan in this period and they said it was forbidden in Spain up to the 1970s, but some Catalan material was published in Mexico.

The students were passionate about Catalan and were all actively involved in promoting the language.

Of course they were very interested in the position of Maori in New Zealand. When I told them that for decades Maori children had been forbidden to speak their own language at school, and even punished for it, they nodded with full understanding.

The story of the Spanish government's decision to ban a language spoken by more than seven million people is not unique. Greek governments banned the use of Macedonian in northern Greece; the British government banned Scots Gaelic after the 1745 rebellion.

No one was sent to prison for speaking Maori in New Zealand, but there is no doubt that speakers of Maori were disadvantaged in this country.

The Catalan teachers were interested to hear about language revitalisation efforts in New Zealand. They understood well that language is a signal of group identity, and also that there are people who still think national unity can be achieved by having everyone speaking the same language, even if it means losing a language to achieve this.

The Spanish teachers asked me whether New Zealand children learnt foreign languages in our schools. I explained that the majority of our population speak English and that we regard it as a high achievement to master another language.

These students spoke fluent English – some of them spoke three or four languages.

One of them said, 'Maybe it isn't important in New Zealand to learn another language. For us it is not a choice, it's a necessity.'

I wonder if it will ever become a necessity in New Zealand?

# Losing the power of words

*20 September 2008*

I ENJOYED WATCHING THE COUNTRY CALENDAR on TV recently about Bendigo Station in Central Otago. My mother's cousin, Dick Lucas, took over Bendigo in 1947 and developed a model run there. I remember visiting the station as a child. The Perriam family, who are the present owners, have brought about changes at Bendigo, including a successful wine-growing venture.

John Perriam described how they had benefited from the process of high-country tenure review, where the government allowed some leasehold land to become freehold in exchange for putting other land into the conservation estate. But some aspects of this process have angered Perriam, and he likened some government initiatives to 'ethnic cleansing'.

The term 'ethnic cleansing' came into English in the 1990s to describe the civil war in the former Yugoslavia, where thousands of people were killed or displaced. It was used for the 1994 massacres in Rwanda, when nearly a million Tutsis were killed. Can changes to high-country land tenure in New Zealand really be described as 'ethnic cleansing'?

As a linguist I find this puts me into a dilemma. I know that the meanings of words often weaken, and our English vocabulary is full of examples. We can say Archie was terribly rich, or frightfully rich, or awfully rich. 'Terrible' once meant something that terrified you; 'frightful' was something that filled you with fear; 'awful' inspired you with awe or dread. These were strong words with a powerful effect. Today they have become weak and insipid. Terribly, frightfully and awfully are now just versions of 'very'.

Once, if you were 'astounded' you would have been rendered unconscious. Something that was 'stunning' could have stupefied you. Today, the word 'scamp' is used of a mischievous child – once it meant a highway robber. In the 17th century if someone was 'naughty' that person was

125

morally bad and wicked. Kate Burridge, an Australian linguist, tells us that 'ratbag' was once highly offensive – on a par with scumbag or slime-bag. Today it has become quite mild in its meaning, even affectionate.

I recently heard a mother addressing her young son as 'you little monster'. In the 16th century this would have meant he was a person of inhuman cruelty or wickedness.

The Toyota ad using the word 'bugger' is a good illustration of this weakening in meaning. I never once heard my parents utter this word. There are people, usually older people, who find it offensive today. But now I constantly see it on Toyota tyre covers, and John Campbell cheerfully uses it in his TV show *Campbell Live*. It has become another word for 'fellow' or 'chap'.

There's one modern usage I do find hard to accept. From time to time we hear people telling us that New Zealand hospitals are becoming 'third world'.

My brother has spent his working life in Africa living among poor people. Once, when he was badly injured, I visited him every day for weeks in a real third-world hospital. It was a harrowing experience.

Maybe some things could be improved in our hospitals, but to describe them as 'third world' is nonsense.

Is the term 'third world' now undergoing semantic weakening and losing its force? Has it come to mean 'not as good as we would like'? And has the same thing happened to 'ethnic cleansing'? Is this just another example of semantic weakening that we have to accept?

Language is always changing, and much of the time we can do little about it. But maybe there are times when we can speak out and say that people are using words inappropriately. To call New Zealand hospitals 'third world' or to say that changes in high-country tenure are 'ethnic cleansing' dilutes the meanings of these powerful phrases. It makes them weak and insipid.

It also suggests that the people who use them in this weakened state have no idea about places in the world where people live in real poverty, or suffer atrocities.

# Recording for posterity

*27 September 2008*

WE'VE ALL HEARD ABOUT THOSE secret recordings of Bill English at a National Party function. I have listened to the tape and it was difficult to hear what was being said with all the background chatter going on.

Collecting tape recordings is something we sociolinguists do, but data obtained from a noisy cocktail party would be no use for our purposes.

I began making tape recordings when I was a student in London in the 1960s. I was writing my thesis on the intonation patterns of church sermons. I asked various preachers for permission to record their sermons, and on Sunday mornings I would set out with a reel-to-reel tape recorder that ran on batteries and was carried in a large leather bag. I had to set this up with the microphone positioned on top of the front pew. The rest of the congregation were always towards the back of the church.

At that time several linguists at University College London were also making tape recordings. They were trying to collect samples of spontaneous conversation. On one occasion I was cheerfully gossiping about the professor and wondering why the people around me were not chipping in as they usually did. Later I found that I had been surreptitiously recorded for research purposes. That taught me never to make secret recordings myself, or to allow my students to do so.

But it's a problem. As soon as you ask for permission and bring out your microphone, people start talking differently. Folk who had been chatting comfortably suddenly become stiff and put on their best linguistic behaviour. Sometimes they sound quite peculiar. It's like people posing for photographs with artificial smiles.

We call this the 'observer's paradox'.

The aim of sociolinguistic research is to find out how people talk when they are not being systematically observed. And the only way to find this out is to systematically observe them.

So it's a challenge when there is a tape recorder on the table to get people to talk as they normally would. Often time can resolve the problem – the first five or 10 minutes of a recording might be unnatural but then people forget and relax.

The students in my third-year New Zealand English class had to collect recordings of casual speech and they found it was not easy. But some were gifted interviewers with a wonderful ability to put speakers at their ease.

The man who is called the father of sociolinguistics, Professor William Labov, always carries a tape recorder with him. When he was on a fellowship at the University of Canterbury he was keen to record New Zealanders. Apparently he got good data at the fire-station.

Labov doesn't bother about getting written permission from his speakers, but we New Zealand linguists are not so casual, even if we would like to be. Today, before any speaker is recorded we must get him or her to sign a consent form allowing the recording to be used for research purposes.

We still have to find ways of dealing with the observer's paradox. When we're collecting New Zealand English data we ask speakers to read a word list with 35 items covering all the interesting sounds. One of the things we're interested in is whether a speaker pronounces words like 'letter' and 'Peter' with a 't' or a 'd'. When they're reading the word list very few speakers use the 'd'. But more speakers use it for the numbers that precede each item on the word list. So 'thirty' sounds like 'thirdy'. This means we know that those speakers do use the 'd' pronunciation when they're not being extra careful.

I'm grateful to people who have let us record them. Maybe in a hundred years time researchers will listen to them and know what New Zealanders sounded like at the beginning of the 21st century. But they will find no incriminating comments from politicians off their guard at cocktail parties.

# Fewer people using 'fewer'

SINCE I BEGAN WRITING THIS column, several people have told me they understand that we have to accept that language changes, even if we don't like it. But there are one or two changes that cause them distress. At the top of their list is the loss of the word 'fewer'. Every visit to the supermarket they see the sign for '12 items or less'. It makes them sad and they want to go out and kick someone.

The National Party billboard calling for 'less bureaucrats' also offends these people.

Dave Kelly has written to me about this:

> I wonder if you could comment on … the different terms used for referring to things that come in discrete units which can be counted (such as people and aeroplanes), contrasted with things that come in bulk and can be divided into arbitrary quantities (such as liquids, powders, etc). For a decrease I would say 'there are fewer people' but 'there is less water'. You often hear people saying 'less people' but that seems to me to be wrong.

Dave Kelly is right. The rule I was taught for standard written English was that you use 'fewer' with things that can be counted, and 'less' with things that cannot be counted. So we can have '12 items or fewer' and some of them might cost 'less money' than in other shops.

Those who get annoyed by 'less boys than girls' or ' less eggs in this recipe' have learnt the rule and make a distinction. However, the brutal fact of the matter is that they are probably now in a minority. 'Fewer' is on a life-support system.

I decided to investigate the current usage of 'less' and 'fewer' so I asked Dr Heidi Quinn in the Linguistics Department of the University of

Canterbury to help me. At the university there is an extensive archive of current New Zealand English collected over the past 15 years. It's called the Canterbury Corpus and consists of 150 hours of recordings of mainly casual conversation. There are equal numbers of males and females, younger speakers and older speakers, working-class speakers and middle-class speakers. All the spoken data has been transcribed, so it wasn't hard for Heidi to pull out every instance of 'less' and 'fewer'.

When I looked at speakers born between 1930 and 1983 I found only two examples of 'fewer' but over a hundred examples of 'less', often in relation to things that could be counted – less picnics, less things, less jobs, less students, less hours and so on.

So why is 'fewer' vanishing? I think there are two reasons. One is that we have only one word for 'more' and we don't make a distinction between countable items – more eggs, and items that can't be counted – more butter. We get along perfectly well with one word. So what's happening is that 'less' is behaving like 'more' and covering everything.

The second reason comes from the evidence in the Canterbury Corpus. Children learn by hearing people using the language around them. But if people are no longer saying 'fewer', and the evidence strongly suggests that this is the case, then we can hardly blame children for not saying 'fewer' either.

So this is the dilemma. In the end we have to accept change, but it doesn't mean we always have to like it. If the loss of 'fewer' troubles you, then I suggest that you clap your hands and rejoice every time you hear people say 'fewer' or see it written. But if you get annoyed whenever you see '12 items or less' then you're probably going to be miserable every time you go to the supermarket. Is it worth the angst?

# When is a woman a lady?

*11 October 2008*

WHAT'S THE DIFFERENCE BETWEEN A lady and a woman? I've been going back through early copies of the *New Zealand Listener* and this was a question people were asking in the 1940s.

The correspondence was set off in December 1942 by someone from Auckland who signed herself 'A Woman'. She stated that she was a woman worker and she objected to the title of a radio series, *For My Lady*.' She said it smacked of lavender (or mothballs) and old lace. 'What's wrong,' she wrote, 'with "For the Women", "About Women" or "For the Housewife"?'

Someone from Kaikoura complained about a programme called *We Work for Victory*, which had interviewed 'lady car-cleaners'. She wrote: 'Please step in, someone, before we have post-ladies, milk-ladies, baker-ladies, butcher-ladies etc.'

In January 1943 came answers to these letters. Someone signed 'For My Lady' wrote: 'I have a very dear friend who is an old lady. Am I to refer to her as an old woman?'

'Pakeha' from Rotorua wrote: 'Let us not lose what are surely two of the most beautiful words in the English language: "lady" and "gentleman".' According to this writer, these terms do not denote people who rely on money, property and fine clothes, but to people 'who display the virtues that come under the heading of good breeding – gentleness, courtesy, consideration for others'.

From Hataitai in Wellington, someone signed 'One of Them' wrote that we should 'instruct our girls a little more in the decorum that befits a lady'.

I think the letter-writers raise some interesting questions. We have two words in English for adult female human beings – lady and woman. Do they have different meanings? If they do, how would you explain the difference to someone learning English?

131

When I've asked my university students about this, they tell me that 'lady' suggests surface features of style, clothes and etiquette. 'Woman' is more fundamental. Ladies don't have babies; women do. My female students did not want to be called ladies. They pointed to the women's movement of the 1970s; it wasn't the 'ladies' movement'. But when I asked them what they would call a group of elderly female human beings they admitted that they would refer to them as a group of 'old ladies' not 'old women'. When I asked why, they said that 'lady' was also the polite term.

When I was growing up my Great Aunt Clara had very firm ideas about social hierarchies. She believed (like 'Pakeha' from Rotorua) that ladies had 'good breeding' – something that women didn't have. 'Ladies recognise those who are ladies,' she would say, 'and ladies can recognise breeding when they see it.' You didn't argue with Great Aunt Clara.

The reason why we have two words goes back to feudal times. The 'lady' was a member of high society, married to a lord. A 'woman', on the other hand, was someone of low birth, working in the fields outside the castle.

The word 'woman' comes from Old English, where 'wif' was the word for a female. 'Mann' originally meant just a human-being. So 'wifeman', later shortened to 'woman', was an adult female human being. Later 'man' changed to mean a male.

I've raised this question before in these columns. We don't live in feudal times today but we have inherited a language that still has words that once related to people and society in feudal times. Does this language influence the way we see the world today? Are there actual differences between 'ladies' and 'women' or are we made to see differences because we have the two words? How would it be if we had only one word for an adult female human being? Would we still see differences? Does 'good breeding' actually exist, or do we imagine it because there are words for it?

# Hard-wired pronunciation

*18 October 2008*

MY YOUNGEST DAUGHTER CAME HOME for a few days in the school holidays – she's a primary school teacher in Wellington. This year she's been attending a course on second language acquisition, with special reference to Maori. I've noticed the care with which she pronounces Maori words in English. She complains when people on TV presenters pronounce 'Tauranga' with the vowel in 'towel' not in 'toe'.

I've had letters from readers on the subject of the pronunciation of Maori words in English. They point to the history of the English language, where there's been a constant inflow of foreign words that have been integrated into English. In a column I wrote last year I showed how ordinary words for breakfast food – bacon and eggs, toast and marmalade, tea and coffee – have all come into English from other languages. They now seem thoroughly English. The letter-writers use this point to ask why we don't allow normal linguistic processes to take place so that Maori words can become totally integrated into English and pronounced accordingly.

In the early history of New Zealand English this is exactly what happened. People today are surprised to find that the word 'cockabully' for a small freshwater fish comes from Maori 'kokopuru', or that 'biddy-bids', those nasty burrs that catch in your socks when you're tramping, come from Maori 'piri piri'. Maori placenames were also given 'English' pronunciations: the Waimakiriri became the Waimak, and Paraparaumu became Paraparam.

The question of the pronunciation of Maori words in English has been debated for decades. It was a popular topic in letters to the editor of the *New Zealand Listener* in the 1940s, and some people then were calling for authentic Maori pronunciations. In 1967 the New Zealand Broadcasting Corporation decided to allow anglicised Maori placenames on the radio and there was such an outcry that the decision was quickly reversed.

For native English speakers it is not always easy to pronounce words in a Maori way. Our brains are hard-wired to use English sounds. This means that when some of us try to pronounce Maori words we might not get them exactly right. It's not because we're racist or because we don't care, but just because pronouncing words in another language can be difficult.

For example, in Maori you can begin a syllable with the sound we write as 'ng'. The rule in English is that 'ng' can only ever occur at the end of a syllable. So it's easy for English speakers to say 'sing' or 'singing'. But it's hard to pronounce the tree name 'ngaio', or the tribal prefix 'ngati' with the initial 'ng'. So we use the nearest English equivalent, which is 'n'. The girl's name Ngaire becomes Nyree.

But there are features of Maori that are not inherently difficult for English speakers. For example, rather than pronouncing the town names Motueka or Motukarara with 'motch-you' we could say 'mo-tu'. We could say Wanganui or Mangere with the 'ng' as in 'singer' not as in 'finger'. And in Tauranga we could use the vowel in 'toe' not 'towel'. It takes an effort because old habits are hard to break, but it's not really so hard and it all helps.

The question of the pronunciation of Maori words in English is a dilemma for linguists who have conflicting loyalties. The non-prescriptive objectivity pursued by linguists as scientists comes into conflict with the cultural and humanist motives of linguists as New Zealanders living in a bicultural society.

British sociolinguist Peter Trudgill has been a regular visitor to the University of Canterbury. He's very aware of these issues because he's often asked the same questions about the way English speakers pronounce Welsh words and Welsh placenames. He applauds those who make the effort to use a Welsh pronunciation, but he would not condemn those who don't. But he's very critical of those who make fun of the people who do make an effort.

# Webster's labor of love lives on

*25 October 2008*

My computer has a handy spell-checker and I need it. If I make a spelling mistake in my language column (and this has happened) there are plenty of people happy to point out my error. But there was a time when I had a problem because my spell checker had a North American disposition. Colour became color, centre changed to center, defence to defense.

So how did it happen that we have two possible spellings of some English words? The answer comes from a man called Noah Webster.

Webster is famous today for his dictionary – *An American Dictionary of the English Language*, published in 1828 when he was 70 years old. He was an unlikely character to achieve such fame. He has been described as crotchety and humourless, a hack rather than a scholar, an unsuccessful lawyer, an obscure school teacher, an itinerant lecturer. He was 'devout, industrious, patriotic, persistent, conceited, perverse'. One account of him said, 'Ignorance never dampened his fire.'

Webster's driving motivation was American patriotism. Before the American revolution all textbooks were imported from England, so he decided to write a 'speller' for American school children. It was very popular and sold millions of copies. He said it was a matter of honour for an independent nation to have 'a system of our own in language as well as in government'.

In Webster's view the language of England was corrupted and already in decline, so one way he could mark the difference between the English of England and of America was through spelling reform.

So the American spellings of words such as color, labor, center, defense and traveler were part of a patriotic attempt to distinguish American English from British English. Webster made some other changes that we too have adopted, such as removing the 'k' from 'musick' and 'publick'. But he failed with his equally sensible imagin, primitiv, thum, hart (heart) and yung. Today Webster is famous not for his speller but for his dictionary, which took him 27 years to complete. Webster's dictionary was notable in a number of ways. It had clear and simple definitions. It included new words in current usage, and for the first time it contained American terms, such as banjo, possum, hominy, skunk, squash, caucus and chowder.

No doubt Webster thought other Americans would be pleased with his work, but he was wrong. He was viciously attacked by the language purists, who said that the addition of new words was preposterous. The newspaper the *Boston Palladium* declared that because the author had included 'the vulgar provincialisms of uneducated Americans' the result was 'a volume of foul and unclean things'. The *Palladium* stated that 'the English language has arrived at its zenith and requires no introduction of new words'.

Webster's first dictionary sold only 2500 copies and he had to mortgage his home to bring out a second edition. He remained in debt until he died in 1842, with his dictionary still unrecognised.

When Noah Webster was writing his speller and his dictionary he was writing for a new nation. He was writing for children who were growing up as American rather than British citizens. And he was writing about the American English.

His dictionary was published by two brothers, George and Charles Merriam. Their firm published only the dictionaries, and they brought out regular revisions. But they didn't secure the sole right to Webster's name, so if you're thinking of buying a Webster's dictionary today be careful. Any dictionary can call itself a 'Webster's dictionary' and many do, even though they have no connection with Noah Webster. The genuine Webster's dictionaries are sold under the name Webster-Merriam.

This month is the 250th anniversary of the birth of Noah Webster, a cantankerous man who helped America to achieve cultural independence. And he's the reason my American English spell-checker wanted me to write center, color and defense.

# Unhappy as a sandboy

*1 November 2008*

LINLEY ASKED ME A QUESTION the other day. She and some of her friends had been wondering about the origin of the phrase 'happy as a sandboy'. This is a familiar expression to me and somehow I'd always pictured a small boy at the beach with a sunhat and a bucket and spade. When I went looking for information I found I was quite wrong. It has nothing to do with happy boys on a beach. Rather it refers to a rather dreary occupation. Sandboys were people who went around selling sand, and they were not necessarily boys. The term 'boy' was used for any worker low down on the social ladder.

So why would someone want to buy sand? In Victorian times it was useful for cleaning pots and pans. Maybe it was a forerunner of sandsoap. It was also put on floors where liquids or other nasty things might be spilt. So it was used in gin shops. I can remember as a child going into the butcher's and shuffling through the sawdust on the floor. Before the days of sawdust it was apparently the practice to lay sand in butchers' shops.

Michael Quinion in his excellent website (www.worldwidewords.org) tells us that being a sandboy was hard work and badly paid. In London sand was dug out of pits on Hampstead Heath and then hawked around the streets, sometimes from panniers carried by donkeys. In Henry Mayhew's book *London Labour and the London Poor*, written in 1861, he recorded the comments of a man in charge of sand excavation: 'My men work hard for their money, sir. They are up at 3 o'clock of the morning, and are knocking about the streets, perhaps till 5 or 6 o'clock in the evening.'

It doesn't sound like a very happy job to me – so why do we say 'happy as a sandboy?' I've looked at various explanations. One suggests that because it was a dusty business sandboys liked to drink large amounts of beer. Another points to Dickens' novel *The Old Curiosity Shop*, where there was a small roadside inn called the Jolly Sandboys. Of course 'happy as a sandboy' might have been used ironically, as people would have understood that a sandboy's life was anything but a happy one.

An Australian and New Zealand expression with a similar meaning is 'happy as Larry'. So who was Larry? Harry Orsman's *Oxford Dictionary of New Zealand English* doesn't see any connection with a person named Larry. He suggests that it comes from a British dialect term 'larrie', meaning a practical joke or a lark. Maybe it's related to another British dialect word that came to Australia and New Zealand – larrikin, for a 'mischievous and frolicsome youth'.

In the late 19th century 'larrikinism' was mischief or practical jokes. In 1963 in New Zealand two 17-year-old workmen were placed on probation for 12 months. They had pleaded guilty to breaking into an implement shed at a golf club, removing a tractor and driving it around the grounds. The magistrate said it was not an ordinary case of burglary but rather irresponsible larrikinism.

I asked my daughters if 'larrikin' was still used. They recognised it but said it was old-fashioned. They then explained to me about 'bogans'. I now know that bogans are Pakeha working-class men who wear tight black jeans and denim jackets and drink Jack Daniels or bourbon and Coke. They have tattoos and listen to heavy metal music.

The female version of the bogan – the bogan chick – likes the gypsy look, with crushed material and lace. Bogans wear 'sharkies', which are wrap-around glasses as seen in the TV drama *Outrageous Fortune*.

One daughter pointed to her skirt, the hem of which was a raw frayed edge. She told me this was 'bogan chic' (as opposed to bogan chick). It's the Misery brand, bought from a shop called Illicit. So I've learned a bit about bogans. One day I'll explain to my daughters about bodgies and widgies.

# It's like old as the hills

*8 November 2008*

'LIKE THE FIRST HOUR I was like totally fine, like I wasn't like drunk'. I didn't invent this sentence. It comes from data collected by Dr Alex D'Arcy of the University of Canterbury Linguistics Department. She's an expert on 'like'. She wrote her PhD in Canada on it.

Several people have asked me about 'like'. Peter Green wrote:

> We older people have all observed the development during the last couple of decades of the extremely widespread practice of randomly peppering all spoken communication with this little word, so that every sentence includes it at least once or maybe even more.

Is Peter Green right? If he is, then the use of 'like' breaks a golden rule of linguistics, which says that language is not random or chaotic. Everything is governed by rules, and the different forms of 'like' in everyday speech are actually used with great precision. D'Arcy says we currently suffer from what she calls 'the forest for the trees syndrome'. Because 'like' can appear in so many places it looks random, but it actually isn't. If we step back we can see that it is used in very particular ways.

Is the use of 'like' a new development? Peter Green says he's heard it in the past 20 years but D'Arcy tells us it's been around for over 200 years. The vernacular uses of 'like' are complex and they are historically longstanding features of English dialects. She has found examples of it in recordings collected in New Zealand in the 1940s. Thomas Steel, born in Te Awamutu in 1874, says: 'Like until his death he used to write to me frequently.' Catherine Dudley, born in Cardrona in 1886, says: 'You know like you would be going to the hotel to stay.' This evidence shows that this feature is not something that originated recently in North America, as some people seem to think. Peter Green has also noticed another use of 'like' and he gives some examples. *I said 'yeah'* becomes *I was like, 'yeah'*. *He said, 'You've made my day'* becomes *He was like, 'You've made my day'*. He asks how this change happened.

'Be like' before speech has a technical name. It's called a quotative verb. Other quotative verbs are 'say', 'think' and 'go'. *He said, 'You've made my day'; He thought, 'You've made my day'; He goes, 'You've made my day'*. And now we also have 'like'.

According to D'Arcy, the quotative 'like' seems to have emerged around 1980 in California, and from there it spread quickly through American English. After about 1990 it started to be heard in other Englishes around the world. So young people in Canada, Singapore, India and South Africa were saying: *I was like, 'Where did that come from?'* And they were also saying this in Australia, Britain and New Zealand.

The quotative 'like' is not confined to English. Apparently it has also appeared in French, German, Swedish and Hebrew. So what we are hearing in New Zealand is part of a worldwide development.

Peter Green asks where quotative 'like' comes from. D'Arcy says it seems to have developed from 'like' as a conjunction before a clause. 'It felt like everything had dropped away.' She thinks it's been successful because it's so versatile. If you use 'say', this can be followed by words only, and if you use 'think' it must be followed by thoughts. But 'like' can appear before words, thoughts, sounds, gestures and even writing. (The same thing can be said for 'go'.)

D'Arcy is a world expert on 'like' so I'll let her have the final word:

These uses are not simply 'a girl thing' or 'a teenager thing', nor strictly 'an American thing'. Instead to a certain extent these forms are everybody's thing.

# Words that wound

15 November 2008

STEVE CARTER WORKS FOR THE Mental Health Foundation. He's written to me about the use of words associated with mental illness, and the stigmatising of the mentally ill.

He is right about the power of language to perpetuate prejudice. I gave myself five minutes to write a list of words to describe the mentally ill. I wrote down over 40, mostly derogatory. I did the same for words to describe the blind and I came up with nothing.

Words relating to mental illness have characteristics in common. One is to present mental illness as a deficiency. The original meaning of the word 'crazy' was 'broken' or 'shattered' (like crazy paving.) Today we hear people described as unhinged, having a screw loose, crackpots, a shingle short, not the full quid, and so on.

Some words for mental illness present it as something funny – words like wacky, nutty, bonkers. People are described as 'a bit funny' or 'funny in the head' and they have to go to the 'funny farm'. In the 18th century it was an entertainment for people to visit the Bethlehem Royal Hospital in London (which gave us the word 'bedlam'). They paid a penny to peer into the cells of the inmates and were allowed to bring long sticks to poke them and enrage them. It was all such a joke.

Mental illness has produced a long list of euphemisms. The word 'insane' originally applied to someone who was generally unhealthy. The word 'mental' meant 'pertaining to the mind' (like 'mental arithmetic'). A 'lunatic' was someone affected by changes of the moon. 'Handicapped' was term from horse racing. Words that were introduced as polite or kindly alternatives quickly degenerated in meaning and became a means of abuse.

I think the use of euphemisms and joke terms camouflages a deep underlying fear of mental illness. Where there's fear there are often euphemisms and joke terms. Think of the way we can talk about death. 'She kicked the bucket'. In World War 2 weapons were given friendly names. Bayonets were called 'tin-openers'. The bomb dropped on Hiroshima was named 'Little Boy'. It's as if a jokey name might reduce a fear of the realities of war. So perhaps for some people fear of mental illness is mitigated by referring to 'crazies' or 'nutcases' or people being 'a sandwich short of a picnic'.

I've read articles on this subject and it's clear that those working in the arena of mental illness are deeply concerned about the power of words to do harm. They ask us not to define people by their mental illnesses. So rather than saying 'Jo is a schizophrenic' we should say 'Jo experiences schizophrenia'. This allows for changes in the condition and the possibility of recovery. I found that the word 'handicapped' is no longer considered appropriate, and some have problems with the term 'disability'. It's good to be warned. But it's also difficult to get people to change deeply entrenched language habits. We saw this with the attempts by the women's movement in the 1970s to get rid of sexist language. The backlash was immediate and 'politically correct' became a dirty word.

I think the answer is in education. When my son John was seven he attended a London school. One day he told me that one of his classmates was a 'paki'. I asked him what he meant – the boy definitely wasn't from Pakistan. John said 'paki' just meant a stupid person. He had no idea that this word came from 'Pakistani' and was a term of racial abuse. Once this was explained he didn't use that word again. If 'handicapped' is no longer an acceptable term, then people need to be educated about this and not blamed if they don't know.

But perhaps the real answer is to get rid of the fear associated with mental illness. Then people mightn't need to use jokes and euphemisms. The current TV advertisements are designed to do this: 'Know me before you judge me.'

# Peggy and her squares

*22 November 2008*

KAREN COFFIN AND HER HUSBAND Chris spent a year in Christchurch. When they were about to go back home to England we talked about different words they had learned in New Zealand. Karen then asked me why New Zealanders called small knitted squares of wool 'peggy squares'. 'Peggy square' seems such a normal everyday term to me. It took an overseas visitor to point out that it is a New Zealandism.

The story of the peggy square began in 1930 with a woman called Mrs Lewis, who used to conduct a radio session about woollen fabrics and fashions on 2YA. She was known as 'the Wool Woman'. When she was visiting some friends on a farm north of Wellington she came across a four-year-old girl called Peggy Huse who was learning to knit. Peggy had made several little squares from scraps of wool and her mother had stitched them together to make a cover for her doll's bed.

This was during the depression and Mrs Lewis, the Wool Woman, had a bright idea. Perhaps poor families could be helped if children would use up the scraps of wool in their mothers' knitting bags and make blankets for needy people.

The Wool Woman then discussed the possibility with 'Aunt Molly', who took the Children's Session on the radio. They asked little Peggy to work out the number of stitches for a 6-inch (15cm) knitted square and to make a sample. They decided that these squares would be called 'peggy squares' after her.

Aunt Molly talked about Peggy and her knitted squares on the radio, and 'Aunt Molly's Sunbeams' (young singers on the Children's Session) began to knit peggy squares. Then the staff at 2YA (including the men) began to knit them too, and Aunt Molly organised a band of volunteers to sew the squares together and to line the blankets.

The idea caught on and peggy squares poured in from all over New

143

Zealand. Several thousand rugs were made and distributed to needy families.

In 1932 the DIC (a department store that older readers will remember) had a window display of rugs and a photo of Peggy Huse. The manager wrote her an official letter:

> For a little girl of six you have become quite famous during the last week, and we have all been much interested in you since we know that you worked out the number of stitches and the size of the needles to use for the Wool Squares the 2YA Children knit, and which have been given your name. That is why we were so glad to have your photograph in our windows with the beautiful bedcovers made from Peggy Squares that are to be given to people who are badly in need of warm blankets. We are sending you an enlargement of your photograph to remind you that you were able to be a real help not only to the poor and needy but to New Zealand farmers in this bad year they are passing through.

Peggy square rugs are still being made for worthy causes. I remember my aunts in Redcliffs having a regular afternoon session when a group of women came together to knit peggy squares and sew up the rugs. A good number were sent through the Save the Children Fund to Africa, and I once saw New Zealand peggy square blankets being distributed to destitute families in Lesotho.

I asked Karen Coffin what she called 'peggy squares' back in England. She wasn't even sure if she had a name for them – maybe just 'knitted squares'. I was glad she asked me about this term because the story of the peggy square is unique to New Zealand and it's a piece of our social history. They say things are going to get tougher in New Zealand. I've got some odd balls of wool somewhere. Maybe I should get knitting.

# Miles of old meanings

*29 November 2008*

I SEE JOHN ABOUT EVERY THREE months and he always tells me I should write a column about the language of weights and measures. Last month he reminded me again and I asked him why he thought it would be interesting. He replied:

> Well, we've changed to the metric system of weights and meas-
> ures but we still use the old terms in everyday language. We
> say 'I had to drive miles to find a petrol station' rather than 'I
> had to drive kilometres'. We're more likely to say 'I put on a few
> extra pounds over the winter' than 'a few extra kilograms'. And
> McDonald's sells 'a quarter-pounder' not 'a one hundred and
> twenty-grammer'.

In these columns I've written about many examples where the language has changed. Is this a case where society has changed but the old language still lurks around?

I decided to remind myself about the weights and measures systems I learned at school. So I dug out an old school exercise book containing my attempts at 'stories' in standard two. There it was, the Classic Exercise Book – 24 leaves, ruled 4 lines to the inch. On the back were set out 'Arithmetical tables'. There was the Sterling Money Table. I remember having to learn that one – four farthings to the penny, 12 pence to the shilling, two shillings to the florin, two shillings and sixpence to the halfcrown and so on up to 21 shillings to the guinea. Have these all disappeared? People in Britain still use pounds and pence, but does anyone know what a florin or a halfcrown are? Do people still 'spend a penny' when they go to the toilet?

The table for Imperial Dry Measure contained some words familiar

145

to me – pints, quarts and gallons. But who measured two glasses to the naggin or four naggins to the pint? The Cloth Measure had two and a quarter inches to the nail, and four nails to a quarter of a yard. Did people still measure cloth by the nail in 1949? Why was that on the back of my school exercise book? And there's the table of Hay and Straw Weight, with 36 pounds of straw to the truss, 56 pounds of old hay to the truss but 60 pounds of new hay to the truss, with 36 trusses making up a load. Did inspectors have to weigh those trusses of old hay and new hay and how on earth did they do it?

John is right, some old words have indeed remained in everyday language, but when I see him again I'll tell him about some of those that have disappeared. So which ones have survived? 'Inches' have been replaced by centimetres as a measurement, but you still hear people say, 'He lost six inches from his waist', or they might 'inch along' a tunnel. 'Yards' is still around in 'doing the hard yards', an expression originally from rugby. A 'fathom' (according to my Table of Lineal Measure) is two yards. We still say we can't fathom something when we can't understand it or get to the bottom of it.

Our word 'mile' came from Latin into Old English. It was originally the Roman measure of 1000 paces. We've changed to kilometres, but when we do extra work for someone we can still 'go the extra mile', and if we don't like something we can 'run a mile'. When we're daydreaming we're 'miles away'. It just doesn't sound right for a dreamer to be 'kilometres away'.

In the past weeks words like million, billion and trillion have been regularly heard. They have little reality for me. But when I was cleaning out a drawer the other day I found a threepenny bit and I was filled with affection and nostalgia. But I guess that's the measure of my age.

# The PM's shtrong views on Aushtralia

*6 December 2008*

In November I gave a talk to a community education class. I talked about some of our university research into early New Zealand English. At first the only evidence we had for the early New Zealand accent came from written comments in newspapers and journals. (They didn't call it a New Zealand accent at that time – it was the 'colonial twang'.) In their annual reports some New Zealand school inspectors expressed irritation and dismay about the pronunciation of New Zealand children. And, even worse, some of the teachers had the new accent too.

People started to notice the 'colonial twang' around 1900, and once they noticed it, they heard it all the time. Soon there were complaints from all over New Zealand.

Luckily for us we found another source of information about the early New Zealand accent. The Radio New Zealand Sound Archive (one of New Zealand's great treasures) had recordings of old people, collected in the 1940s. This meant we could listen to the voices of people born in New Zealand as early as the 1850s. From a research point of view this was like finding gold, and it makes New Zealand English the only variety of English in the world with recorded evidence of its whole history.

From these recordings it is clear that the early New Zealand accent was around long before 1900. There are recordings of people born in the 1870s – even in the 1860s – who sound like old New Zealanders. Some speakers born in Otago in the 1870s sound like some speakers born in the Waikato in the 1870s. And you would have no idea where their parents came from in Britain.

This shows that a new language feature can be around for a long time before people actually notice it. It can exist unnoticed for 20–30 years. So if you hear a pronunciation that troubles you, it's likely to be well entrenched.

In my talk I mentioned the interesting sound change that John Key demonstrates so clearly. For the consonant combination 'st' he uses 'sht'. So 'Australia' sounds like 'Aush-tralia' and 'strong' sounds like 'sh-trong'. This is not a new development. I have a recording made in 1993 of a young woman who uses this pronunciation. She tells us that she was cooking a 'roash-t' and the dog snatched it and went running down the 'sh-treet'.

We know that this sound change has been quietly working its way into New Zealand English (and Australian English) for some time. Someone told me after the lecture that her grandchildren in Australia were being encouraged to get rid of their 'slushy s's'. And now we have a prime minister who demonstrates this change. I told the class that John Key would have no idea he was using a sound change, and I explained that it was a change that had not yet achieved public awareness. 'But give it a few more years,' I said cheerfully.

But now I must eat my words. The day after I made that prediction, M. Quin wrote to *The Press*:

> I cringe at the prospect of [John Key's] appearance on the international stage, perplexing world leaders with statements that sound like, 'I have ek-shtremely sh-trong views on sh-tudents from sh-truggle sh-treet who go to Osh-tralia.'

Quin says this mangling of language is laziness and sets a bad example to children. Quin says that John Key sounds drunk or ignorant and neither is acceptable.

These strong words sound rather like the complaints about the early New Zealand accent – that 'odious colonial twang' with its 'mangled vowels' and 'wretched consonants'. But the letter-writer is wrong. This pronunciation is not caused by laziness or inebriation. It's a sound change, and because it's a sound change there's nothing anyone can do about it. You might not like it, but you'll have to get used to it. You'll be hearing it a lot for the next three years.

# Losing our linguistic heritage

*13 December 2008*

IN SEPTEMBER I RECEIVED AN email from Professor Tony Deverson, who said he was about to give his last lecture. Normally that wouldn't be surprising – it was the time of year when a lot of academics were giving their final lectures. But in Deverson's case it really was his last lecture. He began teaching in the English Department at the University of Canterbury over 40 years ago, and, although he's formally retired, he has continued to teach a university course on the history of the English language. Now he's calling it a day. But, significantly, this lecture was also the last lecture on the history of the English language at Canterbury University.

When I began teaching in the English Department in the 1960s, students doing a BA had to take a language paper, and English (language and literature) counted as a language. We repeated each lecture four times to over 200 students in every class. The history of the English language was a compulsory part of stage one English. In those years, students in the English Department could also study Old English, Middle English and Old Norse, with papers also on Beowulf and Chaucer. The university had some fine teachers – some will remember Dr Robin Barrett's scholarly approach to Old English and his dry humour. Literature lecturers (such as Archie Stockwell and Ray Copland) also taught Old English.

So I'm tempted to sing, 'Those were the days, my friend, we thought they'd never end.' But we were wrong. Everything changes. The English Department is now The Department of Culture, Literature and Society. There's been no Old or Middle English, Chaucer or Beowulf for some time, and now the last lecture on the history of the English language has been delivered. There are new courses on creative writing, children's literature, Australian literature, love and desire in the English Renaissance and more. As the poet Tennyson wrote, 'The old order changeth, yielding place to new.'

But the decision to drop the language papers can't be because of lack of interest. Since I've been writing this column I've received many letters and emails from readers of *The Press* wanting to know more about the origins of words, and about language changes over time. The nine-part BBC TV series *The Story of English* won an Emmy Award and continues to be replayed. Does it matter that these subjects are no longer offered for study at the university? I suppose that depends on your point of view.

I was recently in Wellington and went to Te Papa, where I saw the splendid exhibitions of early Maori history and the arrival of people from the Pacific. The purpose of my visit was to attend the production of the end-of-year play at Clyde Quay School where my youngest daughter teaches. I watched eight- and nine-year-old children acting out the history of Wellington, beginning with the Maori myths associated with the area, telling the story of Kupe and his canoe, describing the arrival of Edward Gibbon Wakefield and so on up to the present day. It was inspiring to see these children re-enacting the history of their own city. They had been studying it and they wrote some of the script themselves. And the history of English, with the arrival of the Anglo-Saxons in Britain, the Vikings, the Norman Conquest and the expansion into the New World is part of their history too.

Of course Deverson won't stop his language work. He is co-editor of the *New Zealand Oxford Dictionary*. Like others, I'll hold on to his excellent handouts on the history of the English language, and I'm grateful for his help when readers of *The Press* ask me questions I can't answer.

And who knows, maybe in the future this early period of the English language will be rediscovered and become a trendy new subject. We can always hope.

# Box of Christmas words

*20 December 2008*

IN OUR GARAGE IS A cardboard carton labelled 'Christmas'. It contains an odd assortment of Christmas decorations, tinsel, lights and streamers. Some things in it go back over 50 years. There are primitive Christmas tree decorations made by small children, and gifts from overseas visitors. And we bring them out only at Christmas.

It occurred to me that we have a similar box of Christmas words that we use only at this time of year. Some go back to the beginning of the English language. Our word 'Yule', for example, predates Christianity in Britain. It originally came from *jol*, a midwinter Germanic pagan feast that lasted 12 days and included the burning of the yule log. (*Jol* is related to another word we hear mainly around Christmas time – 'jolly').

We can see the origin of 'Christmas' in its spelling. In Old English it was Cristes Masse – the mass of Christ. The 't' sound has long been dropped, as it has in other words like 'listen', 'hasten', 'moisten', and place names like 'Christchurch' and 'Westminster'.

Father Christmas first appeared as a character in a masque written by Ben Jonson in 1616. He turned up in various guises over the next two centuries as Sir Christmas, Lord Christmas and Father Christmas. It was only in the Victoria era that he became associated with children and carried gifts. When I was a child and put out my Christmas stocking I also left out a pen and paper for his autograph. In the morning, in a shaky script, I found he had written 'St Nicholas'. I suppose I should have expected that, growing up in a vicarage. But I didn't know then that St Nicholas was the origin of Santa Claus. He was a fourth-century Greek Christian bishop, famous for his care of the poor. In America the name Santa Claus evolved through a Dutch dialect from 'St Nicholas'.

In the Christmas word box are other words we bring out only at Christmas. There's Noël – 'The first noël the angels did say.' What were they saying? It's a French word meaning Christmas. It's come through Old French from the Latin word *natalis* meaning 'birth'. 'Noël' is also sometimes used in France as a name for people born around Christmas time.

The words of the King James version of the Bible have been added to our Christmas vocabulary. I can remember one of my children asking what 'abiding' meant. What were the shepherds doing, abiding in those fields by night? Were they just waiting around, or did they actually have a camp? And there's the manger, and the swaddling clothes. Then there are reindeer and sleighs. The 'rein' part of reindeer was Old Norse *hrienn*. It's a bit like our word horn. A reindeer was originally a 'horn animal'.

'Carol' comes from an Old French word for a hymn or a joyful song. I like the irreverent way children have rewritten some familiar carols, with shepherds washing their socks by night, and the mysterious place called 'Orientar' where we three kings came from – one on a scooter, tooting his hooter, following yonder star.

Last year I attended a Christmas lunch in a retirement home. I sat next to an elderly woman whose bewildered stare showed she didn't know where she was or even who she was. But when the music of 'Silent Night' came on I saw her lips moving with the words.

Here in New Zealand our box of Christmas words includes words and customs that go back to the very origins of the English language, combined with our own customs of barbecues and Christmas at the beach, Christmas lilies and the New Zealand Christmas tree, the pohutukawa.

Hymn writer Shirley Murray has captured this in a New Zealand carol that begins:

Carol our Christmas, an upside-down Christmas;
The snow is not falling and trees are not bare.
Carol the summer and welcome the Christ Child,
Warm in our sunshine and sweetness of air.

# Hokey-pokey hanky-panky

*27 December 2008*

MARIE HAS ASKED ME WHERE the term 'hoity toity' comes from. She said she liked the sound of the word. It means arrogant or self-important. Lady Catherine de Burgh in Jane Austen's *Pride and Prejudice* had a 'hoity-toity' manner of speaking. So did Lady Bracknell in Oscar Wilde's *The Importance of Being Earnest*. They looked down their noses as they spoke.

'Hoity-toity' is formed through reduplication with the meaning in the first word. 'Hoity' originally came from 'hoyden', meaning a rude or boisterous girl, but it's changed in meaning considerably along the way. It was pronounced 'heighty', so you can see how it became associated with 'highness', and it's not too difficult to see how it acquired the present meaning of 'haughty'.

There are some good English words made through reduplication. Think of fuddy-duddy, harum-scarum, helter-skelter, hurly-burly, mumbo-jumbo, happy-clappy, hanky-panky, higgledy-piggledy. The oldest example I can find is 'willy-nilly', meaning something that occurs whether it's wanted or not. The term dates from around 1000 AD. 'Nilly' comes from a very old word, nill, which is long gone from English. 'Will' meant to want to do something and 'nill' was the opposite – to want to avoid something. So the original phrase 'will he, nill he' meant whether it is 'with his will' or 'against his will'.

Another old reduplication is 'riff-raff'. This dates from the 14th century and comes from Old French. The French verb *rifler* meant to plunder, or to strip, while *rafler* meant to carry off. So the original French phrase referred to the practice of going through the possessions of dead bodies on a battlefield and taking anything of value. We can see evidence of rifler in the sentence 'He rifled through my jewellery case,' meaning he was looking for something to steal. *Raffler* (with 2 'f's) was later used as the name of a game where the winner apparently grabbed the winnings, giving us our word raffle. The term 'riff-raff' remained tainted by those early corpse robbers and eventually came to mean the dregs of society.

When I was a student studying the English Reformation I was told that the term 'hocus-pocus' came from the point in the old Latin mass where the communion bread was raised and consecrated and the priest said 'Hoc est corpus meum' meaning 'This is my body'. Uneducated people at the time knew this was a significant point in the service, but because they didn't understand Latin the words came to mean a magic trick.

I liked this story and passed it on to my students, but I've now discovered that it's highly dubious. It first appeared in an anti-Catholic sermon given by John Tillotson, the Archbishop of Canterbury, in the 1690s, so we should take it with a pinch of salt. According to my dictionaries 'hocus-pocus' could have come from a kind of dog-Latin used by jugglers and conjurers. By the 17th century the term was used for a trick or a deception. It's also the origin of our word hoax.

Another example of reduplication is 'hokey-pokey'. Apparently 'hokey-pokey' was first applied to icecream sold in Britain in the late 19th century. According to Michael Quinion (www.worldwidewords.org) it could have come from the 'hokey-pokey men' – Italians who went around selling icecream from handcarts. They called out 'Gelati, ecco un poco!' meaning 'Icecream, here is a little!' or 'O che poco!' meaning 'O how little!' This was because the icecream was cheap and you didn't get very much. I remember an Italian man selling icecream from a horse-drawn cart in Sydenham in the 1940s, but he rang a bell.

Quinion also gives another explanation, which is that 'hokey-pokey' might have come from 'hocus-pocus' because this early icecream was made from inferior materials. So there was the idea of trickery again. Both of these explanations suggest a cheap, inferior product – nothing like the wonderful New Zealand hokey-pokey icecream that all visitors to this country should try.

# Children copy peers, not parents

3 January 2009

My father-in-law, Chris Gordon, came to New Zealand at the age of 18 from Northern Ireland. He spent his adult life as a dairy farmer in Waipu, Northland, milking 40 cows – all with names. Chris lived in New Zealand until he died at the age of 93, and the whole time he retained his strong Irish accent.

No doubt when he went back to Ireland for the occasional visit, family members there would have noticed changes in his accent, but in New Zealand you noticed his Irish accent. Curiously, when my husband was growing up, he had no idea that his father spoke with an Irish accent. It was only at secondary school, when friends commented on it, that he realised his father spoke differently from other people in the district.

This is a common phenomenon and it's been given a name – the Ethan Principle. The theory was developed by a Canadian sociolinguist, Professor Jack Chambers, who came to the University of Canterbury in 2001 on a fellowship. It's named after a boy called Ethan, who was born and raised in Toronto. Ethan's parents were Eastern European immigrants who spoke English with 'medium to strong' accents.

But Ethan didn't speak English with the sort of accent his parents used – his English was the same as his other Canadian classmates'. And Ethan was well into his school years before he was even aware that his parents spoke English with a foreign accent.

Chambers has suggested that children like Ethan are equipped with an 'innate language filter'. When Ethan heard his mother pronounce an English vowel with her foreign accent he heard it as a Canadian vowel. The foreign-sounding vowel was filtered out. Even as a pre-schooler Ethan never acquired his parents' accent features – not even in isolated words. Chambers found that this was not unique to Ethan and it was not at all unusual. Children think their parents sound normal, and they don't become aware of any differences until about puberty.

When Chambers talked about this to a sociolinguistics class at the University of Canterbury, one student came up after the lecture and told him her father had a cleft palate that affected his pronunciation. She told Chambers she hadn't realised there was anything unusual about her father's speech until school friends commented on it.

A different example is of an American family who moved from the rural south to West Virginia. The parents with their daughter (who had been brought up in the south) all retained their southern accents. But their son, brought up in West Virginia, sounded like his classmates in West Virginia. When the boy was questioned, he insisted that everyone in his family sounded exactly the same.

In studying the origins of the New Zealand accent we've found that those very first settlers who arrived in New Zealand spoke English with a variety of accents, but it wasn't long before people all over New Zealand were complaining that children were speaking with 'a colonial twang' – early New Zealand English. So perhaps this innate language filter was at work. New Zealand-born children were not aware of their parents' Irish or Scottish accents. They heard only the accents of the children around them.

We know that the New Zealand accent emerged very quickly, probably between 1870 and 1890. We have a recording of Mrs Annie Hamilton, born in Arrowtown in 1877, whose parents came from Ireland. She sounds very similar to Miss Maryanne Turnbull, born in Morrinsville in the Waikato in 1875, whose parents came from Scotland. Both sound like old New Zealanders. Because of the Ethan Principle, they had filtered out the accents of their parents.

This is why I cannot agree with John from Rangiora, who thinks that the way John Key pronounces 'strong' as 'sh-trong' could have come from his Austrian mother. And it's why my husband doesn't have an Irish accent like his father.

# The challenges of English spelling

*10 January 2009*

WHEN OUR CHILDREN WERE AT primary school there was a morning ritual after breakfast when we'd say, 'It's time to hear your spelling.' Out came those battered spelling lists. I hope it helped, though sometimes I had my doubts.

Not all languages have the spelling difficulties we have with English. Spanish has a consistent spelling system – if you read a Spanish word you know how to pronounce it. But it doesn't always work that way in English. Think of the punctuation possibilities for a final '-ough': enough, though, through, thorough, bough and cough.

So why is it harder to spell in English? The answer lies in history.

The earliest form of English was Old English (sometimes called Anglo-Saxon), which dates from the fifth century. When Old English was written down the spelling was quite sensible. A letter represented a specific sound. Our word 'queen' was written 'cwen', 'king' was 'cyning'.

Then came the Norman Conquest, in 1066. William the Conqueror and his followers spoke Norman French. For the next 300 years the powerful people in England spoke French in their castles, while out in the fields the peasants continued to speak English. And the French had their own way of spelling. That's where the 'qu' in queen came from, and the 'k' in king. Have you noticed that the only difference between 'mouse' and 'mice' is in the vowel sound? Yet 'mouse' has an Old English 's' and 'mice' has a French 'c'.

At the time of the Renaissance, learned people changed the spelling of some words to show their Latin origins. This was considered sophisticated. In Old English the river Thames in London was spelt 'Temes'. This was later given the Latin spelling of 'th', though the pronunciation didn't change. Today you can pronounce the name Anthony with the original 't' (with the shortened form Tony) or with the Latin 'th'.

Up to the 14th century 'debt' was written 'dette'. Then it was changed to 'debt' to show that it came from Latin *debitum*. A 'b' was added to 'doubt' to show it came from Latin *dubitum*. You could say this was an early spelling reform, but it only made matters worse. Sometimes the reformers got it wrong. English had a word 'iland', which came from Old English. The reformers mistakenly thought it came from Latin *insula*. This is why we have the odd spelling 'island' today.

We also have some Flemish spellings added by the printer William Caxton, such as 'gh' in 'ghost' and 'ghastly'. And there were some Greek spellings – 'ph' for 'f' and 'rh' for 'r'. Chaucer spelt 'rhyme' as 'rime'. I'm sure a lot of teachers regret that change.

Some changes in spelling had purely practical reasons. Early writing was angular and spiky and the letter 'u' looked a bit like a 'v'. When it was beside 'n' or 'm' this could be confusing, so scribes solved this problem by changing 'u' to 'o'. That's why we have come, love, won, done, son, some and so on.

Today we can identify people by their handwriting. Once you could identify people by their spelling, because variation was commonplace. There was variation in the printed word, also: some printers liked to use a lot of capital letters, some didn't. Type was set with moveable blocks, and typesetters trying to get a straight margin would alter the length of words to make them fit the line. If space was limited they wrote 'goodnes' but if there was room to spare they added some extra letters: 'goodnesse'.

So the spelling mistake is comparatively recent in the history of English. It came with standardisation, and that happened only about 200 years ago.

Pronunciation has changed over the years but old spellings have not. Those silent letters in words like castle, listen, walk, gnaw and knife once used to be pronounced.

Our English spelling is a wonderful guide to the history of the English language, but this isn't much use to children learning their spelling lists today.

# Demystifying academic writing

*17 January 2009*

I'VE RECENTLY FOUND A COPY of my father's MA economics thesis. It was written in 1923 at Canterbury University College and is entitled 'The Production of Gold in New Zealand'. It's a carbon copy with 127 pages of double-spaced typing. The bibliography is half a page. My father was awarded first-class honours for this thesis by an examiner in England.

My daughter has recently finished her MA thesis at the same university and there is no comparison between the two pieces of work. Hers is twice as long (after being considerably cut back), the bibliography is 11 pages and she has chapters of theoretical analysis and detailed discussion of both primary and secondary sources.

It's obvious that standards and expectations of student writing and research are higher today.

My father's thesis is also strikingly different from those written today in another way. His was easy to read. My experience of the subject of economics is limited to Economics I about 50 years ago. But I could read his thesis without difficulty, and I also found it surprisingly interesting. If I were to pick up a thesis today on gold production in New Zealand I would not expect it to be so accessible.

I taught at the University of Canterbury for many years, and I learned about academic writing. I've also spent a lifetime reading academic books. Now from the safety of retirement I can say that academic writing (and I've played the game myself) often seems designed to exclude most readers and inhibit easy understanding.

I remember hearing a lecturer once telling me it had taken him a year to understand one page of a particular writer in his field. Why would you bother? There seems to be an unwritten rule that if something is hard to understand then it must be brilliant. If something is easily understood, it's not scholarly; even worse, it might be 'popular'.

I am not questioning the use of specialist vocabulary. Technical terms are the tools of our trade. Linguists need phonemes and morphemes, allophones and allomorphs. Sociolinguists need diglossia and code-switching. But my concern is about the way in which straightforward material is often converted into something that is convoluted and difficult to understand.

I took an academic book at random from my bookshelf to find some examples for this column. The book was on the subject of politeness. In the first chapter I read about 'first-order politeness conceptualisations'. What are they? Well, they're the ideas or beliefs that ordinary people have about politeness. People having a conversation are 'participants in verbal interaction' or even 'participants in socio-communicative verbal interaction'. And this verbal interaction is 'situated spatio-temporally'. Well, there's a time and place for everything. The author tells us that politeness is thought of as 'the deployment of linguistic structures of politic behaviour in ongoing social practice'.

Fortunately the book had a glossary, so I looked up 'politic behaviour'. Now I know it means 'that behaviour, linguistic or non-linguistic, which the participants construct as being appropriate to the ongoing social interaction'. Thank goodness for that.

As a university teacher I used to spend tutorial time doing guided readings of academic papers, helping my students to understand what the authors were trying to say. This was sometimes a struggle, and when they were eventually enlightened, some students would say, 'Oh, is that all it meant?' Students learned to play the game too. One told me she thought she could raise her mark in an essay in any arts subject if she could get the phrase 'competing discourses' somewhere into her text.

I recently read an article in an American journal about eco-friendly houses. The author advocated the use of outdoor solar linear fabric dehydrators. I'm thinking of writing to that man to tell him that in New Zealand we have rotating as well as linear outdoor solar (and wind-assisted) fabric dehydrators. But in this country we call them clotheslines.

# Shifting the boundaries

*24 January 2009*

A READER HAS ASKED ME ABOUT the word 'pinny'. That's a word that takes me back to my childhood. 'Put your pinny on,' my mother would say if there was any chance I might get dirty. In those days when washing was a whole morning's work and involved lighting the copper and turning the wringer, every effort was made to avoid getting things dirty. (My mother used to sew 'dress preservers' inside the sleeves of her dresses. They absorbed perspiration and could be taken out and washed separately to save washing the dress itself.)

'Pinny' is a shortened form of 'pinafore', which began life as a garment that could be pinned onto the front of (afore) a dress. A pinafore didn't have buttons and some were quite elaborate with frills. Alice in Wonderland wore one. In Gilbert and Sullivan's comic opera *HMS Pinafore* it was a humorous touch to give the naval warship the name of a girl's apron.

Today pinafores and even pinnies are old-fashioned, but the apron remains. My mother had a collection of these – sacking aprons for some kinds of work, and elegant aprons with embroidery for more genteel pursuits. The word 'apron' has an interesting history because it began as 'a napron'. With 'napron' it's easy to see the family relationship to other English words like 'napkin' and 'nappy'. Some other English words have had a similar shift in their word boundaries. 'Adder' (a type of snake) comes from 'a nadder,' 'umpire' comes from 'a noumpere'. (If you want someone to adjudicate you need a 'non peer'.) 'Orange' came into English from Arabic *naranj* but in this case the 'n' was lost in French before it was borrowed into English.

Sometimes the word boundaries shifted in the other direction. A newt was once 'an ewte'. In Middle English 'eke' meant 'also'. So an additional name – an 'also name' – was 'an ekename'. Say it quickly and it becomes 'a nickname'. In Shakespeare's plays men were sometimes addressed as

'Nuncle'. This came from 'mine uncle'. The name 'Ned' was formed from 'mine Ed' and Nelly from 'mine Elly'.

If you say 'icecream' quickly it can sound like 'I scream'; if you say 'an aim' it could be confused with 'a name'. So it's not surprising that people speaking Early English who couldn't read or write might get their word boundaries mixed up and the changed version eventually became the accepted form. The farewell 'God be with you' became compressed into 'Goodbye'. The old-fashioned expression 'prithee' was 'I pray thee'; 'blimey' was a shortened form of 'gorblimey' from 'God blind me'; 'howdy' was a 16th-century shortening of 'How do you do?'

It's not always easy to draw sharp lines between the elements within a word, and sometimes people make mistakes. The word 'minimum' comes from Latin *min* meaning little. (The same element is found in minor and minus.) The second part of minimum – '*im*' – means most. But people connected 'minimum' to the totally unrelated word 'miniature' and before long there was a new prefix in English – 'mini', with the miniskirt, the minivan, the minipill, the minibar and of course that nifty little car, the Mini. So although some new words came about as mistakes, they are still good and useful words.

Writing this column has made me think about aprons. We can be tied to our mother's apron strings. In the theatre, the apron is the part of the stage in front of the curtain. And it's also the front of an aircraft hangar and an air terminal building.

Maybe, instead of throwing our clothes into the washing machine every time we've worn them, we could put on an apron – or a pinny – and it would save power and water. And that would surely be a good thing.

# Purr words and snarl words

*31 January 2009*

'TRADITIONALLY BUILT' – THIS IS how Alexander McCall Smith describes his leading character, Precious Ramotswe, in his novels set in Botswana. It sounds so much kinder than saying she was fat or obese or overweight.

American linguist S. J. Hayakawa invented some useful terms for the different slants we can give to the same referents – to show them in a positive or a negative light. He called them 'purr words' and 'snarl words'. 'Traditionally built' is a purr word, whereas fat, overweight and obese are 'snarl words'.

It's an interesting exercise to identify other purr and snarl words – he's thrifty but she's mean; he's conceited but she's confident; she's shrewd but he's cunning. Is she a free spirit or is she just irresponsible?

It can matter whether you say a person is skinny or slender, fat or traditionally built. And it can matter whether you describe a person as a terrorist or a freedom fighter.

At election time we saw some nice examples of purr words and snarl words. Those purr words were streaming out – common sense, balanced, robust. We were told that 'the fat in the bloated state bureaucracy will be removed by a cabinet expenditure control committee'. A different version might have been: 'Our excellent public service will be slashed by a razor gang.' In Britain the Conservative government of Margaret Thatcher resolutely referred to the 'community charge', but on the streets it was always the hated 'poll tax'.

I thought of Hayakawa's purr words and snarl words when I read a front-page article in the *Sunday Star-Times* just before Christmas. It was headed 'Schools earn F for failure in report jargon'. The basis of the article was a complaint by a mother about her five-year old son's school report. The teacher had written: 'James finds self-management quite challenging.

He needs to use appropriate mediation skills when solving conflicts, and practise safety procedures.' James's mother said he had recently broken his arm at school, and she thought this might account for the reference to safety procedures. She said this report was 'next to useless' and she wanted teachers to give her clear details about her son's progress.

It's true that the extract from James's report was written in bland, anodyne language. It was written with purr words. But what was the alternative? I showed it to some teachers and asked them if they could interpret the comments and describe James and his behaviour in the clear way his mother required. The results were not flattering to James, who was described in various ways as a badly behaved child, and a pain to have in the classroom.

A correspondent to the *Sunday Star-Times* carried out the same exercise and a week later wrote:

> The report James brought home is very easy to understand and I'm happy to translate it for the benefit of his mother: 'James is an ill-behaved little brat. He either doesn't know the rules or chooses to ignore them and reacts badly when things don't go his way. He argues, shouts and pushes other children to get what he wants, and runs around causing mayhem with predictable results. (I hope his arm is better now.)'

At the last election a move towards clear, jargon-free report writing was part of the government's education policy. But it could be tricky. If the teacher had written 'James is a disobedient and difficult child' would his mother have been satisfied? Maybe she would have complained to the *Sunday Star-Times* about that too. The journalist who wrote the article didn't talk to the teacher who wrote the report, or to other practising teachers who every year have to perform the exercise of presenting children's work and progress to parents in ways that are truthful but not damning. 'James finds self-management quite challenging' is an example of purr words. Would parents really prefer the snarl-worded alternative?

# Oh, well, it's a thingamajig

*7 February 2009*

L ESLEY HAS NOTICED THAT WHEN people are talking they sometimes say 'and that'. She's given me some examples. This one comes from a
short story by Owen Marshall:

> 'Look,' says his father, 'it's a matter of things being more serious
> than the doc first thought. There's some more tests to be done
> and that, but he reckons there's no sign of anything really bad.'

The use of 'and that' is a nice example of the difference between spoken
English and written English, because it's a feature of speaking, not writing.
When people see their own speech accurately transcribed they're often
surprised and think it looks dreadful. They're conditioned to seeing writ-
ten English, not spoken English. Spoken English is different from written
English and should not be judged by the standards of written English.

We can plan what we write, but when we speak we need to think on
the spot, so we use simple constructions. When people are chatting,
you wouldn't expect someone to say, 'Robin supposed Sam to be unwell.'
That's a written sentence.

In speech you'll hear words and phrases you won't find in writing.
'Where's that thingamajig for getting tops off bottles?' or 'I need a what-
chamecallit to put on the end of the curtain rail.'

We also have useful phrases to indicate that we could say more but
we're not going to. 'Our teacher just told us there were nouns and verbs
and adverbs and blah blah blah – you know.' Why bother to spell out
conjunctions, pronouns and prepositions? You've got the general idea.
A relative who comes from Ireland says 'la la la'. It has the same effect.
So this is where 'and that' fits in. It's another version of 'blah blah blah'.
'There's nouns and verbs and that.'

One feature of speech that is often condemned is the use of the 'ums' and 'ers' – what we call 'voiced hesitations'. But these are useful devices when you're thinking on the spot. They give you time to plan the next section of your speech, and they also give your listener time to absorb your message. I know voiced hesitations are frowned upon in public speaking, and when they occur constantly they can be annoying. But language read from a script that is dense with information, and has no hesitations or repetitions, can be hard to take in. I find this when I'm listening to the weather forecast on the radio. It has so much information that I mentally switch off until it's time for Canterbury. But then I miss Canterbury and find myself listening to the forecast for the Chatham Islands.

Another feature of spoken English is the use of small words that we don't use in writing – words like 'well' and 'oh' and 'just'. Here's part of a transcript of some people learning to play a board game. 'Oh well, I'll just put this down. Oh, I'll just take one of these. Oh no, hang on. Oh, what do I do? Oh well, you take that card. Oh oh, well – I'll just see what happens.'

'Well,' 'oh,' and 'just,' don't fit into the grammatical categories we're taught at school. Take 'well', for example. In 'she isn't well' it's adjective. In 'he's well qualified' it's an adverb. But what about, 'Well, what do you think? Well, I'm not sure?' This needs a different category. We call them 'discourse markers' or 'conversation markers'.

Little words like 'well' and 'oh' and 'just' are hard to translate into another language but they occur all the time in speech. When you hear second-language learners using them it's a good sign that their English is becoming more fluent. And when writers use them in written conversation it sounds like genuine spoken English. It's a mark of Owen Marshall's skill as a writer and his good ear for New Zealand speech that he uses the phrase 'and that'. It rings true. And it's a mark of Lesley's sharp observation of language that she noticed it.

# TV is not to blame

*14 February 2009*

A LIVING LANGUAGE IS A CHANGING language. This is one of the first things we taught our linguistics students at university. Whether we like it or not, language changes. Some people write to me to tell me I'm far too accepting of language change – they want me to do something about it. But I can't stop the inevitable.

As a sociolinguist I've always been interested in the 'how' question. How does language change? We've been tracking the changes in New Zealand English from its beginnings. But there's another big question – why does language change? I know that I speak differently from my parents, my children don't talk like me, and my grandchildren are different again. We didn't *need* to change the language, so why does change happen? It's a question I can't answer.

Some people believe very strongly that language change has direct causes, and the main culprit is the media. In the 1940s and 50s there were complaints about the bad effects of radio on children's speech. Then TV became the villain. This view was strongly voiced in the 1970s over a children's TV programme hosted by a young Englishman called Stu Dennison, who dressed as an untidy schoolboy and spoke in a London accent. The programme was called *Gizzago*.

I wonder how many people still remember Stu today. In 1976 many letters appeared in the *Listener* about Stu and his speech. The correspondence was started by a Christchurch man who was concerned that his four-year-old son was saying 'yeah' instead of 'yes' and, while watching his father fixing the washing machine, said, 'Arrkardeadgizzago,' which the father interpreted as meaning 'Please may I try'. He blamed his son's speech on Dennison, whom he described as 'a long-haired pseudo Cockney/Liverpudlian with defective adenoids'. This was followed by 36 more letters before the correspondence was closed.

Apart from a few letters, mainly from children, saying they liked the programme and enjoyed its cheerful host, most were from parents deeply worried that the programme would damage their children's speech for life. TV1's attitude was said to be irresponsible; the language on *Gizzago* was described as 'prostitution of the English language', which would have 'harmful effects on children's speaking habits'. A mother from Palmerston North collected signatures asking for a new host for the show.

The belief that TV has a bad influence on children's speech is a deep-seated and widespread popular conviction. It's the same all over the world. But it's a myth. Yes, children might pick up words or phrases. My own children adopted Homer Simpson's 'Duh!' *Wayne's World* in the 1990s gave them 'it was a great party, not'. But pronunciation is a different matter. Children can listen to hours of American TV without developing a trace of an American accent.

One strong piece of evidence that this is a myth comes from the hearing children of deaf parents, who cannot learn language by listening to the radio or to TV. In a famous case a boy called Vincent was encouraged by his deaf parents to watch lots of TV in the hope that he would learn to talk from it, but Vincent remained speechless. At the age of three, when other people began to talk to him, his speaking ability was badly impaired. He had picked up no language skills at all from the TV, because he could not interact with it. It didn't answer him or talk to him. In the jargon of language acquisition, there was no 'face-to-face interaction'. And that is essential for language development.

So those anxious parents in the 1970s needn't have worried about *Gizzago* and its cheerful host. While some of those preschoolers might have picked up some phrases from the television – 'Nice one, Stu' – I can state with certainty that not one of them today will speak like Stu Dennison.

# Linguistic treasures in Papers Past

*21 February 2009*

OVER A YEAR AGO I was invited to write a chapter for a book called *Varieties in Writing: The written word as linguistic evidence.* It's about what we can learn about different varieties of English from written accounts, and my topic was New Zealand English. I completely forgot about this request until I received a last-minute reminder that it was due, so Christmas plans were shelved while I put my head down.

Twenty years ago I had spent a happy time going through old journals and magazines looking for any written comment I could find on the early New Zealand accent. I ended up with three filing boxes of material. There was gold in the reports of New Zealand school inspectors. Some of them had a special interest in pronunciation and wrote about it with passion. They were appalled by the way the children were speaking in New Zealand schools.

When I'd almost completed my chapter I went to the University of Canterbury library to look for some missing references. There I met Dr Colin McGeorge, an expert on the history of education in New Zealand. He was the person who first introduced me to those old school inspectors' reports. He told me about a wonderful new source of historical data called Papers Past. It's the work of the National Library and it contains more than one million pages of digitised New Zealand newspapers and periodicals. The collection covers the years 1839 to 1920 and includes 40 newspapers from all regions of New Zealand. The plan is to make all old New Zealand newspapers searchable.

This is an amazing research tool for anyone studying New Zealand history. I thought of the hours I spent in the university library copying out relevant passages by hand onto cards. And doing the same on visits to the Alexander Turnbull Library in Wellington. Today I can sit at home with my computer and search away through old newspapers to my heart's content.

Now, thanks to Papers Past (http://paperspast.natlib.govt.nz), I have managed to find many more written comments about the way people spoke in this country a hundred years ago. It was too late for my chapter but it's certainly added to my collection of data. For example, in the *Otago Witness* in 1898 is an account of an end-of-year display at the Christian Brothers' School. The visitors had to watch a lengthy series of gymnastic exercises and then listen to six boys reciting poetry for the junior elocution contest. The judge of the contest, Mr A. H. Burton, made a speech before he announced the result. He didn't mince his words:

> There is an evil against which I am determined to wage war. Whenever I find that evil coming up I must strike it. It is prevalent in some parts of the country and in some schools. I refer to what is called the colonial twang. I trust that all parents and teachers will do their utmost to put it down.

This was greeted with applause.
'Women and Whine' was a headline in the *Evening Post* in 1913:

> In the streets one may hear near twos and threes of young women a disagreeable mixture of drawl and whine with the nose as an important instrument in the shocking orchestra … the girls have the school habit of mangling words – drawing them out in tortured flatness between the teeth, reluctant to let them slip through. Probably the blame rests with the parents, who did not bother to check the slovenliness of speech into which any child easily lapses.

People in New Zealand have been writing to the paper about our speech since newspapers began, and no doubt they will go on doing so. Maybe letters written today will find their way into some future academic research project.

# Get used to it, eh

*28 February 2009*

WE'VE BEEN TRAVELLING AROUND THE North Island with Peter Trudgill and his wife Jean Hannah. If you knew about sociolinguistics you might think I was name dropping because Trudgill is one of the big names in this subject. He is Britain's foremost sociolinguist and dialectologist, and he also has a great interest in New Zealand English. That's why he comes here every year.

On our travels we visited family members in Whangarei. We were sitting on the deck of their fine house with our cool white wine, gazing out over the hills, when the conversation turned to language. Rosemary said, 'What I really can't stand is when people say "eh".' Joan said she hated this too.

I didn't take much notice, as I hear things like this often and in the interests of domestic harmony I usually try to ignore them.

But Trudgill wasn't going to let it pass. 'Why do you hate it?' he asked.

The answer came, 'Because it sounds so ugly.'

Trudgill didn't give up. 'Why is it ugly?'

'Because it just is.'

Trudgill then asked, 'Do you dislike the first letter of the alphabet?'

'No,' they said, 'but that's different.'

'But it's the same sound.'

Sometimes you just can't argue with people. We changed the subject.

All around the North Island I heard people using 'eh'. It's quite infectious. In a small shop in Te Kaha on the East Cape the woman behind the counter said, 'It's really hot, eh.' And I found myself replying, 'It is, eh.'

It didn't surprise me that I was hearing more of it on the East Cape, because research at Victoria University in Wellington in the 1990s showed that the 'eh' was most common in the casual speech of young Maori men and women, and also young Pakeha women. It was not so common with older Pakeha.

The technical name for 'eh' is a 'tag'. In English we use tag questions all the time. 'It's been very warm, hasn't it?' 'It hasn't been very warm, has it?' No one teaches us that a positive statement must have a negative tag question, and a negative statement has a positive one. That's a rule we learned when we were learning to talk. Take some more examples: She likes plums, doesn't she? Christopher can't swim, can he? That was such a good film, wasn't it? Don't be late, will you?

I could go on, but I hope this shows how tag questions can be quite a challenge for people learning English. They have to work out the correct tag for each sentence.

'Eh' is different and it's useful because it's an invariable tag. It's always the same. She likes plums, eh? That was such a good film, eh? Christopher can't swim, eh? Don't be late, eh?

When I was in London four years ago I noticed young people using a tag question in an odd way. It was the tag 'innit?' You can see it comes from 'isn't it?' 'It's really cool, innit?' But I was hearing young people saying things like, 'They're going to Hackney, innit?'

When we were living in London in 1990 my 14-year-old daughter wrote down some examples of this: Tottenham rules, innit? We're having beans and chips, innit? 'Innit' has changed from being a form of 'isn't it' to being an invariable tag like 'eh'. Paul Warren of Victoria University has alerted me to a guide to youth slang written for the British supermarket chain Tescos to assist its staff. For 'innit' it gives the meanings 'Isn't it?' 'Is it?' 'You know?' and 'Oh really?'

We don't need 'innit' in New Zealand because we have our own invariable tag, 'eh'. I hope Rosemary and Joan get over their dislike of this handy little conversational prop. Last year my three-year-old grandson took my hand and said 'Apples are good for you, eh Granny?' And what can a granny reply? 'They certainly are, eh Frankie!'

# Wife-beater shirt hard to take

*7 March 2009*

DAVID SMALL SENT ME AN interesting correspondence about a company selling 'wife-beater' shirts on TradeMe. Small said this was 'an outrageous trivialising or even glorifying of violence against women'. His complaint was ignored by TradeMe and the advertisement for the shirts was re-listed unaltered. But when he contacted the *New Zealand Herald*, action was immediate and the auction was withdrawn.

I hadn't heard the term 'wife-beater shirt' but my children knew it. 'It's a T-shirt that's like a singlet,' they told me, and they said that it had been around for some time. In the film *Once Were Warriors* Jake 'the Muss' Heke wore one.

When I began looking for more information I was relieved to find that this term was not a New Zealand invention – it came here from overseas. The first written citation dates from 1996. In my searches I found many overseas references to these shirts, including instructions on how to fold one properly.

Random House's *The Maven's Word of the Day* says:

> The name 'wife-beater' is growing more and more popular, rais-ing the concerns of many victims' rights groups that naming a popular article of clothing after an incident of domestic violence desensitises young people to violence against women.

But it goes on to add:

> Many slang experts argue that this tongue-in-cheek name mocks the self-conscious machismo of the upper-class teen as he strug-gles to evoke the blue-collar image of another time and place.

The correspondence about wife-beater shirts reminded me of an incident over 15 years ago when a young relative was explaining to me that she was saving up for some 'fuck-me boots'. I must have gasped but she continued as casually as if she was talking about Doc Martens. I've since found out that these are tight boots that go at least to the knee. A British friend in her fifties said she knew about 'fuck-me shoes' when she was growing up. They had spiky heels. I must have led a sheltered life.

In another column I wrote about the way in which words can lose their intensity. 'Terrible' today has nothing to do with terror, and 'astonished' no longer means struck by thunder. These are just everyday words today. There's no question that some words give offence and that they're sometimes used deliberately to offend. But in time, with regular use, their ability to shock is weakened. Gordon Ramsay's use of the F-word in his TV series has become tedious and, for me anyway, suggests a pathetic lack of verbal skills.

Teenagers like to use new slang – it's part of being a teenager. These slang terms are then picked up by their younger brothers and sisters. But maybe they don't always realise that some words can be highly offensive to older people. Or perhaps using them is part of teenage rebellion. David Small wrote that the word 'gay' now means stupid or uncool, and is applied to clothing, music and behaviour. He said that it's become common, even among primary school children. I've heard accounts of words like 'spastic' or 'handicapped' also being used to mean stupid.

Some years ago a student in my university New Zealand English class did a small project on slang in Pacific Island English used by teenagers in Christchurch. There were two slang terms that startled me. If you told someone that you saw them at Eastgate Mall on Saturday afternoon the response could be 'Ah, stalker!' And if a boy was seen annoying a girl you could say 'Rapist!' My son taught at a secondary school in South Auckland in the 1990s and he confirmed that the words 'stalker' and 'rapist' were in common use at his school in this weakened sense.

As a linguist I have to accept that language changes. And I think it's important that we know about the changes. But it doesn't mean we always have to like or approve of them.

# Between you and I, it's hypercorrect

*14 March 2009*

ANNABEL IS ALMOST TWO AND she's been delighting her parents by trying out words. Every week new items are added to her vocabulary. Her parents have also changed the way they speak to her. They are now saying things like, 'Mummy's going to brush Annabel's hair.' Or 'Daddy's going to get Annabel's highchair.' Until a few weeks ago they would've said, 'I'm going to brush your hair' or 'I'm going to get your highchair.'

No one has told them to use proper names. It's as if they know instinctively that pronouns – I, me, you, my etc – are tricky for small children because they can't be imitated. If I say, 'I'm going to brush your hair', from Annabel's perspective this means 'You're going to brush my hair'. Different pronouns are involved, which is complicated for a toddler. The easy way around this is to avoid the pronouns altogether and use a proper name.

Native speakers of English use pronouns without even thinking about them, even though some complex rules are involved. If I ask, 'Who won?' you could answer 'They did.' You wouldn't say 'They'. If you don't use a verb, you have to answer, 'Them.'

We say 'Frank likes me' and not 'Frank likes I'. We say 'Frank likes her' and not 'Frank likes she'. We say 'Frank sent it to me' and not 'Frank sent it to I'. We say 'She sang' not 'Her sang'. Annabel will soon learn these rules without anyone teaching her.

So why is it that I get letters from people who are troubled by the use of some pronouns?

One difficulty seems to come when a verb has more than one subject and one of those subjects is a pronoun. Take these sentences. Me and John went to town. John and me went to town. I and John went to town. John and I went to town.

Standard English requires 'John and I went to town'. But you'll commonly hear the non-standard forms 'Me and John went to town' and 'John and me went to town'. The most unnatural form is 'I and John went to town'.

Graham Mansell has written to me about this. He was taught the standard English usage of 'John and I' and was told that 'me and John' was bad grammar. He's been correcting his children (which he says is a losing battle). However, recently he heard the old song 'Loch Lomond' with the chorus, 'But me and my true love will never meet again, on the bonny, bonny banks of Loch Lomond.' This is a good example of the fact that there has been considerable freedom and variation with pronouns between dialects. As he says, you wouldn't say, 'I and my true love will never meet again.'

Glenn Metcalf has seen this sentence in *The Press*: 'It caused a rift between Dave and I.' And she heard a TV presenter say, '... encouraging you and I' ... John Williams saw an acknowledgement from 'Roger and I'. He asks if it should be 'I' or 'me'.

I've noticed these usages too. Why do people use pronouns in what seems such an unnatural way? They say 'He told Dave and I about it' when they wouldn't say 'He told I about it',

I think there's a reason for 'the rift between Dave and I'. We're taught that 'Dave and me went to town' is 'incorrect' or 'bad' English. We must always say 'Dave and I went to town'. So I think people get a bit uncomfortable about 'Dave and me' altogether and change 'Dave and me' to 'Dave and I' wherever it occurs. They start saying, 'He showed it to Dave and I.' Or, 'He's causing a rift between Dave and I.'

This is technically known as a hypercorrection – a mistake that comes from a confused attempt to avoid another mistake. And hypercorrections can catch on. The expression 'between you and I' is now becoming so common that when Annabel is older it might be the norm.

# Politics, religion and saving face

*21 March 2009*

WHEN I WAS GROWING UP there was an unwritten rule about conversations: you shouldn't talk about religion or politics.

Some of the best discussions I've ever had were about politics and religion, so why did we have this prohibition? I think it was to avoid giving offence. Keep to the weather and other uncontroversial topics and no one will be offended.

In our educational system we were not taught rules about conversations. This is because conversation seems so natural that we think it doesn't need any formal teaching. We concentrate on the written word. Yet there must be underlying rules also for conversations, because we know immediately when these rules are broken: Jim always hogs the conversation. Mary talks far too loudly. Nathan keeps changing the subject. Ruth never listens.

Good conversation involves skill and work; it involves sensitivity and co-operation. Sociologist Erving Goffman says people are willing to put effort into conversation because they want other people to like them. He uses the Chinese concepts of saving face and losing face. We don't want to lose face; we help others to save face. We want to appear considerate and we want people to like us. So we don't say, 'Goodness, you've become very fat.' It might be true, but the stout person will lose face and it could mean the end of a friendly relationship you might have had. Don't go out of your way to praise the Labour Party to a die-hard National supporter – well, not if you want to stay friends.

Of course people do get into arguments about politics and religion, and they do say rude things to each other. Someone might be rude to a politician speaking at a street-corner meeting, but in this case it doesn't matter because there's no relationship to preserve. And family members will cheerfully expose one another's weaknesses. 'You're surely not going out dressed like that?' We can say things like this if relationships are strong.

I once heard a friend address someone as 'you horrible hairy-legged South African git'. That would seem appallingly insulting unless you knew that they were the closest friends. In a way it was a measure of their friendship that they could say such nasty things to each other.

The need to save face can also affect the way we make requests. If you said, 'I'm going away tomorrow so I want you to feed my cat,' it could result in a blunt refusal. 'Who does she think I am? No I won't.' It wasn't a polite way to ask. It would be better to be humble and apologetic. 'I know this is short notice, and I really hate to be a nuisance, but is there any chance you might be able to feed my cat tomorrow night?' This helps to maintain the face of the person being asked. If she can't do it, she might say, 'I'm really sorry – I'd like to, but I'm going away myself.' So no one's feelings are hurt.

Philippa showed me a letter sent to 'Mary who solves problems' in the British magazine the *Spectator*. A 44-year-old man, single for five years, had just acquired a girlfriend. He knows people ask him to dinner because they want a spare man at their table. So how does he let them know he now has a girlfriend without putting them on the spot?

In her answer, Mary suggested that he reply:

> Oh, no, I'm busy that night, but maybe I can get out of it. The thing is, I've just left a message for my new girlfriend asking her to do something that night but she hasn't got back to me yet to say yes or no. Tell you what – I'll chase her now and if she's busy, I'd love to come.

Whatever the outcome, everyone saves face.

# Slips of the tongue tangle

*29 March 2009*

Someone from Radio New Zealand was trying to contact a lecturer in the Linguistics Department. As a last resort he rang me at home, even though I'm retired, to see if I could help. I explained that the Linguistics Department no longer has a separate secretary and this was the reason for his difficulty. I then said, 'It's to do with cust-cotting.' I realised at once that I'd got into a verbal tangle, but 'cost-cutting' just wouldn't come. My brain was stuck with 'cust-cotting'.

We call these mistakes slips of the tongue, and there are two sorts. There's the one I made where I had the right words but I had trouble putting them together. We say 'par-cart' for 'car-park'. William Spooner, an Anglican clergyman who was warden of New College Oxford, gave us the name 'spoonerism' for these errors. When toasting the Queen he was reported to have said, 'Let us raise our glasses to the queer old dean.' He was said to have admonished one of his students: 'Young man, you have hissed my mystery lectures and tasted your worm.' (Today it's accepted that these and other 'spoonerisms' attributed to Dr Spooner were actually the mischievous inventions of other staff members, who no doubt had fun making them up.)

The second kind of mistake is where we actually get the wrong word. It's as if we select the wrong item from our mental word store. John Key at the National Party conference last year said, 'I want to send the clearest of messages. Under the Labour government I lead ...' It certainly wasn't what he intended to say. It was a slip of the tongue. It's what happens when someone says, 'Teachers shouldn't use capital punishment' instead of 'Teachers shouldn't use corporal punishment'.

Sometimes I have difficulty with people's names – even people I know well. Their name is on the tip of my tongue. Psychologists call this 'the tip of the tongue (TOT) phenomenon'. Even more embarrassing is my

179

inability to name my own children accurately, and I find myself addressing my granddaughter Kathleen as Charlotte, the name of my youngest daughter. My mother-in-law could run through the names of three or four different granddaughters until she got to the right one. When she was over 90 she would address them all as 'Girlie'.

The inability to find the right word is one of the most common symptoms of aphasia suffered by people who have had severe head injuries or strokes. A man who had recovered from aphasia described it in this way: 'I often had the impression that I had the word within my power but through a tempestuous cleavage another element would come and take its place and this would give to my speech a quality often incomprehensible and fantastic.'

In a number of cases the problems aphasic patients experience are exaggerated forms of the kind of difficulties all normal speakers have. I had a problem saying 'cost-cutting', or I might say 'put the fish in the cupboard' when I meant 'put the fish in the fridge'. Someone's name is on the tip of my tongue. For aphasics this happens all the time.

Researchers are very interested in slips of the tongue. But how do you collect data? Do you carry a notebook around and write the tongue-slips down? Would it be more accurate to use a tape-recorder? Would you have to keep the tape-recorder running for hundreds of hours just to pick up a few tongue-slips? Then there's the problem of interpreting the data. If you say, 'We had an interesting conservation' instead of 'an interesting conversation' is that a slip like 'cust-cotting' or is it the wrong choice of a word?

Studying slips of the tongue can help us to understand more about the workings of language and the human mind. But it certainly is not easy research. I'm just grateful my husband knows what I mean when I ask him to put the fish in the cupboard.

# Regatta and gondola, pizza and pasta

*5 April 2009*

ONE OF MY FAVOURITE DETECTIVE story writers is Donna Leon. Part of the pleasure of her books comes from her descriptions of Venice where her stories are set, and also her accounts of the food eaten by her hero, Commissario Guido Brunetti. Sometimes Brunetti speaks in Italian but sometimes he switches to the local language of Venice, Venetian.

Ronnie Ferguson, a scholar from St Andrew's University in Scotland who has a Venetian mother, has recently written *A Linguistic History of Venice*. Although Venetian is usually described as a dialect of Italian it's actually much older than Italian. Italians find Venetian hard to understand, which is not surprising as it's as different from Italian as Italian is from French and Spanish. And it has survived in spite of the fact that Italian is the only language used in Italian schools, media and government offices.

Some English words have come from Venetian. You might expect to find 'gondola' and 'lido' from the Lido island bathing beach near Venice. 'Regatta' is a 17th-century English borrowing from boat races on the Grand Canal.

There are other words we wouldn't necessarily associate with Venice. The word 'ballot', for example, comes from Venetian *ballotta* meaning a little ball. An early method of secret voting was by means of small balls put in a box. 'Pantaloon' (the origin of our word 'pants') comes from Pantalone, a local nickname for a Venetian. This probably came originally from San Pantaleone, a fourth-century Venetian saint, and it became used for a Venetian character in early Italian comedy who wore distinctive tight trousers. Another English word possibly from Venetian is 'ghetto', the site of the first ghetto in Venice. 'Zany', meaning comical in an endearing way, comes from Venetian Zanni, which was a nickname for Giovanni, the Italian equivalent of John. It was one of the traditional names for a clown.

181

The greeting *ciao*, which you can sometimes hear for 'hello' or 'goodbye', is a shortened form of the Venetian acknowledgement *Vostro schiavo*, meaning 'your humble servant'.

When I started to investigate words from Venetian I also became aware of the large number of English words that have come from Italian. Some have arrived in my lifetime, many through Italian American immigrants – cappuccino, espresso, lasagne, mafioso, pasta, pizza, ravioli, spumante, zabaglione, zucchini. I looked for these words in my 1964 two-volume *Shorter Oxford Dictionary*, which I keep close at hand when I'm writing these columns, and not a single one appears there. It's hard to believe that when I was a university student in the 1960s 'pasta' and 'pizza' were not even in the dictionary. What on earth were we eating then?

Two medical borrowings from Italian reveal early beliefs about illness. Malaria came from the Italian *mala aria* meaning bad air, from the time when people thought malaria came from the bad air in swampy areas.

'Influenza' is Italian from the medieval Latin word *influentia*, meaning influence. It was used for the outbreak of a disease that people thought was caused by the influence of the stars. In the 18th century an epidemic of catarrhal fever spread across Europe, and was known in Italian as *influenza di catarro*. Before long only the first word in the foreign phrase was used in English, and by the 19th century it had been shortened even further to 'flu'.

Our word 'bank' comes from Italian *banca*, meaning a bench, which was the counter where the money changers carried out their business. Bankrupt comes from *banca rotta*, which means literally 'the bank is broken'.

Many of the Italian words that came into English relate to food, music and culture. What would life be like without pianos, cellos, violins and operas; or for that matter, broccoli, macaroni, salami and spaghetti? From Italian we get novels and scenarios, balconies, studios and umbrellas. But we also get volcanoes and casinos, arsenals and contraband, and words that go with them – alarm and risk.

# Yeah-no – it's a discourse marker

*11 April 2009*

IN 1887 A SCOTTISH SINGING teacher called Samuel McBurney travelled around Australian and New Zealand towns giving concerts of 'songs of all nations', accompanied by his wife on the zither. Their concerts were not well attended and the McBurneys' travels would be long forgotten if it weren't for one thing. McBurney had taught himself phonetics on the sea journey to Australia, and wherever he went he carried a notebook and wrote down pronunciations he heard.

This information is like gold for language researchers today. When McBurney was in Brisbane two Englishmen pointed out to him that people in Australia said 'citee' or 'simplicitee', rather than ending the word with a vowel like the one in 'sit' – 'cit-ih', 'simplicit-ih'. Thereafter, McBurney heard the 'citee' pronunciation in every Australian and New Zealand town he visited.

McBurney's experience is a common one. He hadn't heard this particular pronunciation until someone pointed it out to him. Then he started to hear it all the time. We had visitors from England this summer and we did a tour of the North Island with them. They pointed out how often they heard people in New Zealand beginning a sentence with 'Yeah-no'. Jenny Collins had also written to me about this. So we started to listen for it and they were right. Soon I was hearing it all the time: so many people were beginning sentences with 'Yeah-no'. It didn't seem to be affected by age, place, social class or education. And what's more, I was using it myself.

So is 'Yeah-no' a New Zealandism? The answer is no – it's one more thing we share with Australia. And we know it's been around for a while because Australian linguist Kate Burridge was collecting samples of 'Yeah-no' in Brisbane in 1998.

What does 'Yeah-no' mean? I don't think it's the same as the 'no no no no yes' said by Jim Trott, the parish council member in *The Vicar of*

183

*Dibley.* 'Yeah-no' is what we call a discourse marker – a word or phrase that keeps a conversation running smoothly.

Now that my interest has been aroused I've been listening for it and I find that it has different functions. Someone says, 'Are you going to Wellington?' and I say, 'Yeah-no, we're going to stay with Susie.' Why did I say just 'Yeah-no' when my intention was to say yes? Perhaps 'no' makes it a strengthened 'yes'. But then I'm asked, 'Are you going to be there for the whole week?' and I answer, 'Yeah-no, just for three days.' Here I'm saying 'no' but I've softened it with 'yeah' as a politeness feature.

Kate Burridge, who has done research on 'Yeah-no', suggests another function. She says it can be a continuity feature. She gives the example of two women talking about a concert on television. One woman then goes off on a tangent and starts talking about taping the concert. The other says 'Yeah-no' to show that she has acknowledged what the woman was saying, but she wants to gets back to the original subject of how good the concert was. So the discourse marker 'Yeah-no' helps her to get back on track, at the same time showing that she was listening to her friend's comments.

Burridge has also noticed that 'Yeah-no' is common in sporting conversations, especially when someone has been complimented. Mr Body-surfer has been told what a great body-surfer he is and he replies, 'Yeah-no,' acknowledging the compliment but showing he is also a modest body-surfer and he wants to play it down a bit.

I've found that some people dislike discourse markers. They write me grumpy letters about 'ums' and 'ahs', 'you know' and 'you see'. Now that I've started to notice the discourse marker 'Yeah-no' I realise how complex and subtle it is. At the moment I know little about it. There's a great research project there for someone. Yeah-no.

# Made in New Zealand

*18 April 2009*

WE HAD ENGLISH VISITORS STAYING over the summer. They were English language experts and the conversation over dinner invariably moved to the subject of language.

I was surprised to find that some of my everyday terms were completely unknown to them. When someone asks us about something we don't like we say, 'I wouldn't have a bar of it.' I didn't know this was a New Zealand expression. I use it constantly. In the *Oxford Dictionary of New Zealand English* Harry Orsman dates it from 1933 and says that although its origin is uncertain, it possibly refers to a bar of music. I haven't worked out that connection yet.

Our visitors noticed advertisements for 'whiteware'. 'What's whiteware?' they asked. An American friend knew 'white goods' but not 'whiteware'. I asked what they called fridges, washing machines and dishwashers collectively in England and they thought they were just called large domestic appliances. However, a Google search revealed that in the trade they are referred to in Britain as 'white goods'. 'Whiteware' (with the stress on the first syllable) is the New Zealand term.

They commented on our pronunciation of 'Guy Fawkes'. When I'm talking about 'Guy Fawkes night' I pronounce it 'Guy Fox'. with the stress on 'Guy.' They thought this was most peculiar. If I'm talking about the unfortunate individual himself I will pronounce it (as they do for both) 'Guy Forks', with the stress on his surname. Fortunately for me my husband also says 'Guy Fox night', so I'm not just an oddity. But maybe this is a matter of our age, as our children don't pronounce it in this way. I'd be interested in readers' views.

Our visitors didn't know what a 'stoush' was. This is a word we share with Australia for violence (especially on the rugby field) or for a robust argument. And they hadn't heard the term 'a beat-up'. 'What does it mean?' they asked. Then comes the fun of defining it. Was it the same as making a mountain out of a molehill? Well, not really. You hear the phrase 'a media beat-up' for a highly exaggerated or even manufactured newspaper report. When Housing New Zealand is described as 'a slum landlord', as I've seen recently, I'd call that a beat-up. The term is not in any British or American dictionary so we can claim it for Australia and New Zealand.

We were really surprised by one everyday term that our visitors questioned. We thought everyone's kitchen had a 'bench'. Apparently not. I was told that for them a bench was only ever something you sat on. Where they came from, the surface where you cut up your vegetables and dried your dishes was a counter or a work top.

A vineyard director in Marlborough wrote to me about a year ago through this column. He said he'd been thinking about New Zealand words all week, especially the ones that were so commonplace they went unnoticed. And he sent me his personal list. It's quite a mixture. It included jandals, hokey-pokey, cark it, pack a sad, piker, bludge, tiki tour, smoko, wop-wops, rattle your dags, chilly-bin, togs, waratah and lolly cake.

He had given the subject some thought because he had another category – English words that have an entirely different meaning in New Zealand. He gave the example of 'manchester' (not the city but household linen or material), 'two-metre stud' (not a fantasy for bored housewives but the height of an internal wall), and a 'warrant', which is a certificate of roadworthiness.

We need people from outside New Zealand to point out those words that are used differently in other English speaking countries and those that are used only in this country. Our visitors reacted every time someone said 'sweet as' or 'it was slow as' or 'it's hot as'. That's a popular New Zealand construction but they wouldn't have a bar of it.

# Softening the sounds of wartime

*25 April 2009*

In the Radio New Zealand Sound Archives there are some wonderful collections of recordings. The Mobile Disc Recording Unit collected recordings during World War 2 of New Zealand servicemen and women serving abroad. Field recordings were made in North Africa, in the Italian campaign and in the Pacific. After the war members of the occupational forces in Japan were also recorded.

I have listened to many of these recordings, and although my purpose was to study the language used by the speakers, it was easy to be caught up by the messages. Recording machines were a new technology at that time and some speakers sounded nervous, obviously reading from a script. They sent messages to their parents, to family members and neighbours, usually telling them that they were fine, or 'better now'. At Christmas time many spoke longingly of Christmas dinner in New Zealand with roast lamb, new potatoes and green peas. One man told us he had seen many wonderful sights in Europe and North Africa, but as far as he was concerned the finest place in the world was Blenheim.

These recordings of New Zealanders in the 1940s give a human face to that war. The speakers were sons and daughters, husbands and wives. And we know when we listen to their voices that some of them did not return to New Zealand.

Recordings like these are helpful because people in power often use language deliberately to remove the human faces of those fighting and those affected by the fighting. Dead soldiers become 'non-operative personnel'. When a terrible mistake is made and people on your own side are killed it is called 'friendly fire', and when civilians are killed by mistake this is 'collateral damage'. Bombing and shelling become 'surgical strikes', civilian targets are 'soft targets'. I remember during the Vietnam war how the number of people killed was always referred to as the body count.

The Bush administration manipulated language cleverly when they declared they had to fight 'the war against terror'. That term stuck and we heard it over and over again. But you don't need to be a linguist to know that you can't wage war against an abstract noun. It makes no sense, but it sounds impressive. In *Politics and the English Language*' George Orwell said that such language was 'designed to make lies sound truthful and murder respectable and to give the appearance of solidity to pure wind'.

I've written before in this column about the way we use euphemisms for things that can be frightening. Perhaps we think that if we give death or mental illness a friendly or joke name this will diminish its fearfulness. So we say that someone has 'kicked the bucket' or is 'a sandwich short of a picnic'. In wartime soldiers coined euphemisms for their weapons. They named their tanks 'rolling kitchens' and they called their bayonets 'tin-openers'. Those involved with the atomic bomb dropped on Hiroshima named it 'Little Boy', and the bomb dropped three days later on Nagasaki was called 'Fat Man'. The first atomic test was called the Trinity Test. Under the Reagan administration in America the MX-missile was renamed 'Peacekeeper'. Today a war-torn country is known as 'the theatre of operation'. Service people have 'in-theatre leave' and 'out-of-theatre leave'.

Every profession has its own language, and knowing the jargon creates the bond that marks insiders from outsiders. But the language of war is also specifically designed to make unpleasant reality more palatable. American soldiers in the Vietnam war weren't told to 'go and kill Vietnamese fathers and mothers, sons and daughters, aunts and uncles'. They were ordered to 'neutralise the Cong'. That sounds far more acceptable.

This Anzac Day I will be thinking about those men and women whose voices I've heard through the Radio New Zealand Sound Archives. They were real people, and however language is manipulated to shield us from this, war always involves real people.

# Language skills that go unnoticed

*2 May 2009*

We were travelling to Wellington on the Cook Strait ferry. It was the school holidays and the ferry was packed so we were pleased to get a seat with a table, even though it was right opposite the children's play area. A family joined us in our alcove – parents with a five-year-old daughter.

We watched them settle in. They had a bag of picture books. The father's reading was animated and lively. As we passed a lighthouse he explained to his daughter that it was like the lighthouse in one of her stories.

The little girl had a case with paper, pens and coloured pencils and some brightly coloured stickers and she carefully traced some words and individual letters. Her parents gave her praise and encouragement. When she was hungry she was given a healthy biscuit, an apple and some water. She was quietly responsive. It struck me how fortunate that child was, and I could predict her bright future in primary school, secondary school and university.

The children's play area opposite us was a noisy place with about eight shouting children leaping off a climbing frame onto some big cushions on the floor. Some of them had chips and sweets. Their parents were somewhere else, sleeping or playing cards. The racket those children made ensured that no one near them was going to have a peaceful journey.

The ferry crossing takes over three hours. As I watched the children in the play area I started to make some sense of what was actually going on. There was a small boy – maybe about six years old – who was organising the others. They were acting out a story about pirates and he was giving the orders. The climbing frame was a ship and the cushions on the floor made the sea. From time to time the pirates had mock battles, made speeches and leapt into the sea with more shouting and laughing.

I then realised that I was watching another set of linguistic skills, different from those of the family sitting beside us. The six-year-old boy, with his bare feet and dirty shirt, was directing a group of children who were presumably unknown to him. He was giving them a story to act out, and engaging them with activity and entertainment. And those children were really enjoying themselves.

It would be easy to predict a rosy future for the little girl with the books and the writing materials. But what about the boy directing the pirates? Could we be so sure about his future? Will teachers praise him for his remarkable verbal talents?

This experience made me examine my own judgements about children's language abilities. I realised how easily I had been impressed by the girl and her parents with their focus on literacy. But it took me much longer to become aware of the remarkable skills of the little boy. The written word always takes precedence over the spoken, and we know much more about it. It was only because I had plenty of time that I could observe how the boy was making others follow his instructions and also making them laugh. I realised that I had reacted unfavourably to the noise, seeing the shouting and jumping as undesirable behaviour. Give me a quiet child writing or reading a book any day. But by the end of the journey I realised I'd got it wrong. I was missing so much.

And what about those all-important tests that tell us how our children are doing in school? We know they will be good at measuring reading and writing, and that's important. The little girl sitting beside us on the ferry will do very well. But will the tests also recognise the amazing linguistic skills of that small boy? One day he could be a leader in New Zealand, or an actor, or a teacher. But it's not guaranteed.

# Getting into phrasal verbs

9 May 2009

A MAN FROM LOWER HUTT WROTE to me, concerned about what he thought was a recent feature of English. People were saying things like 'the auctioneer knocked down the painting' instead of what he thought was correct: 'the auctioneer knocked the painting down'. Letters like this still surprise me. The writer has suddenly taken notice of a feature of English and assumes it must be a new development.

The example he used reminded me of a time when I was a student at London University in the 1960s. Linguistics students were encouraged to work over the summer as tutors in the University of London Summer School of English. So I found myself in front of a group of students from all parts of Europe wanting to improve their English. In the first session a student asked me about the meaning of 'get in' and 'run up'. Why could we say in English, 'She got in the train' but also 'She got in the washing'? Why could we say, 'He ran up a hill' but also 'He ran up a bill'? It was a sharp lesson to me that being a native speaker did not mean I knew how English worked. This was when I had to learn about 'phrasal verbs'.

'Ran up a hill' can be analysed into two parts. 'Ran' is the verb and 'up the hill' is a prepositional phrase. We can say, 'He ran down the hill' or 'He ran around the hill.' Both sentences have a verb followed by a preposition. But when we say, 'He ran up a bill' the sentence is structured differently. The verb here is 'ran up'. We call 'up' a particle. Verbs like 'run up' or 'get in' are called phrasal verbs.

I had to explain to my students in London that you can have sentences that look similar but have different meanings. One is a verb followed by a prepositional phrase –'Jim turned off the road'; the other is a phrasal verb – 'Jim turned off the light.'

My letter-writer from Lower Hutt had noticed a feature of phrasal verbs. With many you can turn the sentence around. (The surprising thing to me is that he disliked this so much.) 'The auctioneer knocked down the painting' and 'The auctioneer knocked the painting down'. 'She got in the washing' and 'She got the washing in'.

You can't do this with verbs followed by prepositions. You can't say, 'She got the train in.'

Phrasal verbs are the linguistic equivalent of wearing slippers or sneakers. When we want to put on our dressy shoes we can often replace phrasal verbs with a single word. I must carry out (perform) my duty. The soldiers gave in (surrendered). They threw out (ejected) the troublemakers.

Those students at the Summer School of English were enthusiastic about phrasal verbs. They needed them if they wanted to speak colloquial English. And there are hundreds of them. Think of what you can do with 'put'. Put on the kettle. Put on your shoes. Don't put down people. We had to put down our old dog. Would you put out the cat. Please put out that cigarette. We put up some friends for the weekend. She put up the hem of her dress. He put up the curtains. You'll have to put up with it. And that's just a sample. There's a *Longman Dictionary of Phrasal Verbs*.

My letter-writer from Lower Hutt thinks phrasal verbs are a recent phenomenon. Not so – we can trace them back to the 14th century. They are common in Shakespeare, and Samuel Johnson discusses them in his *Dictionary of the English Language* (1755), noting that they give foreigners 'the greatest difficulty'. That's true, but when they get into them they can come up with some comfortable, everyday English.

# Inexorable demise of dark 'l'

*16 May 2009*

THE MAN ON THE PHONE said his name was 'Cow'. I've heard some strange names in my time, but this one was new to me. I asked him to repeat it and it was definitely 'Cow' —and he sounded as if I should know him. It was when he said 'Cow Gordon' that I recognised my husband's nephew. We hadn't heard from Carl for a while but we had plenty to do with him when he was a student at Lincoln University. I was ashamed of my confusion because I knew exactly why his name gave me trouble. It was because of the 'l' at the end of it. Carl and his name are feeling the effects of a New Zealand sound change.

What we write down as 'l' covers some different sounds. But native English speakers have no idea that there are different 'l' sounds until these are pointed out. If you listen carefully to the word 'little' you should be able to hear two different 'l's. Phoneticians call the 'l' sound at the beginning of the word a 'clear l', and the one at the end is a 'dark l'. Dark 'l' occurs in front of consonants: milk, child, railway, and at the end of words: feel, mile, bottle. And it's dark 'l' that's changing in New Zealand English.

In New Zealand we're losing dark 'l' and replacing it with a vowel. The replacement vowel is hard to describe in ordinary spelling – this is where you need a phonetic writing system. But the best I can do is to say that it's rather like the vowel in 'put' or 'foot'. So it's not that we're just losing our 'l's. That would have made Carl's name sound like 'car'. The 'l' is being replaced by a vowel.

New Zealanders are not lying awake at night worrying about their dark 'l's. For the most part the demise of dark 'l' goes unnoticed. When I put on my linguist's hat and listen carefully I hear the same speakers using both pronunciations. Sometimes they pronounce the dark 'l' and sometimes they use the vowel. I know I do this too. This kind of switching is a sure sign that our language is in a state of change. I predict that sometime in the future, the end result will be the loss of dark 'l.' Clear 'l' at the beginning of 'light' or 'little' will remain as it is today. And 'l' between vowels in words such as 'feeling' and ' melon' will stay the same. It's just those dark 'l's' that are changing.

In phonetic terms the 'l' sound and the 'r' sound have quite a lot in common. Once English people sounded the 'r' in words like 'fear' and 'feared'. They still do in some dialects. But about 200 years ago in the English spoken around the London area people stopped pronouncing 'r' at the end of a word ('fear') or before a consonant ('feared'), though it remained between vowels ('fearing'). In New Zealand today it looks as if 'l' is going along the same path.

We are not alone with this sound change. A feature of the London dialect of Cockney, it has been carried into the variety recognised from the 1980s as 'Estuary English', spoken in areas around the river Thames.

The change with dark 'l' has been around in New Zealand for a while. In 1973 someone wrote to the *Listener* complaining that 'lovely words like jewel and children had become "joo" and "choodren".' In 1999 the *Listener's* Jane Clifton described Bill English's pronunciation of 'I meddle' as 'Oi med-ooow'. I've had several letters complaining about the pronunciation of 'vulnerable'.

I visited Carl in Northland a few weeks ago. He told me that since our phone conversation he's become conscious of the way his name is pronounced. He's a dairy farmer, and he really doesn't want to be known as Cow.

# Which witch?

*23 May 2009*

Ken Downes wrote to *The Press* about the pronunciation of English words beginning with 'wh'. He asked why 'wh' was pronounced 'by using a puffing or blowing sound' in words like 'what' or 'when', whereas in Maori it was pronounced as 'f'.

That's an interesting question. To answer the first part I need to go back into history. The earliest speakers of English were able to combine sounds at the beginning of words that we can't combine today. The evidence is still there in our spelling: 'w' was once pronounced in 'wrong', 'k' in 'know' and 'g' in 'gnaw'. There were combinations with 'h' that we've lost today. 'Ring' was 'hring' in Old English, 'loud' used to be 'hlud' and 'neck' was 'hnecca'. Words like 'which' and 'white' were pronounced with an initial 'hw' that was later spelt 'wh'.

The change from 'hw' to 'w' for words like 'white' began in the Middle Ages, but 'hw' also continued to be used in some places. By the 18th century educated people in the south of England were pronouncing both 'which' and 'witch' with 'w'. In time this became the standard. Scottish and Irish speakers continued to make a difference between them.

The reason why some New Zealanders pronounce 'hw' in 'which' and 'white' is because of the Scottish and Irish settlers to this country. The 1881 census shows that around 20 per cent came from Scotland and 17 per cent from Ireland. So in the early days there were plenty of 'hw' users around.

Over the years the 'hw' pronunciation diminished in New Zealand, though it can still be heard in the speech of a few people. In 1939 Professor Arnold Wall wrote that all the main radio announcers in New Zealand maintained the traditional 'hw' but he thought the change to 'w' was inevitable. People still write to the paper complaining about a lack of distinction between 'whales' and 'Wales' but I think it's probably a lost cause.

The second part of Ken Downes' question asks why Maori pronounce 'wh' as 'f'. The answer involves an understanding of different sound systems and the problems of writing down an unwritten language.

Sounds in one language don't necessarily match those in another and this can cause difficulties. Our 'th' sounds cause headaches for second-language learners. French students pronounce 'the' as 'ze'. Cantonese students pronounce 'three' as 'tree'.

The Maori sound system is different from English. In early maps the name of the Northland town Kerikeri was written Kedi Kedi. This was because the Maori sound was neither exactly English 'r' nor English 'd'. Missionaries had to choose what they thought was closest.

The Maori sound that the missionaries wrote down as 'wh' had five variants, including 'f'. By far the most common pronunciation was a sound technically known as a 'bilabial fricative'. It's made with the lips together and the air escaping with some friction.

The problem was that English didn't have bilabial fricatives, and this was a difficulty for missionaries trying to write the language down. It's likely that a number of them came from places in Britain that retained a distinction between 'witch' and 'which', so they chose the spelling 'wh' for this non-English sound. And Maori pronunciation also varied. Some names, like Whenuapai were pronounced with 'f' and some, like Whangarei, were traditionally pronounced with 'w'. The matter is further complicated by dialectal variation. Listen to the way Tariana Turia pronounces 'whanau' – it's nearer 'hw'.

Over the years what was spelt 'wh' in Maori has generally become pronounced as 'f'. The loss of variants and the focusing on a single sound is a natural process. Also it was easier for teachers to have one sound for one spelling.

Ken Downes' question looks simple but answering it requires an understanding of language change and of the sound systems of different languages. Writing down any unwritten language is not easy. It was inevitable that features of Maori would be lost in the process.

# Yeah-no, it's confusing

*30 May 2009*

A FEW WEEKS AGO I WROTE about our overseas visitors identify-ing distinctly New Zealand words and phrases. David Elms told me he had problems when he came to New Zealand with the expression 'to flog something'. In Britain if you flog something you sell it. I can remember my brother's concern as a young Anglican curate in Yorkshire when members of the youth group told him they had flogged some bicycles. As a New Zealander he thought they were confessing to stealing them.

Elms also told me about a newcomer to New Zealand who was short of money and wanted to build his own bookcases so he ordered some white pine. When it arrived he was distressed to find how expensive it was. What he had been given was kahikatea, New Zealand white pine, a native timber, not the common pine he was expecting.

Several people have commented on my statement that in Britain a bench is only something you sit on. They have pointed out that in Britain you can have a carpenter's bench or a workbench. They are quite right and I should have seen the connection between these and our New Zealand kitchen benches.

Dave Gough came to New Zealand from South Africa. The first time he tried to get money from an ATM machine in New Zealand it was out of order. He received a friendly but to him incomprehensible message on the screen that it was 'crook' and that he should try again later. He told me that Westpac later changed this because of 'migrant bafflement'. In his first week at work he was asked to 'uplift' some documents. He only knew of 'uplifting experiences'. He was also asked to have 'oversight' of various areas. This use of 'oversight' as a noun from 'oversee' was quite foreign to his South African English dialect, where the only meaning of 'oversee' is 'overlook'. He was also puzzled by a New Zealand gesture of greeting where the greeter cocks the head. He said that when he attempted this it was described by a competent practitioner as 'resembling a severe tick'.

Gough (who is also a linguist) made an interesting comment about 'yeah-no', which I wrote about in an earlier column. He tells me that in South African English there is a similar usage, 'ja-no'. There is speculation in South Africa about its relation to the Afrikaans *ja-nee*, which is in common usage, but is more general than 'yeah-no', meaning something like 'oh well'. Several people have suggested to me that 'yeah-no' could have come from 'you know'. I can see why they thought this – 'yeah-no' and 'you know' are superficially similar. Both are discourse features, assisting continuity and connecting the speaker and the listener. But because of semantic differences and the difference in the stress pattern we can say that the similarity is purely coincidental.

Bevan Rogers followed the TV series *Dancing with the Stars*, in which the announcer said over and over again, 'Will [the dancers] take to the floor.' Bevan had always thought that dancers 'took the floor'. For him 'taking to the floor' involved a demolition man with a sledgehammer.

I checked with Tony Deverson, editor of the *New Zealand Oxford Dictionary*. He agrees that 'take the floor' is the usual idiom in the dancing context. But he suggests that there has been confusion with and interference from the phrasal verb 'take to' meaning 'to repair to or resort to (a region or a place)'. So we might take to the hills, or take to the bush.

But the term has lost the meaning of escaping somewhere and is now used more generally to mean going somewhere. So maybe that's why dancers now take to the dance floor.

I was taught ballroom dancing by Miss Comyns Thomas in her Saturday morning classes in the Orange Lodge Hall in Christchurch. She always told us to 'take the floor'. But then those classes were nothing like *Dancing with the Stars*.

# Jane Austen and the flat adverb

*13 June 2009*

A LETTER-WRITER TO *The Press* THINKS we're losing our adverbs. He's troubled by phrases such as 'wanting something bad' and 'breathing easy'. He says bad and easy are adjectives, which need '-ly' to turn them into adverbs.

He's in good company. I've read a number of accounts by people concerned about the demise of the adverb. The Apple advertisement 'Think different' was seen by some as a sure indication of the adverb's death.

But the correspondent and the others have got it wrong. The adverb is not on the way out. 'Wanting something bad' is not losing an adverb. 'Bad' might look like an adjective, and it doesn't end with '-ly', but in this example it is an adverb.

It's a matter of function.

Jan Freeman wrote about adjectives and adverbs in the *Boston Globe*: 'Merely cutting off an adverb's tail – cropping really to real – doesn't make it an adjective, any more than a similar operation would turn a monkey into a chimpanzee.'

Words like 'bad' and 'easy' in these situations have a technical name: flat adverbs. Adverbs are not dying, but some of them are 'flattening'.

The correspondent wrote: 'The modern approach is [that] near enough is good enough.' But are flat adverbs a new development? The answer is no. The *Webster-Merriam Dictionary* shows that in the past they were once common. Samuel Pepys wrote in his diary (1667): 'I was horrid angry.' Daniel Defoe wrote in 1719: 'The weather was so violent hot.' Language reformer Jonathan Swift wrote in 1712: 'The five ladies were so monstrous fine.' Another language reformer, John Dryden, wrote in 1672: 'It was exceeding harmless.' Jane Austen used the same flat adverb in a letter in 1796: 'It was an exceeding good ball last night.'

How did things change? When did the flat adverb fall out of favour?

Some of the blame must be put on the 18th-century grammarians, who decided flat adverbs were undesirable. In 1762 Bishop Lowth wrote *A Short Introduction to English Grammar*, which was widely used. It set out a rigid set of rules for English, and Bishop Lowth did not like flat adverbs. The poor flat adverb was given a bad name that it still cannot shake.

Some flat adverbs persisted in spite of Bishop Lowth. 'He played fast and loose.' 'I was turned down flat.' And some flat adverbs continue to exist beside their '-ly' counterparts. It's all a question of function. 'He sang very loud' or 'he sang very loudly'. 'Pull the rope tight' or 'pull the rope tightly'. 'Hold it close' or 'hold it closely', And, for the record, deep, wide and direct were adverbs before anyone added '-ly' to them.

One old flat adverb is 'hard' – 'hit the ball hard'. See what happens when it's changed to 'hardly'? Journalist Mike Crean wrote to me about travelling with a group in Italy that was held up by roadworks. Their enthusiastic young Italian driver, who liked to try out his English, explained: 'They are hardly working to finish the new motorway before Christmas.' Crean wondered whether it would it have been less confusing if he had said, 'They are working hardly.' As he pointed out, there are plenty of minefields for students of English.

One of our difficulties is that the adverb belongs to a rag-bag word class. It can modify verbs, adjectives and even other adverbs. This sentence has five adverbs: '*Yesterday* the band played *very loudly outside here.*' It's certainly not just a matter of adding '-ly' to adjectives.

I can advise those who think the adverb is on its way out not to despair. It's alive and kicking. Does it really matter if people say 'Come quick' or 'come quickly', 'go slow' or 'go slowly'? I think we can cope. And if you're unhappy when things are 'real good' or for that matter 'doing bad' – well, that's language change for you.

# Maori English the way of the future

*20 June 2009*

WHEN I DID MY SECONDARY teacher training at London University in the 1960s I wrote an essay on Maori education. The library at New Zealand House provided me with material and I made a case for the preservation of the Maori language.

My tutor said I'd written rubbish. Maori should stop clinging to a useless language; they should speak English. Other students in the class agreed. They said we were just being sentimental about Maori. Anyone who wanted advantages in life should be speaking English.

This response was the standard wisdom of the time. I've heard older Maori admitting that they deliberately avoided speaking Maori to their own children because of the greater advantages of English.

Today we've witnessed a Maori renaissance. The efforts in New Zealand to save the Maori language are an international success story. And over the years I've thought about my London tutor's comments as I've watched the remarkable efforts of Maori language revitalisation.

But since the 1960s we've seen another development in New Zealand – the growth of Maori English. Maori who don't necessarily speak te reo can still mark their Maori identity linguistically by a distinctive way of speaking English.

Maori English has a different rhythm. English is a 'stress-timed' language with a combination of stressed and unstressed syllables. You can hear this rhythm in nursery rhymes. 'This *is the* house *that* Jack built.' Maori English (like French and many other languages) is 'syllable timed'. Every syllable has some stress, producing a different rhythm. And some Maori English vowels and consonants are different.

Maori English has spread over the past 50 years. I have a 1958 recording of six young Maori talking about moving to Auckland from the country. Only one of them has a slight Maori accent. Today we would expect similar young people to have Maori English accents to a greater or lesser degree.

Years ago when I tried to record Maori English it was impossible because the young speakers would switch to general New Zealand English in the presence of a Pakeha university teacher holding a microphone. They could change varieties of English according to the company they were keeping. But for some speakers today Maori English is not a style – it's their mother tongue.

There's a film showing in Christchurch at present called *Trouble is my Business*. It's a documentary filmed at Aorere College in South Auckland over a period of six months. It follows a remarkable teacher, Mr Peach, as he works with troubled teenagers. We hear them speaking Maori English and Pacific Island English.

For me it was interesting to observe this teacher changing his own New Zealand English when he was talking to these teenagers. His rhythm changed to syllable-timing. Sociolinguists call this 'accommodation'. Sometimes I find myself doing this unwittingly. I don't mean to use a Welsh intonation pattern when I'm in Wales – it just comes out that way. Prime Minister Jim Bolger developed a reputation for accommodation, especially in the company of Irish English speakers. So Mr Peach accommodates to the speech of the children he's talking to. It shows his identification with them and it's one of the ways language change happens.

My son taught for three years at Aorere College and I noticed that his language changed. He was saying say 'fru' for 'through', 'muvver' for 'mother'. He's not teaching now but he still sometimes says 'wif' for 'with'. These things can be catching.

I recommend *Trouble is my Business*. It shows a picture of life in New Zealand that might not be so familiar in Christchurch, and in the end it's an optimistic film. And in it we hear varieties of New Zealand English that are not restricted to South Auckland.

I still believe, as I did in the 1960s, that the preservation of the Maori language is a crucial aim. But Maori English also carries cultural significance, and it's the way many New Zealanders will be speaking in the future.

# The spread of the counterfactual

*27 June 2009*

DEBORAH WILLIAMS TEACHES ENGLISH TO overseas students so she needs to know the rules of English. It's frustrating for her when she finds these rules broken in newspaper articles.

A headline that offended her was: 'Beacon may have saved kayaker's life'. The story then showed that the kayaker died. Williams points out that this would have been clear if the headline had been 'Beacon might have saved kayaker's life'.

Students learning English will have no problem with 'may' and 'might' if they stick to the present tense. 'It may rain this week' and 'It might rain this week' are both fine. The fun begins when the sentence is in the past tense. We can say, 'We hoped we might have a fine day' but not 'we hoped we may have a fine day'.

It gets even more tricky when we come to 'might have' and 'may have'. The standard rule is that 'we might have won the match' and 'we may have won the match' have different meanings. In 'we might have won the match' we could have won if the goalkeeper hadn't broken his glasses. In 'we may have won the match' we don't know what actually happened. It's possible that we won, but also possible that we didn't.

The technical name for 'might have' in 'we might have won the match' is 'counterfactual'. It tells us not what actually happened, but what could have happened if things had been different. According to this rule, the headline 'Beacon may have saved kayaker's life' means that we don't know whether the kayaker's life was saved or not. But the meaning intended in the article was counterfactual. If the kayaker had carried a beacon, his life would have been saved.

Was the newspaper headline about the kayaker wrong or is the use of 'may have' changing in New Zealand English? Can we use 'may have' counterfactually in this country? When Andrew Carstairs-McCarthy, a university colleague of mine in the Linguistics Department, first arrived in New Zealand in 1981 he was puzzled by the New Zealand use of 'may have'.

I did double-takes on reading things like 'Beacon may have saved kayaker's life'. In my type of British English, that implies that the kayaker may still be alive. Likewise, sentences such as 'If the bus hadn't gone over the cliff, the passengers may have survived' caused my syntactic processing mechanism to emit graunching noises. I don't recall encountering this usage in the USA.

Fortunately there are people at the University of Canterbury studying New Zealand English. In 1996 Dr Heidi Quinn administered a question-naire to 90 students when she was collecting data for her PhD. She gave the students this sentence: 'Regular maintenance of the structure may have saved four lives.' She asked them if it meant 1) The people would not have died if the structure had been maintained properly or 2) It seems that the good maintenance of the structure prevented four deaths. Almost all the students chose the first meaning – which is the counterfactual 'may have' that Deborah Williams complained about.

The students were also asked to complete a sentence, choosing between 'may' and 'might'. 'Sarah ___ have fallen down the cliff if I hadn't managed to hold on to her leg.' Of the 90 students, 65 chose 'might'.

So while many students used 'might have' in the counterfactual exam-ple about Sarah, which is the standard rule, most were also happy with 'may have' in the earlier counterfactual example about the maintenance of the structure – the non-standard usage.

This provides a difficulty for the English language teacher. I'm sure Deborah Williams will continue to teach the standard usage for 'may have' and 'might have' but I think it's also useful to understand that usage in New Zealand English is changing. More people are accepting the coun-terfactual 'may have'. When New Zealanders travel overseas this might explain why they are not always understood.

# Mr Brown's round vowels

*4 July 2009*

ONCE A YEAR 'OLD GIRLS' from my school get together for a luncheon. It's a way of registering the passing of time.

At the last such gathering some of the conversation was about changes since we were at school, and this included language. So much of our everyday school vocabulary of the 1940s and 50s has now been dumped in the antique basket. The old girls reminisced about 'indoor shoes' and 'outdoor shoes'. There were panama hats, tunics, sockettes (summer) and lisle stockings (winter). Underneath the tunics were garments my mother called bloomers, with long legs that had to be rolled up for sporting activities on Cranmer Square, under the watchful eye of dubious men leaning on their bicycles. Some vocabulary items I'm glad to have let go.

Looking back on my school days I can see that the teachers wanted to teach us the 'right way' to do things. There was a right way to wear your hat, a right length for school tunics, a right length for hair, and there were rules about when you had to wear your gloves.

There was also a right way to speak. Once a week the elocution teacher came into our classroom and instructed us in what she believed were the right vowel sounds. I've met many old girls who can still recite her little poems: 'Round by the cow house Mr Brown fell down. Poor Mr Brown fell down and broke his crown.'

Today when I think about those elocution lessons they seem like a complete waste of time. No one ever spoke like that outside the classroom; we would have sounded silly. Nevertheless, I think they left us with a feeling of linguistic insecurity. We had the idea that somehow the way we spoke normally was inferior and lazy, and we really should try to do better. But the teacher's model of speech wasn't a New Zealand way of speaking. It was based on the speech of middle-class people in the south of England.

It's easy to make fun of those elocution lessons and the vowel sounds we were taught, but that teaching was totally in keeping with the thinking of the time. In 1939 Professor Arnold Wall wrote a book called *New Zealand English: How it should be spoken*. In his preface Wall wrote:

> This book is designed for use by residents in New Zealand who wish to speak 'good' English or 'standard' English, as spoken by the 'best' speakers in the old land; it is not intended for those who wish to develop a new dialect of English for this country.

Teachers trained at Christchurch Training College were taught by Miss Janet McLeod, author of the book *Rhyming Roadways to Good Speech*. She wrote about 'Good Speech City' and its opposite – 'Slum Town', where the bad speakers lived. She gave instructions about the production of vowel sounds as if she were teaching a foreign language. In the introduction to her book Professor Frederick Sinclaire of Canterbury University College said that in every New Zealand classroom he would like to place a gramophone record of the Christmas broadcast given by the late King George V 'so that all our children might have sounding in their ears a model of easy, unaffected and pleasantly articulated speech'.

So it's not surprising that at my school in the 1940s and 50s we were encouraged to talk like members of the British royal family.

I'm glad that today people no longer feel the need to apologise for speaking with a New Zealand accent. My youngest daughter pleaded with me to be allowed to have speech lessons. I agreed reluctantly. But thankfully there was no attempt to make her produce unnatural non-New Zealand vowel sounds. She was encouraged to speak confidently in public, and that's something I think all New Zealand children should be able to do.

# What's in a name change?

*11 July 2009*

MY SISTER-IN-LAW DECIDED TO CHANGE her name. She no longer wanted to be called Jill: please would we now call her Emily. The reaction of the family was predictable. Some said changing names when you were nearly 60 was a stupid idea. Why did she want to do it? What was wrong with Jill? Others said they would try to oblige but it wouldn't be easy. Some addressed her as Emily but referred to her as Jill behind her back. The name change was a main topic of conversation among family members when they got together.

We know that language changes all the time. We now have 'global warming', the 'credit crunch', 'toxic assets' and 'subprime mortgages' – words and phrases that have quietly crept into general usage without any fuss. But a deliberate and conscious attempt to change language is often greeted with hostility and resentment. The women's movement in the 1970s found this with attempts to get rid of sexist language. Some people were enraged by the title 'Ms' or the use of 'chairperson.'

A name is highly personal. We can forgive the mispronunciation of an ordinary word, but it can be annoying and seem disrespectful to have one's name mispronounced. As a teacher I had to take extra care to remember whether Sandra rhymed her name with 'ham' or 'harm', and if Sarah rhymed with 'air' or 'are'.

People have written to me about the pronunciation of 'Rolleston' and 'Ellesmere'. They ask whether these names should have two syllables or three. I remember a great debate in the letters to *The Press* over the pronunciation of Rolleston. Do we base our pronunciation on common usage or on some other standard? In Christchurch, Antigua Street is not pronounced like the country, where it's 'Anteega'. The name of the North Canterbury town Cheviot isn't pronounced with 'sh' like the Cheviot Hills in England. Does it matter?

Some people certainly think so. From October 1945 until January 1946 there were 26 letters published in the *Listener* about the pronunciation of two British placenames. The correspondence began with the name of the East Anglian town Yarmouth. Some said it should be pronounced the way the locals pronounced it; others said it should be pronounced as it is spelt. Ludovic McWhirter wrote:

> It is time that someone pointed out that the slovenliness of English dialect and its variant forms derives either from illiteracy, or lack of adequate training in childhood in the proper use of tongue, teeth, throat and palate in articulation.

In other words, don't trust the locals – they've got it wrong.

Ngaio Marsh then complained about the pronunciation of Marlborough – shouldn't it be 'Mawlborough'? The correspondence that followed was passionate and acrimonious. I suppose it was a safe diversion from the miseries of the war.

So far in these columns I've avoided the topic of Wanganui/ Whanganui, though people have written to me about this. Dr Jeanette King, who taught for many years in the School of Maori and Indigenous Studies at the University of Canterbury, was asked to talk about it on Jim Mora's afternoon programme on Radio New Zealand National. She pointed out that there were good arguments on both sides and went on to discuss these.

She (and other academics) were then accused by 'The Panel', later in the programme, of sitting on the fence. If she had been asked her personal opinion no doubt she would've given a different answer. And that's my position too. There are arguments on both sides. I support the spelling change to 'Whanganui' but that's my personal opinion. And I know it isn't an easy matter.

It's nearly five years since my sister-in-law changed her name to Emily. Some family members still grumble about it, but most have come to terms with it. Some refer to her as Emily-Jill. Younger family members who didn't know her as Jill have no difficulties at all. But it has required give and take on both sides.

# Yelling at the TV

*18 July 2009*

I'VE HAD SOME INTERESTING QUERIES in the past few months. Colin McCready has noticed that more people are saying 'a large amount of people came' instead of 'a large number of people came'. Other people have also complained about this and pointed out that 'number' should be applied to things that can be counted and 'amount' to things that can't be counted. 'A number of apples were bad.' 'Put a small amount of milk into the cup.'

I think those concerned about this are probably the same people who are anxious about the loss of 'fewer' and its replacement by 'less'. We often hear 'there are less students' rather than 'there are fewer students'. The rule for 'fewer' and 'less' is the same as the rule for 'number' and 'amount.' A number of (or fewer) apples (countable). An amount of (or less) water (uncountable).

I wrote about this in a column some time ago, and received a lively response. At the time I said that 'fewer' was on a life-support system, and that those who are concerned about this should be pleased when they hear it; if they get angry every time they hear it replaced by 'less' they will have unhappy lives.

So I will offer the same advice about 'number' and 'amount'. Just as 'less' is crowding out 'fewer', so 'amount' is taking over from 'a number'. I can regret this, but I can't change it.

I received a letter about 'among' and 'amongst'. The writer said her family had been discussing this. One family member insisted that there was a difference between ' I am among friends', meaning these people are my friends, and 'I am amongst friends', meaning the group of people are friends of one another but not friends of mine. I tried these sentences out on a group of my friends and family, who disagreed. They all reported that the two sentences had the same meaning but 'amongst' was a bit more fusty. What do other people think?

Jay asked me to clarify the meaning of 'louche'. In an article in *The Press* Nigel Slater wrote: 'Today's jam maker is obsessed with setting, which is favoured over the softer, more louche style of jam preferred by the rest of Europe and the Middle East.' In Jay's dictionary 'louche' is defined as being untrustworthy, and derived from the French for 'squint'. 'Do we want to eat untrustworthy, squinty-eyed preserves?' I checked 'louche' in my dictionaries and found that it does indeed come from the French for squint-eyed, but it seems that its more recent meaning is 'decadent'. Nigel Slater's jam might be decadent – my jam is still ordinary jam.

Sharon Whitmarsh wrote to say she was constantly yelling at the television when singular nouns were used with plural verbs. She was distressed by a trade union ad in *The Press* announcing: 'Air New Zealand are ripping us off.' Surely, she wrote, it should be 'Air New Zealand is ripping us off.' She says she has long argued for 'the committee is meeting tonight' not 'the committee are meeting tonight'.

Well, Sharon is right about one thing – in New Zealand you do hear both singular and plural verbs with collective nouns. 'The government is' and 'the government are'. Part of the problem is the difference between American and British usage. In American English a collective noun takes a singular verb. Americans would say 'The committee is meeting tonight.' But in British English you can say, 'The family is coming to tea' or 'The family are coming to tea'. But in both British and American English you would say, 'Twenty dollars is too much to pay for a fly swat.' Here 'twenty dollars' is taken as a single sum, not as twenty individual dollars.

Sharon was pleased with the answer I sent her because she's American – now she knows why she's been yelling at the television.

# The usefulness of 'yous'

*25th July 2009*

JEFF HAS WRITTEN TO ME about the use of 'yous' for the plural of 'you'. He and his family have visited the West Coast regularly for many years and they're familiar with hearing 'yous' from service people. 'What would yous like?' Jeff noted that some Christchurch friends who had recently noticed 'yous' on a visit to the West Coast had labelled it 'common' or 'ignorant'.

English speakers could once distinguish between singular and plural 'you'. In fact 'you' was originally the plural form – the singular was 'thou'. I've written in an earlier column about how English lost 'thou' and 'thee' and how the plural 'you' took over everything.

'Yous' comes from Ireland, and areas where there has been extensive Irish migration. Professor Lesley Milroy carried out sociolinguistic research in Northern Ireland, recording people in their homes. When she was visiting the University of Canterbury she told the students that 'yous' was almost obligatory among her informants. She played us a tape of a woman saying: 'So I said to our Trish and our Sandra, "Yous wash the dishes." Sure I might as well have said, "You wash the dishes," for our Trish just got up and put her coat on and went out.'

I liked this example because that Irish woman was able to make a useful distinction that's not available to me in my variety of English.

There were many Irish settlers on the West Coast, which explains why Jeff hears 'yous' so often on his visits there. But 'yous' is now far more widespread than this. It's also a feature of Maori English. In a short story called 'Encounter' written in 1971 Noel Hilliard gives this exchange between Paul (a Pakeha) and Jason (a Maori):

> Paul knew things were not going his way. He said 'Can't we just leave it at that then? Can I buy yous all a beer?' [Jason replied]

211

'Why did you say *yous all?* ... Is it because you think that's a Maori way of talking? Are we supposed to fall in love with you because you suddenly start talking Maori English like we do – or like you suppose we do?

Some years ago I was discussing 'yous' with some teachers in Auckland. A primary school teacher from Mangere told me about a six-year-old boy in her class called Conor. The children were learning a song in Maori, greeting one person, two people, and three or more people. 'Tena koe, tena korua, tena koutou.' Conor sang loudly, 'Greetings to yous' for 'tena korua' and 'tena koutou'. Then he put up his hand and said firmly to his teacher, 'You'll have to fix your chart, 'cause in English one person is "you" but two or more has an 's' and you have to say "yous".'

Conor has a different pronoun system from mine and his usage gives him greater flexibility. I personally think we need a plural 'you'. In the American southern states you'll hear 'y'all'. I frequently hear 'you guys' for plural 'you' – for both males and females.

Jeff's friends described 'yous' as 'common' and 'ignorant'. This doesn't surprise me. When I talk to community groups, 'yous' is frequently given as an example of a hated usage.

I think there are several reasons for this. The obvious one is that 'yous' is not standard English and in my experience some people greatly dislike non-standard English forms. It's also a spoken form that has not yet developed a conventional spelling. Is it yous, youse or you's? But I think the stigma also comes because of the perceived status of those who use the word. Putting it bluntly, 'yous' is associated with lower-class people.

But I think things might change. I'm hearing it more and more and I'm getting used to it. In casual speech some of my family now say, 'What are yous doing?' Their farewell is 'See yous!' I'm tempted to use it myself. It fills a gap in our pronoun system. Who knows? Perhaps one day it will be part of standard English.

# Comparative grammar teaching

*1 August 2009*

ONCE OR TWICE IN MY university career I've become involved in politics – the politics of English teaching. In 1986 a committee was set up to revise the 6th and 7th form English syllabus. The 21 members included representatives of the teachers' union and other unions, independent schools, the Employers' Federation, teachers' colleges, universities and several Maori organisations. Over three years the committee met three times a year, for a week at a time, in residential hostels.

I represented university linguists, who wanted to bring back grammar teaching in the English class. Students were studying topics like 'the language of advertising', and 'the language of conversation', but linguists were concerned that many students had no technical vocabulary to describe the features of language.

The terms of reference for the committee required it to acknowledge New Zealand's biculturalism, and the Maori committee members did not want this to be mere lip service. What did this mean for the teaching of English language and literature?

Arapera Blank, a teacher and poet from Ngati Paroa, spoke passionately. She said that only the Maori language belonged in New Zealand, while the English language belonged in England. I argued back that New Zealand English certainly had its origins in England, but it was a variety of English unique to New Zealand. Arapera then stood up and linked arms with me saying: 'From now on Elizabeth and I will work together.'

So we had to learn how to work in a partnership between Maori and Pakeha. The committee decided to move away from the dominant influence of Britain and aim to produce an English syllabus that was distinctive to New Zealand.

One of the proposed areas of study was the pronunciation, syntax and semantics of English. This is exactly what the university linguists wanted.

But how should it be taught? Teachers were unhappy with the way traditional grammar had been taught in the past. Many said the only grammar they ever learned came through learning a foreign language.

So the committee took up this point and suggested a different method for grammar teaching. It could be done by comparing examples of English with another language, and the obvious choice was Maori. The purpose of this approach was not to make pupils or teachers fluent speakers of Maori. It was purely a method of teaching about the structure and categories of language.

How would it work? In the structure of the English sentence, the verb comes between the subject and the object. 'Stephen (subject) has washed (verb) the plates (object).' In Maori the verb comes at the beginning. 'Kua horoi (Has washed) a Tipene (Stephen) i nga peretai' (the plates). So students would learn about sentence structure and the categories of subject, verb and object.

In English, the adjective goes before the noun – 'the dirty plates.' In Maori it's 'nga pereti paru' (the plates dirty). So students would learn about adjectives and the structure of the noun phrase. Through examples like these we believed that students would gain the terminology and understanding to describe English grammar. They would also learn about language.

In a questionnaire 75 per cent of the English teachers approved the scheme and 25 per cent expressed varying degrees of opposition.

However, the outraged critics were vocal and well organised. They misrepresented the programme, saying it would replace the teaching of English in the classroom with the teaching of Maori. It would be 'Te English'. The committee was accused of social engineering. Maori was a 'useless stone age language'. (I sometimes wonder if it would have been different if the grammatical comparison had been English and Latin or English and French.)

By 1989 an election was approaching. The Labour government didn't want to rock any boats and the draft English syllabus was quickly abandoned. Looking back, I think perhaps we were naïve. We should have offered the comparative approach as an option, and we should have spent more time talking to the general public.

Today I see that a comparative method of grammar teaching is being heralded as a great new idea overseas. And we were nearly there in New Zealand 20 years ago. It's something to think about in Maori language week.

# Growing our vocabulary

*8 August 2009*

Since I began writing this column two years ago I've received many letters from people who are unhappy about changes in the English language. They tell me they know in their heads that language must change but in their hearts they don't like it.

I understand their concern. As I get older I see many changes around me and I don't always like them. But if I mention this to my children I will probably be told to 'get a life!'

What surprises me is that many of the disliked usages have been around for a long time. And people have been complaining about them for a long time. One reader wrote:

> I am frequently irritated by the pronunciation of a prominent TV1 newsreader. Instead of saying 'picture' and 'pictures' she always says very distinctly 'piksher' and 'pikshers'. This has continued over a number of years. Can you help?

I went back through my files and found a letter to the editor of the *Education Gazette* in 1924 from the headmaster of Havelock School in Marlborough. He set out a list of 'common mistakes made by children and adults in New Zealand'. And there it is: 'pick-cher for picture; na-cher for nature; furnit-cher for furniture ...' So this pronunciation has been around in New Zealand for at least 80 years.

Another reader is troubled by the expression 'for free'. She says 'It instinctively feels and sounds incorrect and offensive to my ear. Surely something is "free", not "for free"? It is either "at no cost", "for nothing" or "free"?' She also wants me to do something about this. (I'm touched by people's confidence in my ability to hold back the tides of language change.)

'For free' is American in origin but British dictionaries include it as a general colloquialism. It is analogous to constructions such as 'for ten dollars' or 'for nothing'. In the *American Dialect Dictionary* there is a citation from 1944: 'Railroads don't haul trash for free.' So it's another expression that's been around for a while.

A more recent bugbear for one person is the expression 'grow your business'. I can also remember being surprised by this usage. I can grow my hair or my potatoes, but not my business. However, when I looked into it I found that it's now well entrenched. The *Oxford English Dictionary* describes it as 'business jargon' and adds that 'it is perhaps better to avoid it in formal contexts'. I think that's probably wishful thinking now. Tony Deverson, editor of the *New Zealand Oxford Dictionary*, tells me you can also grow profits – but not losses.

Many language changes take place so quietly that we don't notice them. The other day my husband and I were walking along the tow path beside the river when a man coming in the opposite direction greeted us. He was wearing a peaked cap and he put his fingers to the peak and said 'Good day'. We both commented on this old-fashioned form of greeting. In my childhood men wore felt hats and it was good manners for them to 'tip their hats' to people they met. The hat tip was a symbolic version of hat raising – another polite male acknowledgement. (The military hand salute is thought to have originated as a stylised hat tip.) But men don't wear felt hats any more and the hat tip and hat raising have pretty well gone.

But as sometimes happens with language change, something might not vanish completely. It might turn up in another guise. The term 'hat tip' now appears in blogs as a way of acknowledging the ideas or words of another person. So for example, when I write about some items of New Zealand vocabulary I could write 'hat tip to Tony Deverson.' It's still a form of good manners and courtesy, even if it's far removed from actual hats.

# Different to, from and than

*15 August 2009*

In the section of *The Press* called 'Putting it right' there's been a debate about grammatical rules. Bevan Dunlop pointed out that in a book review Professor David Gunby had written that it was 'different to' another book on the same topic. Dunlop wrote:

> I was always taught that it was correct to say 'different from' not 'different to'. As a professor emeritus in English, Gunby is above question in matters of usage, but I wonder why the alternative was drummed into us over 40 years ago.

In response, *The Press* quoted the English language expert H. W. Fowler, author of *A Dictionary of Modern English Usage*: 'That "different" can only be followed by "from" and not by "to" is a superstition.'

That should have been an end to it, but a week later another reader was quarrelling with the referee, saying that there *was* a rule that 'different' must always be followed by 'from' and not 'to'. He said Fowler was wrong.

Those arguing for the use of 'different from' have the traditional grammar on their side. I found a grammar book written in Christchurch in 1968 by Dr John Moffat, a teacher at Christchurch Boys' High School and later at the Christchurch Teachers' College. Moffat said that when he was young everyone knew about grammar but sex was a closed book. Now the young knew all about sex and nothing about grammar. He wrote *The Structure of English* because of student demand.

So what does Moffat say about 'different from' and 'different to'? He tells us that the error 'different to' is a hardy annual – not just a mistake in grammar, but a mistake 'in common sense and ignorance of standard usage'.

Those are strong words. According to Moffat the traditional rule for

217

standard usage is 'different from', and anything else is wrong. But where does this rule come from? Presumably it wasn't written on a tablet of stone. Moffat gives this explanation:

> The word 'different' is simply the present participle of the Latin verb *dif-fero* and means, syllable by syllable 'dif-' = away, 'fer-' = bear, 'ent' = ing ... 'The very meaning of the word: bearing away, requires that it be followed by 'from' not 'to'.

Is this a good argument? Does 'different' really mean 'bearing away'? If we say that the meaning of a word today is determined by its etymology we could get into quite a pickle. For consistency's sake we must also say that 'cretin' really means Christian, alcohol really means eye-shadow, and atom really means indivisible.

The alternative view is that the meaning of a word is established by current usage. And when usage changes (as with the word 'gay', for example) then the accepted meaning changes.

In everyday speech you'll hear three variants. There's 'different from' (chalk differs from cheese); there's 'different to', which is like 'similar to' or 'superior to'; and there's 'different than', which is like 'better than' or 'worse than'. 'Different than' is American and also Scots dialect usage.

In the 1970s when I taught a university course on the development of linguistic ideas I gave my class a small test on traditional grammar. Equal numbers chose 'different from' and 'different to' and a few chose 'different than'. I think I would get the same result today.

I hope we can be more tolerant about language variation. If a large percentage of the population says 'different to' how can this be wrong? Fowler, writing in 1926, said the rule demanding 'different from' was a superstition, and in 1951 Sir Ernest Gowers, another English language expert, while recommending 'different from', also said that there was good authority for 'different to'. Neither of these men was a descriptive linguist but they were realists. Do we need to obey a dogmatic rule based on the meaning of a Latin word used hundreds of years ago? Or do we accept current practice?

# Where a weta is a taipo

*22 August 2009*

BRUCE BANKS HAS WRITTEN TO me about an experience at Christchurch Teachers' College in 1958. After he had been reading aloud, his English lecturer asked him which part of the West Coast he came from. When Banks replied 'Reefton' the lecturer informed him that he needed special speech lessons. Banks wrote that he was also confused by a lecture on wetas until he realised that 'a weta was really a taipo'.

In 1972 Mary Durkin, an MA student in English at the University of Canterbury, wrote her thesis on the language of the West Coast. My father came from Ross in South Westland and as a child I thought his speech was different, so this topic really interested me. We thought this thesis would capture a West Coast dialect.

Durkin went to Westport, Reefton and Greymouth and recorded the spoken English of 30 children (aged 10–12) in each town. In the end we were disappointed. Durkin concluded that the pronunciation of the children was not distinctive to the West Coast. It didn't differ from that of children from a similar socio-economic background in Christchurch.

A small grammatical exercise elicited some non-standard English. The children were asked to fill in the space. 'Today I do my work. Yesterday I ___ my work.' Thirty-two per cent said: 'Yesterday I done my work.' The plural of 'you' was often 'yous'. They used constructions like 'I lost me book' and 'I don't know nothing'. (There was a story circulating on the West Coast at that time of a local body candidate who was elected on the platform: 'I'm not promisin' nobody nothing.') But these constructions can be heard throughout New Zealand.

However, Durkin did find some distinctive West Coast vocabulary. She placed letters in local newspapers that produced a good response. There were some words and expressions found only on the Coast, some that were more common on the Coast, and some that had a different meaning on the Coast.

A natural clearing in the bush was called 'pakihi'. However, some of the children thought this meant swampy land, and others thought it was land being developed by the government. The Maori word ponga for a tree fern had changed on the Coast to 'bungy', and a weta was indeed a 'taipo'.

In Otago and Southland a bach is a 'crib', but on the Coast a crib was a miner's lunch and a 'crib-tin' was a lunch-box. Durkin found that most of the children in Reefton knew this, though the meaning of 'crib' had been extended for some to include any lunch or picnic eaten in the bush or away from home.

Some West Coast expressions were Irish in origin. There was the card game 'forty-fives'. People said 'the girl of Smith' rather than 'Smith's girl'. People from other parts of New Zealand were 'from away'. And the name for the letter 'h' was 'haitch'. (Almost half of Durkin's sample pronounced it in this way.)

The term 'barber' (also used in Canada, Nova Scotia and Newfoundland) was used for a cutting wind. In Greymouth the children thought this was a mist, rather than a wind.

Another West Coast term was 'lammy', for a long grey woollen shirt worn in the bush. (This comes from a British dialect term for a thick woollen overgarment worn by sailors.) The word 'possie' (or 'pozzie'), a shortened form of 'position', was used in connection with whitebaiting – though some children thought it was a secret hiding place. (That particular meaning was also familiar to me in my childhood.) A 'scunge' was a mean or miserly person. This was also used instead of the verb 'to scrounge': 'He scunged something from me.'

I don't think we realised it at the time, but Mary Durkin's study was pioneering work, and it is frequently cited by researchers today. Even in 1972 some of the children didn't know these West Coast terms and some words had changed meanings. It would be interesting to know how many of these 'Coastisms' are used – or even understood – today.

# Textes from John Key

*29 August 2009*

JOHN KEY IS A GIFT to linguists. He has such an interesting way with words. Some people find it endearing and others find it infuriating. Personally I rather like the image of a patchwork quilt of cycleways.

Before the election I wrote about his sound change in words like 'strong' and 'Australia', which he pronounces 'shtrong' and 'Aushtralia'. Someone signed only as 'Mary' accused me of being part of a left-wing conspiracy trying to undermine John Key by criticising his pronunciation. Silly me! I thought I was defending him from charges (made by others) of laziness and inebriation.

We can all get caught up in sound changes and I hope readers will know by now that I have no wish to be judgemental. The new cycleway might be called the 'Sir Edmund Hillary Explorator', 'Explorator' is a fine new word. And the 'Afghanistanian government?' Well, we know what he means.

In an interview where he was being questioned about Richard Worth, John Key used the word 'textes' as the plural of 'text'. It wasn't a slip of the tongue because he repeated it a number of times. This is an interesting development and people have commented on it. He has chosen the plural that gives us 'tax/taxes' rather than 'fact/facts'.

Maybe John Key has performed English speakers a service. 'Texts' is a difficult word. It has a wonderful consonant cluster – 'teksts' – four consonants in a row. And English speakers don't usually appreciate long consonant clusters, although some languages have them. I understand that Georgian has a single syllable word, *prtskvnis*, which means 'he is peeling it'. But we struggle to get our tongues around 'strengths' or 'fifths'. The longest sequence of consonants possible in English is seven, but over two words: 'The text's stupid' and 'She tempts strangers'.

If you listen to English-speaking people saying 'postman' and '*West*

*Side Story*' you'll hear 'pos-man' and 'wes-side story'. We drop a consonant. Consonant clusters can also be split up. In some dialects 'wasps' is 'waspes'. That's what John Key has done with 'tekst-es'. I think it does make it a bit easier to say.

A word I've heard a few times (not from John Key) is 'incidence'. Something is happening here, too. We have one incident and two incidents. But somehow 'incidents' has become a singular, spelt 'incidence'. Now we hear 'one incidence' and 'two incidences'.

There have been similar changes in the history of the English language. Today we eat 'peas', with a single 'pea'. But originally the word was a singular noun 'pease'. It's in the children's rhyme: 'pease porridge hot'. Kate Burridge, an Australian linguist, has discovered an ancient rhyme that goes 'Every pease has its vease [fart] but every bean fifteen.' People assumed that the 's' ending on 'pease' was a plural, so a new singular 'pea' was formed.

Some other examples are 'quince', which was once the plural of 'quin'; 'chintz' (that printed cotton fabric), which was the plural of 'chint'; and 'bodice' (the upper part of a woman's dress), which was once the plural of 'body'. Today we have quinces, chintzes and bodices. We say 'the die is cast'. 'Die' was the singular and 'dice' was the plural. But I think today you'd be more likely to hear 'one dice, two dices'.

In 1968 British sociolinguist Peter Trudgill made an urban dialect survey of the spoken language of Norwich in England. At that time he noticed an unusual pronunciation of 'r' but he took no notice of it – it was just an oddity. In 1983 he went back and redid the survey, in 'Norwich Revisited'. He found that what he had dismissed as an oddity in 1968 had become a widespread feature of the English of that area. So although we might think 'textes' is an oddity today, there's always the possibility that in 20 years' time many people will be saying this.

# The legacy of Arnold Wall

5 September 2009

When I was at school in the 1950s our English teacher had us listen to a radio programme called *The Queen's English*. The speaker was Arnold Wall, a retired professor from Canterbury University College. In this programme he answered listeners' language questions. Professor Wall was knowledgeable but acerbic, and didn't suffer fools gladly. One of the pleasures of listening to him was for his public put-downs of people who annoyed him.

Today we see Arnold Wall as a pioneer in the study of New Zealand English, even though he would have rejected such a description. He was personally opposed to the development of what he called 'a new dialect of English for this land'.

Wall was an Englishman who came to New Zealand in 1899 to be the Professor of English at Canterbury College. He became the public face of English language study in New Zealand with newspaper columns and broadcast talks, later converted into books.

Wall's love of language was all-consuming. When he was teaching in England on an annual salary of £30, he spent £3 7/6 on an Icelandic dictionary. Icelandic was not on the university curriculum but, as he said, 'learnt by me for the sheer love of it'. As a student in London he taught himself Icelandic, Danish, Gothic and what he describes as 'similar useless languages' that had nothing to do with the subjects he was studying for his university exams.

In New Zealand, Wall achieved a reputation as a botanist and a mountain climber, and some people admired his poetry. But his fame came from his work on language after he retired from the university in 1931 until his death in 1966.

His book, *New Zealand English: How it should be spoken* (1939), has the subtitle: 'A guide to the correct pronunciation of English with special reference to New Zealand conditions and problems'. And what is the correct pronunciation in New Zealand? He tells us in his preface that it is 'that spoken by the best speakers in the Old Land'. But he also said he didn't want to criticise New Zealand speech unkindly, because some of his young students 'whose speech left much to be desired, yet died gloriously at Gallipoli'.

Wall's lists of common pronunciations (labelled 'essential faults' and 'common errors') give us a useful picture of New Zealand English in the 1920s and 1930s. From him we know that people were pronouncing 'milk' and 'silk' as 'mulk' and 'sulk'; 'result' was 'resolt'. People write to me today saying they've recently noticed 'rain in the elps' or 'in Wallington'. Arnold Wall was writing about this in the 1930s.

He noted the vowel in unstressed syllables: 'Alice' becomes 'Alus'; 'is it?' becomes 'is ut?'. 'Philip' is 'Philup or even Phulup'. This pronunciation he said was the result of original sin: 'Well, it is sheer laziness, and I make bold to call it a sin in the everyday, not the biblical sense.'

Wall also commented on the ending of words like 'dirty' and 'city'. 'The peculiar ee,' he wrote, 'is almost universal, is indeed very distressing, and seems likely to resist all attempts to eradicate it.'

Arnold Wall and I have different attitudes towards New Zealand English and to language change, but I think all serious students of New Zealand English should read what he had to say.

# Intonation conveys intention

*12 September 2009*

RICHARD STUDHOLME HAS ASKED ME to write about intonation in speech. In the 1960s I wrote a thesis on intonation and it's a subject dear to my heart. But it's tricky to write about because it involves the melodies of English. I can sing 'Twinkle twinkle little star' – but I can't convey the tune in written words.

Every language has melodies in it – no language is spoken in a monotone. The voice goes up and down and these different pitches make up the tunes of the language. In some languages the tune belongs to the individual word. If you change the tune, the word has a different meaning. In standard Mandarin Chinese 'ma' said with a level pitch means mother but with a rising pitch it means horse.

In many other languages, including English, the tune belongs to the word group. So you can say 'It was awful' in a way that sounds definite or hesitant, angry or kindly, enthusiastic or dull. All these different shades of meaning are made largely by the tunes we use. If I say 'no' in various ways, it still means 'no' but the tune reveals what I feel about it.

In each group of words is one word that is more important. This word usually comes at the end of the group. 'Fred likes RUGBY.' This is the normal placement. But you can make almost any word important if the sense demands it. 'Fred LIKES rugby' (you said he didn't). FRED likes rugby (but no one else in his family does).

The important word in the group is a bit louder, and it also has a change in pitch. The most common pitch change is the falling tune. We use this most of the time at the end of a phrase – it shows we're finished. A rising pitch is the tune we use for questions, for uncertainty, and to show that we haven't finished – there's still more to say. There are other tunes and combinations of tunes that enable us to express our feelings and our attitudes but I'm giving only a very simple version here.

The tunes of English are not chaotic – there are a certain number of them and they have specific uses. We don't pick them at random and they are not just fancy embellishments; they're significant. We learn these tunes in childhood, before we begin to speak. Babies can babble 'bub bub bub' with a tune so that it sounds a bit like proper speech.

In written English we use punctuation as a fairly rough and ready method of conveying intonation. Compare the way you would say: 'She's going to marry Jason?' and 'She's going to marry Jason!'

English has its own intonation and it is not the same as intonation in other languages. This can create problems for people learning English, who might use the wrong tune in English and not realise it.

Think of how we say 'thank you'. When we get our change from a shopkeeper we use a tune that acknowledges the transaction but doesn't express gratitude. We use a different tune when someone brings us a tin of homemade biscuits tied up with a ribbon. If we used the shopkeeper intonation on 'thank you' for the biscuits, the giver would be hurt and think we didn't care. If we used the gratitude-conveying tune to the shopkeeper, people might wonder what was going on.

Most English speakers don't realise they use intonation. When foreigners get the tunes wrong they are not forgiven as readily as they would be if they made a mistake in pronunciation or grammar. They can be seen as ungrateful or bad-tempered, even if that wasn't their intention.

In New Zealand English we now hear a tune where the voice goes up at the end of a phrase. It's a friendly connecting device – like 'you know?' or 'you see?' But it's the same tune as our questioning intonation, so it gets misinterpreted. And that's a good topic for another language column.

# A curl in the middle of her forrid

*19 September 2009*

ENGLISH SPELLING CAN BE A nightmare at times – especially with names that sound nothing like the way they are spelt. You need local knowledge to pronounce Chomondley as 'Chumly' or 'Marjoribanks Street' in Wellington as 'Marshbanks'.

Frank Paine lives in Berwick Street, but when he asks taxi drivers to come to 'Berrick Street' they reply, 'You mean 'Ber-wick' Street?' Richard Potez from Marlborough has sent me some examples of curious placename spellings from England. He writes:

> London ladies who lunch in Beauchamp Place behind Harrods
> direct their taxi to 'Beecham Place'; Yorkshire workers from
> Rieuvaulx return to their homes in 'Riv-iss'; in the New Forest in
> Hampshire the main town of Beaulieu is 'Bew-lee'.

He also points out that in Marlborough the centre of the wine district is Renwick, named (according to the locals) after a 19th-century doctor whose name was pronounced 'Rennick'. (That one was news to me – when we visited Renwick in the summer with friends we all referred to it as 'Ren-wick'. But then we didn't have local knowledge.) I remember being surprised to find that the place I knew as 'Harden' was actually spelt 'Harwarden'.

Over the years names change. Familiarity can shorten them, sounds change and syllables are smoothed over. The area in London called Marylebone, famous for the MCC (Marylebone Cricket Club), was originally St-Mary-by-the-Bourne. The 'bourn' was the Tyburn stream, which flowed beside the Tyburn gallows. But the original name is quite a mouthful and over time it's been shortened to something like 'Marilibin', with the stress on the first syllable (though one dictionary gives nine possible pronunciations).

We lived for a year in London in Bloomsbury near Theobalds Road.

We used what's known as a 'spelling pronunciation' – 'theo-bald' – but then we heard local people pronouncing it 'Tibbalts Road'.

Spelling pronunciations have been around ever since the arrival of free compulsory education. People who don't know about the old pronunciations have to rely on the spelling. My older brothers would taunt me with the rhyme about the little girl who had a little curl right in the middle of her forehead. 'When she was good she was very very good, and when she was bad she was horrid.' If that rhyme is to work you need to use the old pronunciation of 'forehead' as 'forrid'. You still hear this sometimes, but it's more likely today to be pronounced with the spelling pronunciation 'fore-head'.

I remember a teacher at primary school saying we should pronounce 'towards' as 'tords' but I don't think anyone says that today. Nor do they pronounce 'waistcoat' as 'weskit', or the man's name Ralph as 'Rafe'. Today I think most people pronounce 'nephew' as 'ne-few' not 'ne-vew'.

Where words are unfamiliar we can expect spelling pronunciations. Once people ground grain with a pestle and mortar. Then easier methods were devised and pestles disappeared. But later the pestle came back as a trendy kitchen tool for grinding spices. Today I hear 'pestle' pronounced with the 't' and not with the silent 't' as in 'castle' or 'thistle'.

My mother's family name was Davies, and this always sounded different from Davis. But when I was in Britain I found that Davies and Davis were both pronounced 'Davis'. And Johnson, Johnston and Johnstone were all 'Johnson' – not with the three pronunciations we hear in New Zealand. The boy's name Anthony has the old spelling of 'th' for 't' (as in 'Thames'). In New Zealand I often hear this pronounced as it's spelt – with 'th'.

When I was marking tests and essays on the English language in the university, one of the most misspelt words was 'pronunciation', which turned up constantly as 'pronounciation'. But now I hear people saying 'pronounciation'. So is this a pronunciation based on a misspelling? Or is the spelling based on a mispronunciation?

When I hear overseas visitors struggling to pronounce 'Gloucester Street' or 'Worcester Street' I sometimes wonder if we preserve these curious spellings as a way of separating insiders from outsiders.

# Hello and goodbye

*26 September 2009*

It was 25 years ago that Naida Glavish, a telephone toll operator, made history in New Zealand by greeting callers with 'Kia ora'. It created quite a storm. The TV programme *Media 7* showed a clip from an interview with the postmaster general of the time, Rob Talbot. Talbot said 'Kia ora' wasn't appropriate because it took too much time. He said busy operators had as many as 30–40 calls an hour so there was no time for a greeting.

Talbot's response was bizarre because it breaks the rules of conversation. We must always begin with a greeting. Even when overseas toll calls used to cost a king's ransom we would still say things like 'Hello, how are you? What's the weather like where you are?' before we got down to the business in hand. We had an elderly friend called Lyn who dispensed with the niceties and would begin a telephone conversation with something like: 'Is anyone in your house going to the meeting on Wednesday?' It was most disconcerting, and my children would joke about Lyn's abrupt telephone style.

Ron Talbot and Lyn were failing to recognise that a conversation has a structure, and that if you break the rules, listeners will think it's peculiar or even rude.

The structure is a simple one – at the beginning of the conversation is the greeting, then comes the business, and it's followed at the end by a farewell.

In English we can be quite creative. A greeting can be the formulaic 'Hi' or 'Good morning' but it can also be 'You're just the person I wanted to see'. Or 'Fancy meeting you here!' Farewells can be 'Goodbye' or 'Cheerio' or the old-fashioned 'Hooray', but they can also be 'Oh, is that the time? I must rush'.

In some languages there is less possibility for variation. In Samoan, for example, variation is allowed in informal speech, but in formal Samoan you have to be respectful to the person you are talking to, according to their status, their gender and their standing. You must only ever use the set formal greetings and farewells: 'Talofa' or 'Talofa lava' for good morning/afternoon/evening, and 'tofa' or 'tofa soifua' for goodbye. (And we wouldn't say 'G'day' to the queen.)

My students sometimes asked me why we bothered with these meaningless phrases. Why do we ask people how they are or talk about the weather before we get down to the nitty gritty? They thought it was inefficient and a waste of time.

But they're missing the function of greetings and farewells. These establish social contact – they deal with the relationship between the people in the conversation. Once the greeting has been exchanged, then the people in the conversation can get down to business.

If we don't have a relationship with a person and we don't want to have one, then we don't use a greeting. We say to a stranger, 'Excuse me, could you please tell me the time?' What we're actually saying is, 'Don't worry, I'm not establishing a relationship – I just want to know the time.'

If the conversation goes badly wrong and the speakers end up arguing, it could finish without any farewell. It could even end with a door being slammed or the receiver being slammed down. This is a sure way of saying, 'My relationship with you is over – it's totally severed'.

We learn about the structure of conversation when we learn to talk. We pick up the rules from listening to other people. So we know that when we greet dear friends who have been away for a long time the greeting can go on and on. But it would be peculiar to greet someone like this when you see them several times a day. In that case even a grunt or a nod will do. But the important thing is that the greeting or the farewell happens. It's what keeps us together.

Soifua, Zai jian, Ka kite, Bye bye.

# Goose/geese – why not moose/meese?

*3 October 2009*

I'VE BEEN VISITING MY GRANDDAUGHTER Annabel. She's two and a half. When I last saw her she was producing single words. Now she can rattle off sentences. And she says things like: 'I holded the little mouses.'

While 'holded' and 'mouses' are technically mistakes, they also show amazing language development. Parents should clap their hands with delight when they hear them. Annabel isn't copying – she's actually generating grammatical sentences. She's learnt that the past tense of the English verb is made with '-ed': walked, lifted. The plural of nouns is made by adding '-s': cats, horses. And she's using this knowledge when she says 'holded' and 'mouses'. But Annabel doesn't know about irregular forms yet – there's more to be learnt.

Adam's Year 11 student has asked him why 'goose' becomes 'geese' but 'moose' remains 'moose' in the plural. And why doesn't 'mouse' become 'mouses'?

For a short answer we need to go back to a time before English came to England – when it was a Germanic language on the European continent. Words like 'goose' and 'mouse' are native English words that go back to pre-Anglo-Saxon times when some nouns made their plural by a vowel change. In English today we have a few survivals of this class of words – goose/geese, foot/feet, man/men, mouse/mice etc.

So why don't we say moose/meese? The answer is that moose is not a native English word. It was borrowed in the 17th century from Native American Indian. No English word borrowed after Anglo-Saxon times has that vowel-changing plural. 'Moose' has what's called a 'zero plural'. It's like deer, sheep and salmon. We can have one moose or a hundred moose.

Alison asks if 'sank' has 'sunk'. She wrote:

I heard on the news tonight about the Tongan ferry which 'sunk', and it's by no means the first time I've heard something similar on the news (e.g. 'swum' instead of 'swam' or 'rung' for 'rang'). I expect better of broadcasters, but I hear it all the time in ordinary conversation. I work with well-educated people, and even some of them say things like 'I rung him last night.'

Alison has identified verbs that also go back to the Germanic origins of English. Germanic languages have two verb classes. There are strong verbs, which have a change of vowel for the past tense – ring/rang, swim/swam, find/found, ride/rode etc. (There are about 60 strong verbs in present-day English.) And there are weak verbs which make the past tense with '-ed' – love/loved, walk/walked, lift/lifted.

In standard English the strong verbs have different forms in the past tense and the past participle. He did it (did = past tense)/ he has done it (done = past participle). But in non-standard English strong verbs often have the same form in the past tense and the past participle. He done it/ he has done it. He rung me/he has rung me. The ferry sunk/the ferry has sunk.

This isn't lazy; it's just a characteristic of non-standard English. You could say that the non-standard speakers are actually making their verbs regular. Weak verbs always have the same form for the past tense and past participle. She danced/ she has danced.

Research at the University of Canterbury suggests that drunk, sunk, swum and rung are commonly used as past tense forms in non-standard New Zealand English. This is what Alison is hearing – and from her observation it's spreading into the speech of educated people.

Most English verbs are in the weak verb category. All newly formed verbs will have '-ed' in the past tense. So that's why Annabel says 'holded'. But there's an exception. Do you say 'he sneaked up' or 'he snuck up'? 'Snuck' first appeared in the deep south of the United States in 1887. Today it's made remarkable progress into all varieties of English. In Canada, Australia and New Zealand today younger speakers say 'snuck'. I've found myself saying it too and I'm not young. It's snuck up on me.

# Thomas Hallam and the yod-droppers

*10 October 2009*

I've sometimes come across people who have a passion for language. In a restaurant when we're contemplating the food, they're working out the origins of the waiter from his vowel sounds. They're always listening to language and thinking about it.

One such language fanatic was Thomas Hallam, an Englishman born in Derbyshire in 1819. He was employed by the local railway company, and in his free time he taught himself phonetics. He once heard Isaac Pitman lecturing about shorthand, so Hallam learnt that too. This meant he had two useful tools. He could take down speech verbatim in shorthand, and where necessary he could transcribe it in a detailed way using a phonetic script. (Along the way he also learnt Old English, Greek and Latin – all this with no formal instruction.)

Because he worked for the railways Hallam could travel around England at no expense, and this is what he did at weekends and on public holidays. Wherever there were public meetings with distinguished speakers, or famous preachers in churches or cathedrals, Hallam would turn up with his notebook and write down what he heard in shorthand and in phonetic script. He also investigated English dialects, visiting almost every county of England, interviewing old identities in these areas.

The time Hallam put into this research almost beggars belief – it's not surprising he never married. When he died he left 70 notebooks – 24,000 sides of paper – which are now in the Bodleian Library in Oxford awaiting the attention of present-day language scholars.

Towards the end of his life Hallam wrote a piece called 'Public speakers from whom educated English pronunciation has been recorded from 1850 to 1895'. By sitting in cathedrals, chapels, churches and public halls all over England he was able to make notes on the speech of over 400 speakers. Among them were two of Queen Victoria's sons, the Duke of

233

Edinburgh and Prince Leopold. There were politicians:– Benjamin Disraeli, Lord Salisbury, Lord Shaftesbury. He recorded Charles Dickens and John Chubb the locksmith. And there were countless members of the clergy.

One pronunciation that interested Hallam was the use of 'cy-' and 'gy' at the beginning of syllables in words such as 'can' (pronounced 'cyan') and 'guide' (pronounced gyuide). We're often unaware of this 'y' sound in words because it doesn't appear in spelling. It's in 'few' (fyew) 'human' (hyuman) 'menu' (menyu), 'volume' (volyume), 'continue' (continyue) and so on. It makes the difference between 'Hugh' and 'who'.

The technical name for 'y' is 'yod', from the name of the Hebrew letter. We know from Hallam's notes that it was once used in many more words than it is today, such as garden (gyarden), again, guidance, kindly, mankind, character and against (agyainst). But even in his day it was highly variable, and it must have been so in New Zealand also.

I've found early letter-writers in New Zealand complaining about the pronunciation of 'Tuesday' and 'tune' as 'Chooseday' and 'choon'; there are complaints about 'pitcher' for 'picture' and 'nacher' for 'nature'. In more recent times the complaints have been about 'assume' being pronounced 'ashoom' or 'assoom', 'consume' being 'conshoom'. All of these complaints are about words that once had yod.

Are you a yod-dropper? You can test yourself with a word like 'enthusiasm'. Do you say 'enthyousiasm' or 'enthoosiasm'? I always thought I was a yod-dropper when I said 'education' – 'edge-ucation' not 'ed-you-cation'. But observant students pointed out that when I was giving some radio talks on the Concert Programme in the 1980s I always pronounced 'education' with yod. So I kept yod for careful speech and dropped it in casual speech.

Thomas Hallam's research has shown us that yod-dropping has been around for a long time and I'm sure it will continue. We haven't yet adopted the American pronunciation of 'student' or 'new' as 'stoodent' and 'noo', but this is all part of the same language change.

# Eggcorns and other language mistakes

*17 October 2009*

THERE ARE SOME TYPES OF language mistake that are frequent enough to be given their own names. In the Australian TV series *Kath and Kim*, Kim says to her mother, 'I want to be effluent, Mum!' And Kim replies, 'You *are* effluent, Kimi ...' Kim's use of 'effluent' for 'affluent' is a malapropism. A word is replaced by one with a similar sound, and the result is unintentionally comical.

The term malapropism comes from Mrs Malaprop, a character in Richard Sheridan's play *The Rivals*, written in the 18th century. She said: 'He is the very pineapple (pinnacle) of perfection,' and 'He gives me the hydrostatics (hysterics) to such a degree!' Hylda Baker, a British music hall star, was known for her malapropisms: 'I can say that without fear of contraception (contradiction).'

Malapropisms are different from spoonerisms, in which the sounds of words are transposed: 'a scoop of Boy Trouts' or 'a kuss and a ciddle'.

I've already written about mondegreens, where people mishear the words of a song or phrase. So The Rolling Stones' 'I'll never be your beast of burden' is understood as 'I'll never leave your pizza burning' and 'hallowed be thy name' in the Lord's Prayer is thought to be 'Harold be thy name'.

Now I've come across another type of language error – the eggcorn. An eggcorn is also a substitution, but unlike the malapropism, where the substitution is so wrong it is funny, with an eggcorn the result is plausible. An example is 'old-timer's disease' for 'Alzheimer's disease'.

The term 'eggcorn' was coined by linguist Stephen Pullum in 2003. He'd been taking part in an online forum where he was told about a woman writing 'eggcorn' instead of 'acorn'. (In her American dialect 'egg' would have been pronounced 'aig'). So Pullum suggested the name 'eggcorn' for the whole class of words similarly misanalysed.

Although the term eggcorn is fairly new to me I find there has been quite an industry of eggcorn collection since 2003. In fact the BBC had a programme about eggcorns in 2007. There's a website devoted to them – the Eggcorn Database. Michael Quinion in World Wide Words (www. worldwidewords.org) has written about them with some nice examples: someone acting 'like a bowl in a china shop', or something costing 'a nominal egg' (an arm and a leg). He quotes a letter to *The Times* where a repairman told a woman that her washing machine had 'given up the goat'.

Some people have written to me about language mistakes that I can now put into the eggcorn basket. There's 'baited breath' for 'bated breath'. I think the use of 'baited' is understandable because 'bated' is an ancient word, not used today. It's a form of 'abated', which once meant holding your breath. If you waited with 'bated breath' you were in a state where you'd almost stopped breathing.

There's the eggcorn 'to hone in on' for 'to home in on'. 'Home in on' is an aeronautical term from the early 1920s and comes from homing pigeons. Pilots were guided back to their home bases by radio beacons. In time it came to mean being directed on to a point or a target. 'Hone' means to sharpen, and there's a tenuous connection.

I sometimes hear 'tenderhooks' instead of 'tenterhooks'. A 'tenter' was an instrument of torture, and also a wooden frame on which cloth was stretched. That's another ancient word now lost (apart from 'tenterhooks') so it's not surprising people imagine they're on 'tenderhooks'. Another old-fashioned word is 'wracking' in 'nerve-wracking', which appears as the eggcorn 'nerve wrecking'. Then there are chickens 'coming home to roast', 'fullproof', a 'damp squid' and the curious request 'Please bare with me'.

I tested some of my university-educated friends. They all thought the term was 'baited breath', the word was 'tenderhooks', and that you 'honed in on' things. So maybe such mistakes are becoming accepted items in our vocabulary.

# Who's there? It is I

24 October 2009

IF SOMEONE CALLED OUT 'WHO'S there?' I'm pretty sure you'd answer, 'It's me.' If a man snatched your bag and ran off, I'm sure you'd point to the thief and say, 'That's him.' But according to the grammar rules I was taught at school you'd be using bad grammar. You should say 'It is I' and 'That is he'.

Patricia Smith has written to me about this: 'When I phone someone I know well, I say, "It's me." Some people say, "It is I," [but that] does not sound right to my ear. Could you help?'

Why do we have a rule that no one follows and that doesn't sound right to Patricia Smith's ear?

Because 'It is I' was never an English sentence. Sentences like 'It's me' and 'That's him' are very old English constructions, but 'It is I' is based on a rule for Latin.

Why does English have to follow a Latin rule? Five hundred years ago if you wanted to write a serious academic work you wrote it in Latin. Latin then was the equivalent of standard English today. Writing something serious or formal in English 500 years ago would have been as ridiculous as writing an academic article today in slang. Latin was the international language of scholarship. It was seen as a superior language, and local vernacular languages were inferior.

The idea that Latin was a better language than English influenced grammarians, and they tried to make the structure of English more like Latin.

There's a grammar rule that we must say, 'He is older than I', not 'He is older than me'. This is another rule based on Latin. In Latin the word for 'than' is *quam*, which is a conjunction joining two sentences: 'He is older than I am.' But then you might ask why don't we have a rule that we must say: 'He came after I' on the grounds that this sentence is actually 'He came after I did'. But the word for 'after' in Latin is *post*, which is not a conjunction – it's a preposition. So we can say, 'He came after me.'

I've already written about the split infinitive in these columns. An infinitive is a base word like 'love' preceded by the particle 'to'. The traditional grammar rule is that you must not put another word between the 'to' and 'love'. So you must say, 'It's hard really to love your enemies', not 'It's hard to really love your enemies'. That would be a split infinitive. Because the infinitive was a single word in Latin – *amare* (to love) – the grammarians said that 'to love' in English must also be taken as a single unit. That's the origin of the rule forbidding split infinitives, even though English speakers have been splitting them for centuries.

Several people have written to me about the rule that says we shouldn't end a sentence with a preposition. We should say, 'I have a car with which I'm pleased', not 'I have a car I'm pleased with'. If you ask where this particular rule comes from we're back again with Latin. In Latin it was considered ungrammatical to end a sentence with a preposition. It's the same with French today. French speakers wouldn't say, 'J'ai une voiture que je suis content de.' But English works differently. In English prepositions are good little words to end sentences with.

It's one of the underlying rules of linguistics that a language should be described in terms of its own structure. We can't impose Latin rules on English. If we do we end up with peculiar constructions like 'It is I' that no English person would naturally say. In the Bible when Jesus says that one of his disciples will betray him and they all ask 'Is it I?' I think to myself: I bet they really said, 'Is it me?'

# 'Oh 'appy 'appy 'ummin' bird'

*31 October 2009*

CHRISTINE KOLLER KNOWS ABOUT H-DROPPING because she comes from the East End of London. She asks why Americans say 'erbs for 'herbs' but pronounce 'hospital' with an 'h'.

The pronunciation of 'h' is not always straightforward. Sometimes 'h' can disappear – as it has done in the East End of London. But it also disappears in casual speech. When I say 'Give it to him' or 'Look at her' it's likely that I'll say 'Give it to 'im' or 'Look at 'er.' That's normal in an unstressed syllable. That's not the kind of h-dropping that people get bothered about.

In some varieties of English the 'h' has been lost over the years – people say 'ouses and 'orses. In other places, such as in Scotland and Ireland, they've always said houses and horses.

There was a time when it was perfectly acceptable to drop your h's. In the King James version of the Bible we find 'an harlot' and 'an hundred'. Because of the indefinite article 'an' which always comes before a vowel, they must have been saying 'an 'arlot' and 'an 'undred'.

By the 1800s things changed and pronouncing h's (or not) became a mark of a person's social standing. London East Enders or people from Lancashire who talked about 'ouses and 'orses were looked down on by those who said houses and horses.

In the early New Zealand school inspectors' reports there was great concern about h-dropping. What was called 'the misuse of the aspirate' was a regular complaint. In 1880 a West Coast inspector said that children in Westland were reciting a poem as: 'Oh 'appy, 'appy 'ummin' bird'.

In 1882 a Wellington inspector wrote about a boy who spoke well in class but in the playground said: 'Old yer ed down. Don't never go no further ner the top of the ill.' He made the remarkable suggestion that teachers should join in the children's games in the playground in order to improve their English.

Over the years the complaints about h-dropping in New Zealand became fewer and by 1913 they had ceased altogether. New Zealand English speakers today pronounce their h's.

Some people thought the efforts of the school teachers had achieved this result. It's a nice idea, but I don't think language change works like that. It's more likely the 'h' pronunciation was influenced by immigration from places where it was pronounced – Ireland, Scotland, Northumberland, the West Country, East Anglia and other places. Together they outnumbered the h-droppers from the southeast of England.

Because h-dropping suffers from social stigma, you sometimes find people overdoing it and adding h's where they shouldn't be. We can see this in a letter written by Jane Oates, who immigrated to New Zealand from Derbyshire in 1857. She uses spelling that reflects her Derbyshire accent:

> We have not got bullocks to plow yet but he as (has) a plow so we must trie to hire bullocks to plow till we have got of hour howne …

So let's get back to Christine Koller's question about Americans saying 'erb but also 'hospital'. The answer is that the 'h' was never pronounced in words like hour, honour and honest, which were borrowed from French. Hotel, hospital and herb also came from French, and came into English without 'h'. But when h-dropping fell out of favour, people overdid it and began adding 'h' to some French words where it didn't belong. So that's why we get 'hospital' with 'h'.

I can remember seeing a television programme of the American cooking expert Julia Child, and hearing her talking about 'erbs. It sounded strange, and rather uneducated to me at the time. But I now realise that she was using the original historical pronunciation. So people who say 'an herb' or 'an hotel' are historically accurate if they drop the 'h'. But when they say 'an hotel' or 'an herb' with a pronounced 'h' it sounds quite wrong to me.

# The sound change no one talks about

Years ago I received a letter from Dr Clarke Hanan of Dunedin. He described his experiences at Wellington College in the early 20th century. At the end of morning assembly the headmaster, J. P. Firth, would 'elocute' lines such as 'As it is a fine bright day today we shall go for a sail around the sounds'. The boys in each form were challenged to say the lines to the satisfaction of the head, and the prize was a half-day holiday at the end of term. Hanan said there was much rehearsing under their English master before the trial. On one occasion a lad named Stoddart broke down at the word 'fine', which sounded like 'faw-een', and another shaky word was 'sail', which sounded like 'sigh-al'. Stoddart received a good deal of abuse, both physical and verbal, after school from his classmates.

This all happened at a time when people were first noticing a distinctive New Zealand accent. Around 1900, complaints began to appear about 'an odious colonial twang'. The problem especially involved the diphthongs in 'house' and 'fine'. Children were saying 'heouse' and 'foine'. In 1904 the Wanganui school inspectors said that children should be drilled every day with the words: house, pound, ground, how, now, brown cow etc. A Napier teacher wrote: 'Ask a colonial child to say "I went down town to buy a brown cow" and you may almost make sausages out of the mangled beef.'

A few years later the diphthongs in 'sail' and 'go' were also giving trouble. Hanan's headmaster was testing all four troublesome diphthongs – in fine, day, go and sounds.

Today when people talk about the New Zealand accent they don't talk about these four sounds. They immediately start talking about 'fush and chups'. That's what separates us from Australians. Historically this sound change is a more recent development. The first references to it in writing were in the 1960s when people wrote letters to the *Listener* complaining about the way a new young cooking presenter called Alison Holst was pronouncing the word 'fish'.

There's one characteristic New Zealand pronunciation that doesn't get any publicity – this is the way we say the vowels in 'nurse' or 'bird'. When I went to University College London in 1964 my former teacher from the University of Canterbury, George Turner, had been there the year before me. People spoke of him with respect and affection, and they always mentioned the way he pronounced his surname as 'Tooner'. New Zealanders pronounce the vowel in 'nurse' with tightly rounded lips. Outsiders sometimes wonder if a New Zealander is saying 'terms' or 'tombs'. For me the British Received Pronunciation version, with more open lips, sounds like 'tahms'; a 'person' sounds like a 'parson'.

This sound change gets no publicity, and it doesn't cause a problem because the context tells us if it's a person or a parson. I recognised the New Zealand change when my youngest daughter came home from school with a skipping rhyme: 'Julie Temple is a star'. I asked her who Julie Temple was and she had no idea. I guessed that the origins of that song were with the American child actress Shirley Temple. For someone who hadn't heard of Shirley Temple, the New Zealand pronunciation 'Shooley' could easily be misunderstood as 'Julie'.

People used to write complaining letters about the pronunciation of 'house' and 'fine' and later about 'fish and chips', but no one ever mentioned the vowel in 'the early bird'.

Does the absence of any comment mean that the current New Zealand pronunciation wasn't there in earlier times? Or does it mean that it was there, but it wasn't noticed? Or maybe it was there, and people noticed it, but they had no way of conveying it in ordinary spelling. Perhaps it just didn't trouble people in the way that 'heouse' for 'house' and 'foine' for 'fine' did. That's an interesting historical puzzle.

# How's your father and other naughty words

*21 November 2009*

WE WERE WATCHING THE RUGBY and the commentator said there was a bit of 'how's your father' going on in the scrum. One rugby-watcher thought this meant a fight – a stoush – but another thought it meant what is euphemistically known as 'sexual impropriety'.

So what was going on in the scrum? Where does this expression come from? I went to Michael Quinion of www.worldwidewords.org and he said it referred to a casual sexual encounter, and it comes from a British music hall comedian called Harry Tate (1872–1940). Whenever Tate couldn't think of an answer in one of his sketches he would say 'how's your father?' as a diversionary way of changing the subject.

Quinion says the term is outdated now in Britain, but I think it's alive and well in Australia and New Zealand. Here it has two meanings. In rugby commentary it has joined other euphemisms for sporting violence.

I've read that the British supermarket chain Tesco changed the name of the traditional British pudding 'spotted dick' because some customers were embarrassed by it. They decided to call it 'spotted Richard', but then later changed it back again. However, the county council canteen in Mold, North Wales, also changed it because of 'several immature comments from a few customers'.

I associate 'spotted dick' with boarding school cuisine. It's a steamed suet pudding made with dried fruit, which is why it's spotted. I don't think anyone knows who Dick was.

When people 'have a butchers' at something it comes from 'butcher's hook' meaning 'a look'. In Australia and New Zealand we have a different version. When someone 'goes butchers', or 'goes butcher's hook' it means 'going crook'.

This is Cockney rhyming slang, which involves an expression that rhymes with a word. Then that expression is used instead of the word. So 'would you Adam and Eve it?' means 'would you believe it?'

Rhyming slang was used in the British underworld and some terms became euphemisms for dirty words. Some of these linguistic fig leaves have moved into polite society and their more murky origins have disappeared. When people say 'he gets on my wick' they probably don't realise that it comes from Cockney rhyming slang 'Hackney Wick' (prick). If you say something is 'a load of cobblers' it's rhyming slang for 'cobblers' awls' – (balls). Blowing 'a raspberry' is from 'raspberry tart' (fart). I think it's old fashioned now, but I've heard respectable people saying that someone is 'a berk'. This comes from 'Berkley hunt', and I'll let you work that one out.

Sometimes we avoid taboo words by using coy expressions such as 'the four-letter-word'. I remember when Tim Shadbolt was arrested in the early 1970s for using 'the eight-letter-word'. People at that time were going around counting out possibilities on their fingers. Later the answer was revealed when he wrote a book called *Bullshit and Jellybeans*. Now we have 'the F-word' and 'the N-word'. *The Press* uses full points (f..k) so that sensitive people are not offended.

In heated moments some people swear. But some use clayton's swear words – words that are not the actual swear words but sound like them and have the same function. Shivers, shoot, shucks, shite, sugar. There are the variations on the name of Jesus Christ – jeepers, jeez, gee, gee-whizz, jeepers creepers, cripes, christmas, crumbs and crikey. I was surprised to find that 'for crying out loud' comes from 'for Christ's sake'. 'Damn' becomes 'darn' and 'hell' becomes 'heck'. You might not actually be taking the Lord's name in vain, but gosh, golly, goodness gracious, for goodness sake, and goodness knows – they all derive from the name of God. They're examples of linguistic ingenuity but do they count as swear words?

# Dunedinites, Aucklanders, Cantabrians?

*28 November 2009*

David Ellison wrote to *The Press* saying that people in England speak English – so why shouldn't New Zealanders speak 'New Zealish'? He is not the first person to put forward a name for the New Zealand way of speaking. Professor Arnold Wall coined the name 'Enzedic'. He used it himself in his broadcast talks in the 1950s but it didn't catch on.

Alex Buzo, an Australian, produced a little book on New Zealand English to assist Australians. He coined the name 'Kiwese' and his book is subtitled *A guide, a ductionary, a shearing of unsights*. I'm sure Australians found his book funny when it was written in 1994, just as they are laughing today about the Australian cartoon on YouTube called 'The beached whale', making fun of the New Zealand accent. The whale is 'beached as, bro' and eats 'plenktun' (plankton) not 'chups'.

But so far we seem to be able to get along perfectly well talking about 'New Zealand English' or 'NZE' for short. And we use the term 'New Zealandism' for a word or a meaning that's part of the distinctive vocabulary of New Zealand English. Obvious examples of New Zealandisms are Maori loan words or terms such as 'the All Blacks' and 'the DPB'. We've even exported some of our New Zealandisms to Australia – 'marching girls', 'the TAB' and 'boots and all'.

Closer to home, it seems we have no special name for the inhabitants of Christchurch. People from Wellington are Wellingtonians, from Dunedin they are Dunedinites, from Timaru they're Timaruvians, and from Auckland they're Aucklanders. But we don't have Christchurchers or Christchurchites.

The nearest we can get to a name for someone from our area is 'Cantabrian'. Some people get annoyed by this name for people from Canterbury. One letter-writer a few years ago wrote:

Unless there has suddenly been a great influx into the Canterbury province of expatriate students from Cambridge University in the United Kingdom, this has to be a gross display of ignorance on the part of those who use this terminology – and those who stand by and let it happen.

But the full word 'Cantabrian' doesn't have a British meaning – apart from referring to someone from the northern Spanish region of Cantabria. When we call ourselves Cantabrians, I doubt whether anyone would confuse us with Spaniards.

In Britain the word 'Cantab.' is a shortened form of 'Cantabrigiensis', meaning 'of Cambridge', from 'Cantabrigia' – the neo-Latin name for Cambridge University. Someone who is BA (Cantab.) has a degree from Cambridge University. I'm reliably informed that a degree from the University of Canterbury is BA (Cantuar) short for Cantuariensis, though I'm not sure how often that's used.

Some New Zealand placenames have been very productive in producing nicknames. TV weather forecaster Jim Hickey talks about 'Palmy' for Palmerston North and 'Dunners' for Dunedin. There's 'Gissy' for Gisborne, 'Hoki' for Hokitika, and 'Whangers' for Whangarei.

My children have introduced me to 'Rotovegas' for Rotorua, 'Ashvegas' for Ashburton and 'Invervegas' (Invercargill). They refer to Taranaki as 'the Naki'. Hamilton has spawned a few variants – Cowtown, Hamiltron, H-Tizzle, the Tron and Hammytron. Auckland is Auk, the big Auk, Dorkland, Jafa City, Jafadom. Wellington is Wellywood, Welly, Wellies and Wello. And then there are the 'Hutties'. An army friend tells me that Waiouru is sometimes 'Waiberia' or 'the Uru', and Burnham is 'the Nam'.

So what is it about Christchurch that it seems to have missed out in the name-calling game? Or perhaps there are nicknames for Christchurch but I just haven't heard them. I hope people will enlighten me if there are. And I can think of only one Christchurch suburb with its own derivative – 'Fendaltonian'. We've had the City of the Plains, the City of Trees and, probably best known, the Garden City. In the 1990s Christchurch became 'the City that Shines'. But its inhabitants are just people from Christchurch (or Cantabrians).

# Out of the mouths of babes

*12 December 2009*

We have a new grandson. Alexander was born at the end of October, and, like all grandparents, we look at him and wonder what the world will be like for him when he grows up.

We know he has been born with many advantages – a loving family who will talk to him and read to him and give him encouragement. And he will have another advantage – his family all speak standard New Zealand English. The language he hears at home will be the same language he'll be expected to use when he goes to school.

It's an amazing experience to watch the language development of a small child. Linguists now believe that the human baby's brain is programmed before birth for language. Language is a biological function, like walking or sexual maturation. All babies that hear normally will talk. Some start early and some take their time, but they all get there in the end. It doesn't matter where the child lives, or how rich or poor, intelligent or less intelligent: that child will develop language. Language is a human function that separates us from the animals.

Alexander is already on the remarkable path of language learning. In the grand design his brain is programmed to learn language, but it is not programmed to learn a specific language. The language he grows up speaking will be the language he hears around him – the language his family and his friends speak. If his family were Chinese he'd speak Chinese, if he were born in France he'd grow up speaking French.

Let's imagine another baby born in New Zealand at the same time as Alexander. We'll call him Zac, and his parents love him and talk to him and want the best for him. Zac's parents speak a variety of New Zealand English that is different from standard English. They say 'We seen it on TV' or 'She come here yesterday' or 'I never did nothink' or 'What are yous doing?'

247

Linguists call this non-standard English – or vernacular English. It's not lazy and it it's not chaotic. It's just as much governed by systematic rules as standard English. And because Zac grows up hearing his family and friends using non-standard English, this will be his mother tongue.

When Alexander goes to school he'll be expected to use standard English and that won't be a problem because that's his mother tongue. But it will be harder for Zac: he'll have to learn standard English. And so he should – he would be shockingly disadvantaged if his school didn't teach him standard English. He'll need it for writing, and he could need it for future employment.

So Alexander will have one variety of English but Zac will have two.

I'm a strong supporter of the teaching of standard English in school. But I'll also defend the speakers of non-standard English. I know this angers some people, who say I'm just being PC. I was once accused of being 'a Marxist who encourages lazy slack-jawed speech'. These critics think I should come out and say it's completely wrong and bad to say 'I seen it' or 'What are yous doing?' But I won't. For some New Zealanders this is their mother tongue.

When New Zealand English was first recognised, people believed that New Zealand children had a choice. They could speak like educated people in England or they could use this horrible new colonial dialect. But what choice was there really? The way New Zealand children spoke in 1900 was not a matter of personal virtue and certainly not a matter of choice.

Alexander and Zac didn't choose their families and they didn't choose their mother tongues. In the world they grow up in I hope there will be tolerance for varieties of English. I hope people won't say that Alexander is good and Zac is bad because of the way they speak.

# The sound of silence

*19 December 2009*

I'VE BEEN THINKING ABOUT SILENCE. In this language column I write about words and talking and conversation – all those activities that fill up silence.

British anthropologist Bronislaw Malinowski lived with the Trobriand Islanders in the Western Pacific in the early 20th century. He came to the conclusion that for them silence was not a reassuring factor. He said that the Trobriand Islanders found silence alarming and dangerous. He wrote: 'A stranger who cannot speak the language is to all tribesmen a natural enemy.' He believed it was a universal fact that taciturnity was seen as a sign of unfriendliness and also a sign of a bad character.

Malinowski invented the term 'phatic communion' for phrases such as 'Nice day today' or the Melanesian 'Whence comest thou?' He said such phrases are needed to get over the strange and unpleasant feeling people get when facing each other in silence.

This theory has interested me. I used to get my students to do a small exercise. They had to work out which strangers they might acknowledge in the course of a day. They agreed that they would greet a person walking on the beach (especially if that person had a dog); they would address someone in a lift; they would address a stranger walking on a country road. But they wouldn't greet a stranger on a busy footpath. It seems we want to make contact with isolated strangers for our own peace of mind. A silent person walking towards us on a dark road at night could be dangerous. So we say 'Good evening' to get the reassurance of a reply.

I think we English speakers often find silence uncomfortable. Our family belongs to an organisation called Servas, where overseas visitors are given free hospitality for a couple of nights in the interests of international understanding. Once we had four young people from Finland staying. They stood completely silently in our kitchen as I was cooking the dinner

249

and it felt strange to me – almost oppressive. I remember how I chattered to fill the silence and struggled with their long pauses. I later read that it is a characteristic of people from Finland to talk less than we do. They are sometimes known as 'the silent Finns'.

This experience showed me that tolerance of silence is culturally determined. In a sociolinguistics class I used to teach, we studied the use of silence by Western Apache American Indians. The stereotype of the American Indian is of a strong silent person who says the occasional 'How'. A study by K. H. Basso has shown that the use of silence by the Western Apache is integral to their culture. Whenever there is a difficult or ambiguous situation their practice is to remain silent. So when Western Apache Indians meet strangers they don't talk to them. Strangers who are quick to talk are regarded with suspicion. The Western Apache Indians observe the strangers silently for hours or even longer – until they feel ready to speak. In their culture courting couples remain silent. The custom is to remain silent around anyone who is drunk or enraged. When they sit with a bereaved person they never talk.

My students found this American Indian custom of silence completely different from our behaviour. But to understand the Western Apache culture the knowledge of when not to speak is as important as knowing what to say.

One of my students was in a stormy relationship and she decided to follow the custom of the Western Apache Indians. When her partner became abusive she remained silent. But her silence made him even more enraged. Remaining silent in our culture can have a different effect. The person who doesn't talk is sulking or stand-offish or ill. There's a saying that goes: 'It is not the case that a person who remains silent says nothing.'

# Thinking outside the square

*26 December 2009*

My Latin teacher at school was Miss Ethel M. Duff. She was a stern teacher who I remember with affection. I can still picture her rubbing the sleeve of her cardigan to explain the Latin word *tritus*, past participle of the verb *terere*, to rub or wear away. 'Remember, girls, that words that are "trite" are "well rubbed".'

I've often thought of Miss Duff's well-rubbed words. So much of our language isn't novel or original – we use the same phrases and words over and over again. When someone asks 'How are you going?' we don't give them a detailed account of our health. We say, 'Fine, thanks.' When my youngest daughter was starting to talk she learned to say, 'Oooh, what's in it?' when anyone was opening a present. This was long before she could produce questions beginning with wh-words. She'd learnt a useful 'word package' to bring out at the appropriate occasion.

We use familiar well-rubbed expressions because they're quick. Socio-linguists call them schemata, or formulaic language. We're not linguistic automata, but at times our use of language can get close to an automatic process. It's as if we have hundreds of pre-packaged instructions about what to say in particular situations. We don't need to create original sentences every time we speak.

It's helpful to have our well-rubbed phrases. People learning a foreign language need to learn these to gain a comfortable fluency – to sound like native speakers. And when we're in ambiguous or difficult situations, especially those involving death or illness, there's a comfort in the familiar words. I remember on the anniversary of the Wahine disaster people said things like: 'He was in the wrong place at the wrong time' or 'We have learned to live with it' or 'Time can be a great healer'.

On the other hand, there are some well-rubbed phrases and words that can be irritating. These are the ones we call clichés. The word cliché came from the printing trade. When a printing plate was cast with moveable type it was a good idea to cast whole phrases that were used repeatedly as a single slug of metal. The French word *cliché* came from the sound of the matrix being dropped into molten metal to make the printing plate. In the 19th century it came to be used for words or phrases that had lost their force through overuse.

Robert Fisk, Middle East correspondent for the *Independent*, has described how he was taught to write in clichés when he was training to be a journalist in Britain in the 1960s. When the police were seeking a hit-and-run driver they 'spread their net' or 'narrowed their search' or 'stepped up their hunt'. Storm-battered ships 'limped' into port; protesters 'took to the streets'; failed council plans were 'put on ice'. Today Fisk rails against writing where 'key players interact with each other' or 'impact society' or 'outsource their business' and 'downsize their employees'.

In these language columns I try to be tolerant and objective, but that doesn't mean I must approve of the constant use of clichés.

So when the ducks are in a row and we've picked the low-hanging fruit and sung from the same hymn book, we might be able to boost our self-esteem or at least seek closure but there's no free lunch. When the scenery or the people are iconic, when ideas are robust and we can see the big picture, or think outside the box, when clean-and-green meets the nanny state – well, going forward and frankly speaking, the reality is that at the end of the day it gives me a pain in the neck.

# How should we talk in church?

*2 January 2010*

WHEN I STUDIED THE HISTORY of the English language at university I found I already had a surprisingly good understanding of Elizabethan English. This wasn't from studying it in textbooks, but rather from growing up in an Anglican vicarage.

From as long ago as I can remember I was taken to church and heard the words of the King James version of the Bible, and the old Anglican *Book of Common Prayer* written by Bishop Cranmer in 1549. I knew that God always spoke in an ancient inflected language. He said, 'Knowest thou?' not 'Do you know?' In the garden of Eden he said to Adam: 'Hast thou eaten of the tree whereof I commanded thee that thou shouldest not eat?' Not 'Did you eat the apple from the tree when I told you not to?'

When I was in England in 1979 there was a lively debate about a new version of the Church of England Prayer Book called 'Series Three'. People like Sir Lawrence Olivier and Prince Charles came out strongly on the side of tradition. They said the modern language of Series Three had removed the beauty and the mystery of the Elizabethan language of Bishop Cranmer. But parish priests came back and said Elizabethan language made the Prayer Book incomprehensible to ordinary people. I certainly remember as a child being puzzled by the prayer that began 'Prevent us good Lord in all our doings'. Why would we ask God to stop us from doing everything? The earlier meaning of 'prevent' as 'go before' had been lost.

In 1979 it wasn't just a debate between the conservatives and the moderns. It was a debate involving the nature of religious language. People carrying out revision pointed out that Bishop Cranmer himself wanted people to be able to understand the language being used. Cranmer said '... the ministers should use such language as the people may understand and take profit thereby'.

The Roman Catholic 'Instruction on Translation of Liturgical Texts', written in 1969, said the language used should be 'common usage suited to the greater number of the faithful who speak it in everyday use, even children and people of small education'.

But what happens when you write in the language of common usage? In the language of the Australian of 'small education', the parable of the loaves and the fishes was told like this:

> After a while the Apostles said, 'It's time to tie on the feedbag
> – but there's not enough tucker for this mob.' Andrew said,
> 'There's a kid with five loaves of bread and two fishes.' So Jesus
> said, 'Righto, bring me the bread and the bream.' He blesses it
> – breaks it into bits and the Apostles take it around. Jesus said,
> 'Collect what's left over or we'll be in strife for littering.' Jesus
> had fed 5000 blokes – that's not counting all the sheilas and
> kids.

This version wasn't acceptable, even though it was pointed out that Jesus was a working man himself who mixed with common people.

In New Zealand the Anglican Church published *A New Zealand Prayer Book* in 1989. For a time I was a member of the revision committee, and I know how challenging this work was. But I think the result was remarkable. The old pronouns were gone – God was addressed as 'you', and the language was inclusive. With Maori as an official New Zealand language, a large part of the *Prayer Book* was in both English and Maori. And there were sections translated into Fijian and Tongan.

As a child I was familiar with the ancient song of creation in the Book of Common Prayer known as the Benedicite. In *A New Zealand Prayer Book* it's been rewritten: 'Kauri and pine, rata and kowhai, mosses and ferns: give to our God your thanks and praise. You Maori and Pakeha, women and men, all who inhabit the long white cloud: give to our God your thanks and praise.'

# What's happened to 'women'?

*9 January 2010*

JOHN PARKES HAS WRITTEN TO me about the New Zealand pronunciation of 'women'. He wrote:

> Since returning to New Zealand two years ago, I have noticed a
> number of people using the singular 'woman', when the plural is
> being referred to. They never use the word 'women'. I have heard
> it on Radio NZ and also from friends, both male and female …
> I was wondering whether this was just uninformed.

In 1990 Tony Deverson wrote about the merger between 'woman' and
'women' in *Te Reo* (the journal of the New Zealand Linguistic Society).
He suggested then that the use of 'woman' for the plural had been around
for 20–30 years.

The first written complaints about it appeared in the *Listener* in 1963.
A woman wrote:

> I am appalled by the mispronunciation of the plural of 'woman'.
> This word 'women' should be pronounced 'wimmin' and not in
> the same way as 'woman'. How can we expect people to speak
> correctly when a professor makes this mistake about fifteen
> times in two minutes?

She then suggested that the pronunciation was a 'sub-conscious non-
acceptance by the New Zealand male of the New Zealand female as his
equal'.

The difficulty with 'woman/women' is that these words are highly idiosyncratic in both spelling and pronunciation. There are no other English
nouns like them. In their spelling the singular/plural contrast is in the
second syllable, wo*man*/wo*men*, but in pronunciation the contrast is on
the first syllable, *wo-*, spelt the same for both words.

The plural 'women' is the only English word where 'o' in a stressed syllable is pronounced 'i'. George Bernard Shaw used this to produce his joke spelling of 'fish' as 'ghoti' – 'gh' (rough), 'o' (women) and 'ti'(nation).

Some people have argued that plural 'women' is a spelling pronunciation – where the pronunciation has been influenced by the written word. I'm not entirely convinced, but it could be contributory factor.

It seems to me there's a much more important reason. It's the New Zealand pronunciation of the vowel in words like 'kit' and 'risk'. In its extreme form we have a sound change that gives us 'cut' and 'rusk'. That's why people talk about 'fush and chups' whenever the New Zealand accent is mentioned. That's why 'women' sounds more like 'wummin' than 'wimmin'. This isn't a problem for Australians whose pronunciation for 'fish' is nearer 'feesh'.

The change could also be reinforced by singular 'woman' being used as a generic. We find 'woman's intuition' and 'the role of woman in society'. And there's the *New Zealand Woman's Weekly* – which is different from the *Australian Women's Weekly*.

So what Parkes is describing is a word which, for a number of reasons, has become a new zero plural. In New Zealand 'woman' has become like deer, sheep or salmon. You can have one woman or five woman – just like one sheep or five sheep. The context usually tells us if there's one or more than one involved.

I think the idiosyncratic form of the word itself and the features of our New Zealand accent are responsible for this change. But I'm sure this won't stop the criticisms of the zero plural 'woman'.

In 1990 Deverson wrote, '... whether this is yet the pronunciation of the average New Zealander might be disputed'.

Today we will have to say that there's no dispute: zero plural 'woman' is heard widely among all social groups. Researchers at Victoria University in Wellington have made an analysis of recent recordings. They report that half the time even the oldest group of speakers failed to make a distinction between 'woman' and 'women', and the younger speakers rarely made a distinction.

The zero plural 'woman' is not uninformed and it's not lazy. It has nothing to do with men refusing to see women as their equal. And like it or not it's probably here to stay.